HIGHER EDUCATION FOR SUSTAINABILITY

Student and employer demand, high-level institutional commitment, and faculty interest are inspiring the integration of sustainability-oriented themes into higher education curricula and research agendas. Moving toward sustainability calls for shifts in practice such as interdisciplinary collaboration and partnerships for engaged learning. This timely edited collection provides a glimpse at the ways colleges and universities have integrated sustainability across the curriculum. The research-based chapters provide empirical studies of both traditional and innovative degree programs as well as case studies from professional schools. Chapter authors illustrate some of the inclusive and deliberative community and political processes that can lead to sustainable learning outcomes in higher education. Exploring the range of approaches, campuses are making to successfully integrate sustainability into the curricula, this much-needed resource provides inspiration, guidance, and instruction for others seeking to take education for sustainability to the next level.

Lucas F. Johnston is Assistant Professor of Religion and Environmental Studies and a Faculty Associate in the Center for Energy, Environment, and Sustainability (CEES) at Wake Forest University, USA.

HIGHER EDUCATION FOR SUSTAINABILITY

Cases, Challenges, and Opportunities from Across the Curriculum

Edited by Lucas F. Johnston

 Routledge
Taylor & Francis Group

NEW YORK AND LONDON

First published 2013
by Routledge
711 Third Avenue, New York, NY 10017

Simultaneously published in the UK
by Routledge
2 Park Square, Milton Park, Abingdon, Oxon OX14 4RN

Routledge is an imprint of the Taylor & Francis Group, an informa business

Library of Congress Cataloging-in-Publication Data
Higher education for sustainability : cases, challenges, and opportunities
from across the curriculum / edited by Lucas F. Johnston.
p. cm.
Includes bibliographical references and index.
1. Education, Higher—Environmental aspects. 2. Sustainable
development—Study and teaching (Higher) 3. Sustainability—Study and
teaching (Higher) 4. Interdisciplinary approach in education. I. Johnston,
Lucas F.
LB2324.H543 2012
338.9′270711—dc23   2012003924

ISBN: 978-0-415-51935-9 (hbk)
ISBN: 978-0-415-51936-6 (pbk)
ISBN: 978-0-203-12304-1 (ebk)

Typeset in Bembo
by Cenveo Publisher Services

Printed and bound in the United States of America on sustainably sourced
paper by IBT Global

CONTENTS

Foreword   *viii*
Paul Rowland

1   Introduction: What's Required to Take EfS to
    the Next Level?   1
    Dedee DeLongpré Johnston and Lucas F. Johnston

SECTION 1
Understanding the Landscape for Change   **9**

2   The Emerging Environmental Sustainability Program
    at Meredith College: Exploring Student and Faculty
    Interest and Participation   11
    Laura Fieselman and Erin Lindquist

3   Understanding Student Environmental Interests When
    Designing Multidisciplinary Curricula   29
    *Jeremy T. Bruskotter, Gregory E. Hitzhusen, Robyn S. Wilson,
    and Adam Zwickle*

4   Learning Outcomes: An International Comparison of
    Countries and Declarations   45
    Debra Rowe and Lucas F. Johnston

SECTION 2
Sustainability Across the Curriculum: Strategies and Tactics 61

5   Systems Study of an International Master's Program:
    A Case from Sweden 63
    Sanaz Karim, Nadarajah Sriskandarajah, and Åsa Heiter

6   Keys to Breaking Disciplinary Barriers that Limit
    Sustainable Development Courses 79
    William Van Lopik

SECTION 3
Educating the Professional 93

7   Strategies for Transforming Healthcare Curricula: A Call for
    Collaboration Between Academia and Practitioners 95
    Carrie Rich and Seema Wadhwa

8   Sustainability and Professional Identity in
    Engineering Education 109
    *Mark Minster, Patricia D. Brackin, Rebecca DeVasher,
    Erik Z. Hayes, Richard House, and Corey Taylor*

9   Implementing Environmental Sustainability in the Global
    Hospitality, Tourism, and Leisure Industries: Developing
    a Comprehensive Cross-Disciplinary Curriculum 124
    *Michelle Millar, Chris Brown, Cynthia Carruthers, Thomas Jones,
    Yen-Soon Kim, Carola Raab, Ken Teeters, and Li-Ting Yang*

SECTION 4
Problem-Based Learning 137

10 Everybody's Business: Addressing the Challenge of
    Team-Teaching Partnerships in the Global Seminar 139
    Tamara Savelyeva

11 The Moral Ecology of Everyday Life 154
    James J. Farrell

12 The Living Home: Building It into the Curriculum   169
     Braum Barber and Leona Rousseau

SECTION 5
Transformational Approaches   **183**

13 Shaping Sustainability at Furman and Middlebury: Emergent
     and Adaptive Curricular Models   185
     Angela C. Halfacre, Jack Byrne, Michelle Horhota,
     Katherine Kransteuber, Steve Trombulak, Brittany DeKnight,
     Brannon Andersen, and Nan Jenks-Jay

14 Stepping Up to the Challenge – The Dalhousie Experience   201
     Tarah Wright

15 Sustainability as a Transformation in Education   214
     Charles L. Redman and Arnim Wiek

16 Toward a Resilient Academy   223
     Richard M. Carp

     Epilogue   238
     Lucas F. Johnston

     About the Contributors   *241*
     Index   *255*

FOREWORD

When you wake up tomorrow, the world will be a bit less hospitable. The earth will be a warmer place, the air will be more polluted, the supply of safe drinking water will have diminished, less food will be available per person, and biodiversity will be reduced. Social, health, and economic disparities will be evident not only in comparisons of national wealth, but even within the richest nations the gaps between the richest and the poorest will contribute to social instability. The planet will be more crowded and still most of the wealth will be in the hands of a few.

The upwelling of concern about society's future based on environmental, economic, and social challenges has made it clear that the creation of a sustainable society of opportunities will require wise decision-making by everyone. It will not be enough to assign responsibility to one sector or one political group or one element of the social structure. A sustainable society can only be attained through the combined efforts of all of society. That is why it is so important that higher education institutions take the lead in ensuring that all their graduates – the leaders, the teachers, the professionals, and a significant part of the workforce – have an understanding of the challenges we face and the tools and dispositions to address those challenges to create a healthy, just, and sustainable world.

During the past two decades, education for sustainable development, or sustainability education, has emerged as a common topic in discussions about higher education curriculum discussions. The inclusion of sustainability in the curriculum, both as a part of traditional degrees and as the foundation of new emerging programs, has become a part of the discussions among individual faculty within department meetings, and among campus committees. Despite these conversations and the efforts of dedicated faculty to address issues of sustainability in their teaching, it is clear that among the thousands of institutions in the United States and Canada, only several hundred of them offer their students opportunities to take courses addressing sustainability. In many of those institutions that do offer sustainability coursework, only a small percentage of the students are able to enroll in it. Clearly, if we are to ensure that the nearly 20 million post-secondary students in the United States and Canada leave their institutions knowing how to make the decisions to shape a sustainable society, we will need to take sustainability education to a higher level. The good news is that there are indicators that many institutions are ready to do so. More than 675 campus presidents and chancellors have become signatories of the American Colleges and Universities Presidents Climate Commitment, which commits their campus to "to make climate neutrality and sustainability a part of the curriculum … for all students."

For better or worse, we have come to realize that the growth of sustainability education has occurred through a wide variety of ways that represent the wide diversity of our institutions and their various missions. Some institutions have been able to embrace sustainability as a core principle and value and have created core requirements for all students. Other institutions have focused their sustainability education efforts on developing graduate programs for sustainability professionals. Another approach has been to develop sustainability workforce programs as new jobs have emerged. Still, others have approached the challenge from a faculty development process that leads to infusion of sustainability across the curriculum among the willing. There has been no single pathway to success (and I would argue that there should not be) in developing and implementing the sustainability education curriculum. This lack of uniformity frustrates some who want to find a blueprint to follow, but it preserves a critical strength of the academy: the ability to create diverse curricula for diverse populations. It also reminds us that as we look at the examples of the successes in this volume, we should carefully evaluate how we make use of them, and the lessons they can teach.

So then, we stand at a point where we have the opportunity to critically evaluate these successes while recognizing that that we face clear challenges in moving forward. In nearly every conversation about sustainability education there is the question, "What do we mean by sustainability?" Some have argued that the term is in need of definition, clarification, branding, and marketing. Likewise, there have been several groups that have struggled with Herbert Spencer's question, "What knowledge is of most worth?" as they have attempted to define the learning outcomes and core competencies of sustainability. Although those outside the academy may consider these issues, well, what else, *academic*, they are of significance. If sustainability is to become an essential part of the fabric of the higher education curriculum it should have recognizable outcomes associated with it. Also, we need to be mindful that our educational institutions were not established nor are they structured to create the healthy, just, and sustainable society we are seeking. Consequently, we need to be looking into the future to envision what higher education might entail and what will be needed to transform our current system into what is needed and desirable. If higher education is to become an integral part of society then there needs to be a radical shift from serving the disciplines to serving society. This has obvious implications for changes in the rewards structure of the enterprise as well as the educational processes.

The transformation of higher education does not imply the rejection of reason, knowledge, and learning; but it does, in a fundamental way, challenge us to think about the role of higher education in ensuring that its graduates are prepared to create a society based on both reason and compassion. It is essential that the people of the future understand how our world works, how things are interconnected, and the complexity of relationships that shape our desired and undesired outcomes. It is less important that we have formulaic processes for saving the earth (which will do just fine without us), but it is critical that our graduates understand how it all works, how we effect it, how it effects us, and how we effect each other. So, knowledge and reason will be important for sorting out some issues but we will need to also care about ourselves and each other as a part of the people of the earth. That is, we will need to care about humanity. A sustainable society must be based on compassion for others and from that compassion, an understanding that we must analyze our actions with concern for our impacts on each other as well as the rest of the ecosphere. A focus on compassion as an outcome is a radical change for much of higher education, although not one that is inconsistent with the goal of providing opportunities for success for all in current and future generations.

This volume helps us review some of the promising practices that have been developed and used in the past decade and that have promise for moving us forward in sustainability education. In addition, some of the authors challenge us to think more deeply about the issues of the present and of the future of sustainability in higher education. It is right that our authors look not just to past successes but also to future challenges – that is an essential element of thinking sustainably. Readers will find in this volume praxis, the nexus of practice and theory that can help us examine where we have been, where we are, and where we are going in sustainability education.

If higher education is to be relevant to our society today and in the future, it must prepare its graduates with the knowledge, skills and dispositions to create a healthy, just, and sustainable society that provides opportunities for success to all its members. Higher education must become a part of that changing society and it must change with the evolving, sustainable society. It is the responsibility of each of us who works in and with the higher education enterprise to ensure that it does.

Paul Rowland
Executive Director
Association for the Advancement of Sustainability in Higher Education

1

INTRODUCTION

What's Required to Take EfS to the Next Level?

Dedee DeLongpré Johnston and Lucas F. Johnston

Student and employer demand, high-level institutional commitment, and faculty interest are inspiring the integration of sustainability themes into higher educa-tion curricula and research agendas. Generally, Education for Sustainability (EfS) has evolved from the study of the environment to a broader study of humans' relationship with the environmental resources that support life on this planet. The growth and expansion of this field has created synergetic relationships between the life sciences, social sciences, humanities, and professional schools. Scholarship is crossing disciplinary boundaries to draw on the resources needed to craft answers to society's most pressing challenges. Organizing principles, like problem-based learning, facilitate this cross-disciplinary work and illustrate the interconnectedness of issues and fields of practice. Because moving toward sustainability requires multidisciplinary collaboration, questions and challenges arise around tenure track and promotional requirements for faculty, funding, budgeting, and academic/disciplinary homes for faculty and students (Rowland *et al.* 2009). Additionally, models of integration vary from infusion into courses throughout the curriculum to the establishment of sustainability as a unique academic discipline.

There is a paradigm shift underway in society. Many have suggested that North American and Western European societies are undergoing a transformation away from twentieth century resource intensive and extractive modes of produc-tion and wealth creation. The culmination of such a paradigm shift, however, requires a citizenry that is radically more (and more accurately) informed than most of the general public today. The predominant Western mode of education is outdated. The most pressing problems across the globe – famines, armed con-flicts, demographic transitions – are the result of dynamic biophysical, social, and psychological processes. Solving such wicked problems requires an educational system that trains students to be adaptive learners who can anticipate disruptions and envision their solutions and attendant opportunities at multiple scales – from the local to the geopolitical. Most classroom experiences do not currently reflect this general need. Often times, in spite of institutional demand, faculty members seem reluctant to cede control over the curriculum to make possible more innovative curricular developments. It is their notoriously conservative and slow response to social and market needs that results in this dearth of graduates who have a vision of what a sustainable career, much less a society, looks like.

Nevertheless there are several levers that are driving change, not the least of which are the faculty leaders who recognize the value of educating students to be interdisciplinary problem-solvers. Perhaps even more important, however, are external drivers such as funding bodies and potential employers. These significant pressures can shape the educational mission and pedagogy of higher education institutions. Funding agencies are, themselves, demanding cross-disciplinary collaboration and an articulation of sustainability-focused metrics from applicants. Employers who are recruiting graduates with interdisciplinary educational backgrounds see a distinct advantage in the competitive global marketplace. They are increasingly interested in taking advantage of the public relations benefits of sustainability, as well as the significant advantages of increased employee retention and productivity. Graduates are articulating a desire for employment in organizations that demonstrate a commitment to shared values.

For students educated in sustainability, theory and practice are coming together at the intersection of classrooms and co-curricular experiences. The leading edge of change in sustainability studies and sciences has begun to provide a vision of a world where the integrity of ecosystem services is envisioned as an important prerequisite for flourishing social systems. Some of the low-hanging fruits in this transition have been the relatively expeditious changes made on campuses, from efficiency gains in physical plant operations to movements underway in student life. Students engaged in co-curricular opportunities are benefitting from the hands-on opportunities to apply principles of sustainability to real-world scenarios. The academe has arguably also, although haltingly at first, begun a similar transition.

Because the curriculum is primarily the responsibility of the faculty, change must also be initiated by them. To that end, the Association for the Advancement of Sustainability in Higher Education (AASHE) has hosted curriculum workshops since 2006 that have reached more than 340 faculty, administrators, and graduate students, representing more than 200 campuses (AASHE 2010: 2). The success of these workshops, according to facilitators Geoff Chase and Peggy Barlett, is the empowerment of faculty leaders on campuses to foster the creativity of their colleagues in creating change. The impact of these workshops at

Barlett's home institution, Emory University, for instance, has been profound. After seven years of faculty workshops, nearly 80% of all departments on campus offer at least one sustainability-related course. According to a recent survey, pedagogical innovations included new readings on sustainability topics (58% of respondents used such readings), generation of new units or modules related to sustainability (64% of respondents), new laboratories, exercises, or research projects (44% of respondents), and transformed courses (34% of respondents). With well over 300 participants from varying institutions in the national workshops, these offerings will continue to initiate positive transformations in campus culture. With a membership of about 1,140 academic institutions and associated businesses, the hosting organization, AASHE, can be considered the nationwide clearinghouse for the most important trends toward sustainability in higher education.

Following a *Summit on Sustainability in the Curriculum* in February 2010 in San Diego, CA, AASHE published a *Call to Action* (AASHE 2010).[1] The *Call to Action* outlines the challenges inherent in curricular change, including the scale of the issue (there are 1.2 million faculty in the United States alone), the multiplicity of curricula on campuses (from general education to graduate education and co-curricular education), the interdisciplinary nature of education for sustainability, and the diversity of types and sizes of educational institutions. Among the opportunities noted in the report is the acknowledgment that the work of faculty is supported by a network that includes "students, staff, administrators, employers, accreditation agencies, foundations, and non-governmental organizations" (AASHE 2010: 3). Collaborative partnerships among these stakeholder groups provide the leverage for expediting the curricular changes necessary to support teaching and research for sustainability.

In November 2010, following the San Diego event, the US Department of Education hosted another sustainability summit in Washington, DC. Speakers at this summit emphasized that the US Departments of Labor and Education are looking toward partnerships between four-year and two-year institutions of higher education to lead the green jobs revolution.[1] While questions were raised about broader workforce demand for graduates educated in sustainability, the clearly outlined expectation was that the educational system would inform the workforce about the case for a transition to sustainability. This expectation was not limited to institutions of higher education. The *Call to Action* was directed at the K-20 system in the US – kindergarten through graduate-level education.[2]

According to Debra Rowe, President of the US Partnership for Education for Sustainable Development, many countries across the globe have national strategy plans in place for education for sustainability (see chapter 4, this volume). US Secretary for Education Arne Duncan acknowledged that educators play an essential role in preparing students for jobs in the green economy, and that they also prepare them for their roles as environmentally literate and responsible citizens. Most importantly, he also acknowledged that the Department of Education had not yet done enough to lead this effort.[3]

This book is an attempt to provide a glimpse of the ways in which sustainability is being integrated into education. The focus is on the ways in which a wide variety of campuses are making positive steps toward EfS. There have been advances in K-12 education, which is important, since the willingness and ability of students to engage effectively in such work at the college level is, of course, affected by the quality and character of their K-12 education. But this volume primarily provides an accounting of undergraduate and graduate education, including elaboration on the role of partnerships with disciplinary associations and accrediting agencies, and raises questions about who creates drivers for change in the short, medium and long term. In addition, it explores different ways of integrating sustainability into the curriculum, from including it as a general education requirement (as at the College of the Menominee Nation, see chapter 6, this volume), to an organizing principle for a graduate program (see chapter 5, this volume). Also included are examples of programs that are preparing professional students for the new green economy (as in some of the professional schools, see chapters 7–9, this volume). Finally, there are examples of effective, sustainability-oriented problem-based learning experiments in post-secondary education (see chapters 10–12).

It is also important, however, to elaborate on what this book is not. It does not aim to be a complete set of answers that will guide a campus in a curricular transformation. It has become clear that many sustainability challenges must be resolved in a manner appropriate for each specific campus culture. Wake Forest University hosted a conference in February 2010 in Winston-Salem, North Carolina, titled, *Taking It to the Next Level: Strategies for Adaptation across the Sustainability Curriculum*, which highlighted the importance of site-specific curricular adaptation. Several cases that were presented at the conference are highlighted in Section 5: Transformational Approaches. The conference challenged participants to consider questions such as:

- Should sustainability be infused into every academic discipline, or should it emerge as a unique multidisciplinary field?
- In the case of multidisciplinary collaborations across departments, where should faculty be housed and how are funds and time allocated?
- Are multidisciplinary fields rigorous enough to stand up to academic scrutiny, or are they less rigorous alternatives to single discipline studies?
- Should faculty be rewarded for researching and publishing across disciplines and for securing cross-disciplinary grants? If so, how?
- How is sustainability different than other multidisciplinary fields? Are co-curricular opportunities for applied learning particularly important in this emerging field? Is career development for sustainability different than general career development?

These are important questions, and ones that must be answered to approach sustainability in any educational institution. This volume does not, nor does it seek to, completely answer these questions; the answers are ultimately local and specific, not generalizable.

What this volume does provide, however, is a foundation for exploring curricular change, or rather some blueprints of strategies that have (or in some cases, have not) worked in particular circumstances. These blueprints may variously provide inspiration, guidance, and instruction for others seeking to take education for sustainability to the next level. In this transition, there is no single answer or silver bullet that will create a learning environment which ensures our species' and civilizations' meaningful long-term prospects. Broad outlines, however, do exist and this volume presents some promising strategies and anticipated difficulties toward those ends. The approaches here are context-dependent and cannot be uncritically exacted and applied just anywhere. But they may help to shape how those working at all educational levels think about the ways in which education can and must be transformed. They illustrate some of the inclusive and deliberative community and political processes that can lead to sustainable learning outcomes.

Outline of Chapters

The volume is divided into five sections: Section 1: Understanding the Landscape for Change; Section 2: Sustainability Across the Curriculum: Strategies and Tactics; Section 3: Educating the Professional; Section 4: Problem-Based Learning; and Section 5: Transformational Approaches.

Section 1: Understanding the Landscape for Change begins with a contribution from Meredith College. The college initiated a sustainability program following a 2010 survey of freshmen, which demonstrated significant student interest in sustainability programming. Although like many colleges and universities Meredith continues to suffer from budget constraints, individual faculty and staff continue to drive change by participating in sustainability-oriented training, and integrating systems thinking and sustainability themes into courses. Next, the contribution from the team from the School of Environment and Natural Resources at The Ohio State University illuminates some of the strategies they have employed to gather student input as they design and grow their sustainability-oriented course offerings (Bruskotter *et al.*). This data may act as a helpful reference for other institutions considering the development of sustainability-oriented coursework. Finally, Debra Rowe and Lucas Johnston's analysis compares the relative successes and differences in approaches between disciplinary associations in the US, Mexico, and Sweden. The chapter concludes with a discussion of a possible international common ground for sustainability learning outcomes.

Section 2: Sustainability Across the Curriculum: Strategies and Tactics details some different approaches to bringing sustainability to educational settings and provides some helpful data about how to actualize curricular developments. In undergraduate and graduate schools, education for sustainability has typically followed one of two patterns: the "infusion" model, in which sustainability is broadly integrated into existing curricula, and the "distinct discipline" model, wherein sustainability or sustainable development is envisioned as a distinctive interdisciplinary field. Karim *et al.* examine the organizational structure of a graduate program that illustrates the latter strategy – the distinct discipline model. Varying interpretations and definitions of sustainability have been obstacles to both program administrators and students. These authors offer a methodology for formulating sustainability-related problems in a contextually appropriate manner, and a framework for communicating the values that are central in education for sustainability. For an example of an alternative model, William Van Lopik's account from the College of the Menominee Nation is particularly instructive. There, the Sustainable Development Program encourages the integration of sustainability themes in courses across the curriculum (the "infusion model"), but also mandates that all students take an Introduction to Sustainable Development course as a general education requirement.

While both of the models above educate students about sustainability in general, historically little attention has been paid to profession-specific education for sustainability.

Section 3: Educating the Professional addresses this lacuna by providing perspectives on educating graduate-level professionals, in various fields, for sustainability competency. Chapters included here detail challenges and opportunities which emerged from novel programs integrating sustainability into education for healthcare (Rich and Wadhwa), engineering (Minster *et al.*), and the hospitality and tourism industries (Millar *et al.*).

Section 4: Problem-Based Learning explores pedagogies related to teaching "big ideas." In the first case, Savelyeva introduces readers to the Global Seminar program, which focuses on intensive and international faculty–student interaction, and includes faculty from the US, Mexico, Costa Rica, Italy, Australia, Sweden, Honduras, South Africa, Germany, Austria, China, and Denmark. Narrowing the focus to the local, Farrell's chapter examines the creation of the Campus Ecology class and accompanying textbook at St. Olaf College (Northfield, Minnesota), detailing some strategies for helping students draw connections between everyday choices and broader scale (even global) environmental impacts. Next, Barber and Rousseau's chapter examines the "living home," an interdisciplinary curricular development at Lethbridge College (Canada) that engages engineering, interior design, and multimedia production students in building homes with attributes appropriate for specific climates. Helping students make such connections will increasingly be the task of teachers who must themselves be able to think and work across disciplinary boundaries. Ultimately, it becomes clear that sustainability may require a shift in cultural and educational priorities, and a new vision of what constitutes a good teacher.

Section 5: Transformational Approaches explores the outlines of such a shift. Angela Halfacre and her colleagues at Furman University (her home institution) and Middlebury College provide a comparison of different tactics for integration. Furman's *emergent* model of integration affords for the development of new programs for studying and implementing sustainability, resonating to some extent with the approach taken by the College of the Menominee Nation. Middlebury's *adaptive* approach, on the other hand, seeks to integrate sustainability through already existing academic units. Also covered in this section is Canada's first College of Sustainability at Dalhousie University, which houses the Environment, Sustainability and Society program, an undergraduate double major program in which students earn simultaneous degrees in sustainability and a more traditional discipline, ensuring that students from across the university's academic foci are exposed to education for sustainability (see Wright's contribution). Next, Charles Redman and Arnim Wiek suggest that a significant transformation in current modes of education is a prerequisite to a sustainable society. Based on Redman's experience as the Founding Director of Arizona State's School of Sustainability, they suggest that student learning outcomes must include a capacity for systems thinking, as well as anticipatory, normative, strategic, and interpersonal competences. To provide these skills, educational institutions need to become more adaptive problem- and future-oriented bodies. Finally, Vice Provost for Undergraduate Academics at St. Mary's College (CA), Richard Carp, concludes the volume by arguing (echoing some of Redman's suggestions) that because the academy is complicit in the practices that are indicative of an unsustainable society, a sustainable culture requires re-imagining the purpose of higher education, and the relationships between teachers and learners.

One of the most important seeds of a sustainable culture is the compassion that Paul Rowland so eloquently highlights in his foreword: a willingness to engage others with distinctly different value sets and priorities from a standpoint of compassion and humility. Whether such a radical proposal will gain widespread traction in higher education, traditionally one of the most insular institutions in the Western world, remains to be seen. But the growing scholarly and popular attention to sustainability signals that the beginnings of such transformations are already underway.

Notes

1   Editor's notes from the summit.
2   See http://www.ed.gov/news/speeches/citizenship-and-pathways-green-economy-remarks-under-secretary-martha-kanter-sustainab, accessed 9 July 2011.
3   See http://www.ed.gov/news/speeches/greening-department-education-secretary-duncans-remarks-sustainability-summit, accessed 9 July 2011.

References

Association for the Advancement of Sustainability in Higher Education (AASHE), 2010. *A Call to Action*, available at http://www.aashe.org/files/A_Call_to_Action_final(2). pdf (accessed 9 July 2011).

Rowland, Paul, *et al.*, 2009. Roundtable: reluctant professors. *Sustainability: The Journal of Record*, **2**(6): 341–347.

SECTION 1

Understanding the Landscape for Change

2

THE EMERGING ENVIRONMENTAL SUSTAINABILITY PROGRAM AT MEREDITH COLLEGE

Exploring Student and Faculty Interest and Participation

Laura Fieselman and Erin Lindquist

Early Development of the Sustainability Curriculum at Meredith College

Meredith College Background

Meredith College, located in Raleigh, North Carolina (USA) is an independent private women's college focused on liberal arts undergraduate education with several coeducational graduate programs. Chartered in 1891 as the Baptist Female University, the college became independent in 1997. In 2011 the College enrolled over 1980 students. Meredith College's history and character introduced several unique elements to campus sustainability work, including the College's heritage as a Baptist institution, the presence of only female undergraduate students, and its location in the southeastern United States. As a women's institution, women's leadership and issues often framed campus conversation and culture. And, like many colleges and universities in the Southeast, Meredith College faced the unique challenge of embracing its Southern heritage and customs while working toward campus change, including curriculum development related to sustainability.

The "Greening" of Meredith College

Students at Meredith College pursued learning about environmental sustainability outside the classroom before faculty talked about integrating the subject matter more formally into the curriculum. Angels for the Environment formed in 1997 as the student environmental club on campus. The club's mission was to create a more sustainable campus and to promote awareness of environmental issues on the Meredith campus and in the Raleigh area.

The concept of "greening" was first introduced to Meredith College campus as a strategic objective in 2001 by Janice C. Swab, Professor of Biology in a document submitted to the Senior Management Team titled "Planning for a 'Greening' of the Meredith College Campus" (Swab 2001). This initial introduction to sustainability began:

> If Meredith College is to fulfill its role to educate its students…for life in the 21st century, it must rethink its values and concepts as they relate to the natural environment. The word "green" implies an attempt to move toward the concept of sustainability – meeting present needs without compromising the ability of future generations to meet their needs.

Five years later, in the fall of 2006, the Meredith Student Government Association President Megan Hembree asked her Executive Committee to focus their attention on the campus' level of "environmental friendliness." Student research found that "Meredith's environmental efforts did not compare favorably with many of the…[other] campuses reviewed" (Thie 2006). The student government unanimously supported hiring a full-time staff position to support the college's environmental efforts, requiring that the position collaborate with schools and departments on campus.

Early Sustainability Curriculum Efforts at Meredith College

In 2007, Angels for the Environment helped Meredith College celebrate its first Earth Day with the signing of the Talloires Declaration by President Hartford. The Talloires Declaration, drafted by University Leaders for a Sustainable Future (1990), was the first official statement made by university administrators of a commitment to environmental sustainability in higher education. At the signing of the Declaration, the College committed to teaching for sustainability, or at least environmental literacy, though no immediate action was taken.

That same year, the university approved hiring a full time Sustainability Coordinator, whose responsibilities included, "work[ing] with the Meredith faculty, the Academic Deans and Department Heads and the Academic Programs Division to integrate sustainability initiatives and practices into their curriculum." The position was filled in July 2008.

In February 2008 and 2009, Meredith College participated in Focus the Nation's National Teach-Ins. In 2008 the event was the largest national teach-in in United States history; the topic of conversation was global climate change. At Meredith College, over 100 faculty, staff, students, and visitors attended a teach-in panel featuring panelists from the Environmental Defense Fund, Greenpeace, North Carolina State University's Department of Forestry and Environmental Resources, and Meredith College. Again in 2009, Meredith participated in the national dialogue. Faculty interest and participation increased from 2008, with six faculty, two guest speakers, and several staff joining over 100 students for cross-disciplinary conversation on climate change through panel discussions, film screenings, and a campus chapel service dedicated to the teach-in.

Annually Meredith College names a campus theme to invite the community to explore complex problems through discussion, reading, and hands-on experiences. In 2008–2009 the theme was "Sustaining our Environment: Developing our Greenprint." Throughout the year, campus focused on environmental issues through the Summer Reading Program selection, Al Gore's *An Inconvenient Truth*, and invited lecture series speakers which included Greenpeace Executive Director John Passacantando, Animal Planet Host Jeff Corwin, and documentarian and environmental ambassador Celine Cousteau. The newly formed Office of Sustainability was tasked with developing the campus Greenprint, the roadmap for integrating sustainability at Meredith College. The sustainability coordinator began crafting the Greenprint by visiting a cross section of campus groups, including Student Government Association, Faculty Council, Deans and Department Heads, College Programs, Facilities Services, Institutional Advancement, and Senior Management Team, in addition to hosting open sessions co-facilitated by a Green Team.[1] The following questions were posed to each group:

- What is the vision for sustainability at Meredith College?
- What are the most pressing priorities?

Groups compiled their responses using the community visioning model.[2] Values, goals, and priorities that arose repeatedly among the groups were compiled into the Meredith College Greenprint by the Office of Sustainability and approved by the Senior Management Team in July 2009. The campus vision for sustainability included the statement:

> We, at Meredith College, are committed to a balance between environmental conservation, social justice, and economic consideration. We are working as a united community to deepen our education and spread awareness of environmental sustainability. We take responsibility to challenge ourselves, think differently and take action accordingly. In considering our legacy, we conserve resources and reconsider our needs. We are creating enduring solutions on our campus that are holistic, collaborative and proactive, and are engaged in crafting a healthy, safe and comfortable future for the globe.

Goal 1 read "Meredith College will educate the campus community about sustainability," with Outcome 1.4 "Faculty will weave sustainability into the curriculum where applicable." Action Steps listed under this outcome included:

ACTION STEP: Identify and promote existing course connections to sustainability.
ACTION STEP: Use sustainability case studies throughout the existing curriculum.
ACTION STEP: Consider one or more of the following: major or minor in sustainability, Summer Reading Program grounded in sustainability, sustainability as an element of the First Year Experience, certificate program in sustainability, or General Education sustainability thread.
ACTION STEP: Expand opportunities for using the physical campus and operations as a learning laboratory.

This goal and outcome first formalized the College's intention to integrate sustainability into campus academics by exploring a variety of curricular avenues.

Cross-disciplinary Faculty Collaboration to Explore Sustainability in the Curriculum

Sustainability Teaching and the Learning Circle

Faculty first came together formally to discuss sustainability across the curriculum at the joint invitation from the Vice President of Academic Affairs and the Sustainability Coordinator. Initially proposed as a faculty working group that "would develop and recommend a 'greenprint' for weaving sustainability into academics at Meredith College," the group was comprised of faculty that already incorporated sustainability into their classrooms by engaging students in understanding and addressing economic, social, and environmental dimensions of sustainability. Eleven faculty joined the group at its beginning in the spring semester of 2009. As the group discussed possible directions for the curriculum, the need to simply share current projects and support each other in teaching and learning sustainability became apparent. The group dubbed themselves the Sustainability Teaching and Learning Circle (STLC), and focused on a variety of sustainability-related classroom and service projects. The STLC faced the challenges of developing an Environmental Sustainability major and minor in fall 2009, and then developed the sustainability conversation across the curriculum in summer 2010. The group grew as it reached out to campus leaders who supported a variety of special programs; by summer 2010 the STLC included twenty faculty.

Some of the faculty started collaborative projects across different courses and disciplines as a result of their participation in the STLC. For example, E. Lindquist and Matthew Stutz in Geosciences have collaborated on two projects. Stutz developed a semester-long curriculum in his Environmental Resources class which involved doing a greenhouse gas inventory for Meredith College using the Clean Air-Cool Planet Campus Carbon Calculator™.[3] E. Lindquist had her Environmental Science class develop carbon education modules for the campus community which used the findings from Stutz's class and individual student-led energy audits to design lifestyle change modules to decrease the campus' carbon footprint. As a result of the incorporation of these learner-centered, civic-engagement projects, the student evaluations of the course as a whole improved (Table 2.1).

Courses Across the Curriculum

The STLC inspired the Meredith Director of General Education, Paul Winterhoff, in concert with the sustainability coordinator, to compile a list of sustainability-related courses offered at the College. The information was gathered initially by targeting specific faculty, and then later by an all-faculty survey:

> For the information of the whole community – and especially students – we are attempting to catalogue all those courses that give substantial focus to environmental sustainability related content and activities. We want to feature a list… that might lead students to your courses because of this content. Meredith does not currently have a sustainability requirement… However, that need not limit us from identifying those courses – across the entire curriculum – that educate students about the variety of areas in which they can study and learn sustainability.
>
> *(Winterhoff 2009)*

TABLE 2.1 Comparison of student evaluations of Environmental Science before (2008, $n = 9$) and after (2010, $n = 5$; 2011, $n = 12$) the incorporation of a collaborative, learner-centered sustainability curriculum at Meredith College. For questions 1–3, students rated each statement on a scale from 1 to 4: 1 = disagree, 2 = tend to disagree, 3 = tend to agree, and 4 = agree. For question 4, the scale ranged from 1 to 5: 1 = much less than, 2 = less than, 3 = about the same, 4 = more than, and 5 = much more. Class averages are given, and the college average is in parentheses for each parameter and year (not available for 2011)

Question	2008	2010	2011
1. I understand the major concepts/principles covered by this course.	2.8 (3.5)	4 (3.6)	3.6
2. I am able to apply the concepts and principles covered by this course.	2.8 (3.5)	4 (3.6)	3.7
3. As a result of taking this course, my interest in this subject matter has increased.	2.3 (3.1)	4 (3.2)	3.3
4. Overall, how much do you feel you have learned in this course compared to other courses you have taken?	3.1 (3.7)	4.8 (3.9)	4.2

Faculty responses required a brief description of "sustainability-related assign-ments, tests, presentations, or other activities … [where] 'other' could include field trips, speakers, artistic displays or products." Screened by this description, a list was first compiled in 2009 which included a diversity of subjects from across campus including foreign language, art, biology, English, design, music, and political science courses.

The listing was problematic because the request to faculty did not define sustainability, nor did it offer parameters for the extent to which sustainability was part of a course. The Sustainability Tracking, Rating, and Assessment System (STARS), a program of the Association for the Advancement of Sustainability in Higher Education (AASHE), was developed to assign institutions credits for achieving sustainability across campus operations, education and research, and planning, administration and engagement. In its Phase 1.0, STARS offered credits for an inventory of academic offerings because such a list provides a baseline and foundation for advancing a sustainability curriculum, can help institutions identify strengths and opportunities for growth, and helps students to find and understand sustainability course offerings. The criteria required by STARS include an institution-developed definition of sustainability in the curriculum that distinguishes between sustainability-focused and sustainability-related courses:

> **Sustainability-focused courses** concentrate on the concept of sustaina-bility, including its social, economic, and environmental dimensions, or examine an issue or topic using sustainability as a lens. **Sustainability-related courses** incorporate sustainability as a distinct course component or module, or concentrate on a single sustainability principle or issue.
>
> *(AASHE 2010)*

To remedy the discrepancies created during the first collection of sustainability courses on campus, the group met during the 2010 fall semester to refresh the course listing to ensure its clarity and comprehensiveness.[4] Specific learning outcomes were defined for the two course categories (sustainability-focused and sustainability-related) and each designated course was expected to meet all outcomes within its category (Table 2.2). The STLC designated a sustainability-liaison for each department (largely STLC members), and as a group they reviewed the course syllabi to determine if courses met either of the two catego-ries' outcomes. In addition to attracting students to the general education courses because of their documented interest in further sustainability education (see Exploring a Sustainability Major and Minor at Meredith College below), the course designations will be used for several campus initiatives including inclusion of new courses into the environmental sustainability major and minor, and future exploration of a sustainability requirement in the general education program.

TABLE 2.2 Learning outcomes for the sustainability-related and sustainability-focused courses across the Meredith College campus. Designated courses are highlighted and coordinated through Meredith's general education program. Outcomes were derived from STARS (2010). Faculty sustainability-liaisons and members of the Sustainability Teaching and Learning Circle (STLC) were asked to review course syllabi to determine what outcomes they met

---

After taking a sustainability-related course at Meredith, students should:

- effectively communicate the concept of sustainability;
- make connections between their chosen course of study and sustainability;
- think critically about existing assumptions, information quality, and data interpretation when identifying and addressing problems related to sustainability.

After taking a sustainability-focused course at Meredith, students should:

- synthesize knowledge of the scientific, social, political, and economic aspects of sustainability and apply it to issues of sustainability;
- use creativity to develop sustainable solutions to complex problems;
- apply interdisciplinary knowledge and skills to the workplace and community.

Living Learning Laboratories

In 2010, encouraged by the growing number of classroom projects and campus spaces related to sustainability, the sustainability coordinator compiled a list of Meredith Sustainability Learning Laboratories, modeled on Furman University's Sustainability Living/Learning Laboratories (see chapter 13, this volume for more on Furman University's contributions). This listing includes the Meredith Forest, student reuse store, and the rainwater harvesting lake, among other featured spaces on campus.[5]

Multi-Institution Trillium Workshop

At the Wake Forest's curriculum conference "Taking It to the Next Level: Strategies for Adaptation across the Sustainability Curriculum" in March 2010, the authors and their interdisciplinary colleagues in the Triangle (Raleigh–Durham–Chapel Hill) and Triad (Greensboro–Winston-Salem–High Point) areas of North Carolina discussed hosting a workshop on sustainability curricula after hearing Dr. Peggy Barlett speak of the Ponderosa and Piedmont Projects at Northern Arizona University and Emory University, respectively. With the leadership of Dr. Charlotte Clark at Duke University, the group hosted Dr. Barlett for a two-day workshop at Duke in May 2010 to train the faculty participants to work with their home institution faculty to develop new sustainability curricula across their campuses. Participants became familiar with the faculty development approach utilized by the Ponderosa and Piedmont projects through varied workshops, which included hearing from local experts and exploring local environments, discussing pedagogical techniques for campus leadership, making interdisciplinary connections, and developing opportunities for students' civic engagement. A focus on place was emphasized throughout the workshop. A diversity of institution types participated, from large (3) and small (1) public universities to large (1) and small (2) private institutions. After the workshop, Clark generated a website where the group – named Trillium by the participants – could continue to share ideas and collaborations.

Meredith College had its Sustainability Coordinator (L. Fieselman), one administrator (Associate Vice President of Academic Programs), and seven faculty (including E. Lindquist) representing seven disciplines (Biology, Child Development, Communications, English, Geosciences, Politics, and Psychology) in attendance at the workshop.[6] At the completion of the workshop, the Meredith group was inspired to return to campus and continue the discussion of how to infuse the sustainability curriculum into all facets of the academic program including general education and special programs such as service learning, research, ethical leadership, and a new initiative in critical thinking. A Piedmont- style on campus workshop was held for Meredith faculty in May 2011 on campus.

While faculty began to address sustainability across the curriculum on campus, student demand for sustainability in higher education continued to grow.

Connecting a Sustainability Program to Student Interest and Perception

National Trends

By 2010, sustainability was increasingly influencing admissions decisions. Almost two-thirds (66%) of 15,722 respondents to The Princeton Review's 2009 College Hopes & Worries Survey indicated that they would value having information about a college's commitment to the environment and that it might impact their decision to apply to or attend the school, with 24% responding that this information would "strongly" or "very much" contribute to decisions about which schools to apply to or attend. A survey by researchers at the College of William and Mary of 1,700 students at a diverse group of nine campuses found that "current freshmen are two times more likely to choose their school based on sustainability concerns than the entering freshman class just 3 years ago (13.5% vs. 6.5%, respectively)" (Scheer-Irvine et al. 2008). UCLA's Higher Education Research Institute conducted a 2008 survey of 240,580 first-year, full-time students at 340 four-year institutions, finding that almost half (45.3%) said adopting green practices to protect the environment is "essential" or "very important" to them. It is clear that potential incoming freshman were seeking colleges and universities which demonstrated a commitment to sustainability in academic programming and facility management.

Sustainability Literacy Assessment at Meredith College

The College began administering an annual Sustainability Literacy Assessment to all incoming freshmen beginning in 2009. The assessment was designed to gauge students' understanding of and beliefs about sustainability, record their participation in environmentally preferable behaviors, and document interest in learning more about sustainability-related issues while in college. Designed as a pre-post survey, the assessment will be given again as the students leave campus as graduating seniors.[7]

Incoming freshmen agreed that understanding environmental sustainability and learning more in this area are important (see Table 2.3). When asked about motivations for engaging in environmental practices, most students responded that they engage because they believe it will make the world a better place or because they find environmental practices economically beneficial. Fewer students, though, responded that they engage in environmental practices because they had been taught, further indicating the need for Meredith to offer educational resources for environmental sustainability (Table 2.3).

Students' understanding of what sustainability meant to them varied greatly (Figure 2.1), which indicated that part of the discussion about sustainability through the curriculum should center on defining the term and forming a common language. From the results, it was apparent that students' understanding

TABLE 2.3 Meredith College freshmen responses to 2009–2011 Sustainability Literacy Assessments

	2009 (n = 332)	2010 (n = 298)	2011 (n = 301)
Percentage of incoming freshmen that agree with the following statements			
It is important for young adults to understand environmental issues.	97.6%	99.3%	96.3%
I would like to learn more about environmental issues and sustainability while in college.	85.6%	83.7%	83.3%
Percentage of incoming freshmen that agree with the statement, "I engage in environmental practices because…"			
I believe it will make the world a better place.	95.5%	92.9%	92.0%
I find it personally or spiritually rewarding.	73.7%	65.7%	65.9%
I was taught by my family or friends.	67.7%	62.2%	64.1%
I was taught by my school.	57.1%	59.3%	59.3%
I was taught by my community and/or religious organization.	49.7%	47.5%	50.3%
I find them economically beneficial.	81.6%	78.8%	80.9%

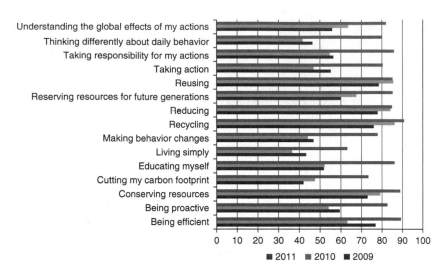

FIGURE 2.1 Percentage of Meredith College students who responded "yes" to the statement, "When I hear 'sustainability' it means to me…" (2009 and 2010). In 2011 the wording of the question was changed to "please rate the importance of how important each of the following are to your definition of sustainability"; data plotted here indicates responses of "important" and "very important." Data was collected from the incoming freshman class in August as part of the Sustainability Literacy Assessment.

of more complex issues related to sustainability, such as carbon footprints, behavioral changes, and living simply, was less developed than their understanding of more basic and popularized aspects of sustainability such as recycling and reusing materials, and reducing consumption. In 2010, the range of variation of students' understanding from simplistic to complex sustainability concepts was even more pronounced (Figure 2.1). Because the more complex sustainability issues fit the institutionally-approved definition of sustainability more than the simple ones, these results emphasize the importance of incorporating the definition and use of sustainability into general education classes.

In 2010 and 2011, five questions were altered or added to the survey to focus more closely on what students wanted from a program in Environmental Sustainability. Data gathered indicate students want to know more about environmental sustainability, but do not necessarily see the classroom as a place to learn this information. Responses to the assessment suggest the college should focus on co-curricular education in addition to classroom sustainability teaching. We see a relatively strong freshmen interest in a sustainability academic program, either minor or major, at Meredith College (60 and 29 people, respectively in 2011) (see Table 2.4).

TABLE 2.4 Incoming Meredith College freshmen responses to questions regarding interest in participating in environmental sustainability education while in college. The survey was administered in August 2010 and 2011

While at Meredith College I would like to...	Percentage of students that agree	
	2010 (n = 298)	2011 (n = 301)
Learn more about environmental issues and sustainability while in college.	83.7%	83.4%
Take a course focused on sustainability.	38.5%	43.0%
Complement my chosen major with the interdisciplinary environmental sustainability minor.	18.0%	20.3%
Either major or double-major in the interdisciplinary environmental sustainability major.	6.2%	9.6%
Participate in a student organization or event focused on sustainability.	61.0%	61.7%

National academic and career trends, combined with the data from the Meredith Sustainability Literacy Assessments, informed the decision to develop an Environmental Sustainability academic program.

Exploring a Sustainability Major and Minor at Meredith College

Program Development at Meredith College

Program development was accelerated in the summer of 2009 when, because of budgetary constraints, Meredith College's Board of Trustees and the Senior Management Team (SMT) proposed eliminating 11 majors that were under-enrolled; the then current BA in Environmental Studies was one of them. Although enrollment in individual environmental classes remained strong, averaging 16 students per class, enrollment in the major itself was low (9 students in fall 2009).

The BA in Environmental Studies major first appeared in the 2003–2004 Meredith course catalog; however the first cohort of students was not enrolled in the program until spring 2007 with the first graduate in December 2009. One of the reasons for the delay was poor marketing of the interdisciplinary major across campus; the majority of the campus believed it was a biology degree because it was administered by the biology department. In addition, the college offered a BS in Biology with a concentration (now career track) in Environmental Science, and most of the students interested in environmental issues enrolled in this major because they had career plans in the sciences. By aligning some of the introductory environmental courses such as Environmental

Science, Environmental Ethics, and Environmental Resources with general education requirements in 2008, faculty were able to attract students to the major through increased enrollment in these classes. Also, during the first years of student recruitment into the BA in Environmental Studies major, as part of a wider departmental program review in 2007–2008, the BA in Environmental Studies program was revised to align the major better with current course offerings across the campus. Key to this process was the interpersonal contact and discussion among the faculty members teaching in the Environmental Studies major. They became more knowledgeable and interested in supporting the major, which had presented an on-going challenge because the Environmental Studies major was housed within the Department of Biological Sciences, despite its interdisciplinary nature.

In fall 2009 faculty redesigned the Environmental Studies major into the Environmental Sustainability major and minor to achieve three goals: (1) to fit with the Meredith College Greenprint's objectives and highlight sustainability education on campus; (2) to emphasize the interdisciplinary nature of the major and attract students from all parts of campus; and (3) to meet the increasing demand for college graduates with a background in sustainability. The proposal was accepted by SMT in late fall 2009, the new major and minor were approved by Meredith's Academic and Faculty Councils in spring 2010, and the Environmental Sustainability major and minor first appeared in the 2010–2011 course catalog.

Given the evidence of green job growth, faculty developed the Environmental Sustainability program to give Meredith College graduates access to a diverse array of potential green careers. Education, conservation, natural history interpretation, design, environmental planning, community planning, sustainability consulting, organizational sustainability, environmental law and policy, public administration, media analysis, and renewable energy are among potential options. The elective structure of the Environmental Sustainability program at Meredith College offered students the choice to tailor a program that fits their professional and career interests.

Environmental Sustainability Program Design

A better balance of scientific, social and economic aspects of sustainability were incorporated into the Environmental Sustainability major compared to the original Environmental Studies major (Appendix A). The revised major reduced the course requirements and total number of credits in the major. This allowed students to double major in Environmental Sustainability and a more discipline-centered major, or minor in other disciplines. It also gave students more choice in electives to cater the major toward their career goals.

The three foundations of the program, (1) science and math, (2) social science, and (3) economics and communication, were developed from a report by the

World Conservation Union (IUCN), "The Future of Sustainability," which recorded that "the core of mainstream sustainability thinking has become the idea of three dimensions, environmental, social and economic sustainability. These have been drawn in a variety of ways, as 'pillars'...or as interlocking circles" (Adams 2006). Faculty incorporated communication courses into the economics foundation because they believed that strong oral, written, and interpersonal communication skills were required for a successful career in environmental sustainability. Careful advice assisted students in selecting the electives across the foundations most appropriate for their career interests. To further develop the interdisciplinary nature of the program and better represent the different environmental disciplines and career options, the pool of faculty advisors was extended beyond the Department of Biological Sciences and students could complete their capstone research or internship experience with a faculty advisor in any department.

Environmental Sustainability Learning Outcomes

After the Environmental Sustainability major and minor were approved by the Faculty and Academic Councils in spring 2010 it was apparent that learning outcomes and methods of assessing the outcomes were needed before students enrolled in the major. Meredith's Director of Research, Planning and Assessment, Dr. Pamela Steinke, facilitated a learning outcome brainstorming session with program teaching faculty. Steinke synthesized the potential outcomes after the meeting into one set of six draft outcomes which were sent to all sustainability teaching faculty for further revision. Students who had completed the program, it was hoped, would:

- understand the balance of scientific, social, political, and economic aspects of environmental sustainability;
- integrate the knowledge and skills from different disciplines and apply this interdisciplinary understanding to issues of sustainability;
- think critically about existing assumptions, information quality, and data interpretation when identifying and addressing problems related to sustainability;
- communicate effectively with people from diverse perspectives and facilitate collaborative relationships to accomplish goals;
- use creativity to develop sustainable solutions to environmental problems;
- act adaptively to apply interdisciplinary knowledge and skills to the workplace and community.

Although there was broad support for the design and learning outcomes of the new interdisciplinary program, there were also unique challenges to creating the major and minor – some financial, and some organizational.

Challenges to the Creation of the Environmental Sustainability Major and Minor

Because the new program was developed in a climate of budgetary constraints, it was created without additional institutional funding for resources, new courses, new faculty, or a program coordinator. The major and minor still remained, therefore, under the administration of the Department of Biological Sciences, even though it was an interdisciplinary major. Because the coordination of the original Environmental Studies major had been done as a departmental duty of the faculty member teaching Environmental Science and advising the students in the major (E. Lindquist), there was no appointed leader for the new Environmental Sustainability program nor course release assigned to the program coordination. As the new major was initiated and faculty involvement in the program grew on campus, it became apparent that the college needed an appointed faculty leader for the sustainability curriculum. In 2011, Meredith College received a generous grant from the Margaret A. Cargill Foundation to support undergraduate research, curriculum development and support, faculty professional development, campus-wide events in environmental sustainability, and a course release for a faculty director of the grant (E. Lindquist). To ensure the grant activities which have the largest impact on student learning, faculty development, and institutional recognition continue after the three-year grant period with college support, assessment of these outcomes will be conducted and documented on an annual basis.

Conclusion and Lessons Learned

As sustainability has become an emerging value at Meredith College in the past ten years, we have begun to integrate sustainability initiatives across campus operations and academics. Sustainability in academics took two distinct directions: the creation of a major and minor in Environmental Sustainability, and the addition of definition and structure to sustainability teachings across the curriculum, with the intention to increase availability of sustainability-related and sustainability-focused courses. The next steps include designing a mechanism to assess student sustainability learning and programming, and adjusting to meet student needs. The academic division must also agree upon a working definition of sustainability for the campus. Through the process of integrating a sustainability curriculum into the Meredith College's major initiatives, we have various recommendations for other academic institutions that plan on initiating or expanding their sustainability programs:

- Begin curricular work by engaging current or latent personal and/or professional sustainability interests of faculty.

- Utilize existing campus expertise wherever possible, inviting outside expertise when appropriate or to re-energize faculty when necessary.
- Actively listen to students' professional interests and create academic opportunities in these areas.
- Initiate and implement changes quickly, as students are eager for sustainability learning opportunities.
- Define and redefine "sustainability" as the campus works together, ensuring students, faculty, and administration are working from a common place.
- Employ AASHE's resource center, events and web conversations for support and guidance.

Notes

1   The Green Team was assembled by the Sustainability Coordinator in the 2008–2009 academic year to facilitate initial campus sustainability conversations. The team was comprised of a voluntary group of interested individuals.
2   Community visioning is a citizen-based process by which the community identifies and defines core values and goals, forming the foundation of a community comprehensive or strategic plan (Mitrofanova 2007).
3   Clean Air-Cool Planet Campus Carbon Calculator™ available at: http://www. cleanair-coolplanet.org/toolkit/inv-calculator.php.
4   See Sustainability Course Offerings at http://www.meredith.edu/academics/gened/.
5   See Meredith Sustainability Living & Learning Laboratories at http://meredith.edu/ sustainability/living-learning-labratories.htm.
6   Meredith's participation in the workshop was funded by a grant from the Margaret A. Cargill Foundation to support the development of the environmental curriculum and research, 2009–2014.
7   The Meredith College Freshmen Sustainability Literacy Assessment is posted online in the Association for the Advancement of Sustainability in Higher Education's Resource Center, http://www.aashe.org/resources.

References

Adams, W.M., 2006. The Future of Sustainability: Re-thinking environment and development in the twenty-first century. Report of the IUCN Renowned Thinkers Meeting, 29–31 January 2006.

Association for the Advancement of Sustainability in Higher Education, 2009. Academic programs in sustainability, Campus Sustainability Resource Center. http://www. aashe.org/resources/programs.php (accessed 1 September 2009).

Association for the Advancement of Sustainability in Higher Education, 2010. *STARS 1.0.1 Technical Manual.* http://www.aashe.org/files/documents/STARS/STARS_ 1.0.1_Technical_Manual.pdf (accessed 19 July 2010).

Focus the Nation, 2008. *Focus the Nation 2008: National Teach-in on Global Warming Solutions.* http://www.focusthenation.org/focus-nation-2008-0 (accessed 21 July 2010).

Focus the Nation, 2009. *Solutions for the First 100 Days: National Teach-in on Global Warming Solutions.* http://www.nationalteachin.org/about.php (accessed 21 July 2010).

Global Insight, 2008. *Current and Potential Green Jobs in the U.S. Economy*. The United States Conference of Mayors Climate Protection Center 2008. http://www.usmayors. org/pressreleases/uploads/greenjobsreport.pdf (accessed 26 July 2010).

Higher Education Research Institute, 2008. Political engagement among college freshmen hits 40-year high. University of California at Los Angeles Graduate School of Education and Information Studies. http://www.gseis.ucla.edu/heri/pr-display.php?prQry=28 (accessed 26 July 2010).

The Meredith College Greenprint: A plan for integrating sustainability, 2009. Meredith College. http://meredith.edu/sustainability/documents/greenprint-plan.pdf (accessed 19 July 2010).

Mitrofanova, Y., 2007. Community Development: Visioning. University of Nebraska-Lincoln Extension in Lancaster County. http://lancaster.unl.edu/community/articles/communityvisioning.shtml (accessed 1 July 2010).

The Princeton Review, 2009. The Princeton Review gives 697 colleges "green" ratings in new 2010 editions of its annual college guides and website profiles of schools. www.princetonreview.com/green/press-release.aspx (accessed 26 July 2010).

Scheer-Irvine, N., Weston, S. and Roberts, 2008. *Campus Greening Efforts: What difference do they make?* The College of William and Mary. http://jtrobe.people.wm.edu/press% 20release%20campus%20greening.pdf (accessed 26 July 2010).

Swab, J., 2001. Planning for a 'greening' of the Meredith College Campus. Unpublished paper, Department of Biological Sciences, Meredith College.

Thie, L., 2006. The Student Government Association's 2006–2007 Budget Request. Unpublished paper, Student Government Association, Meredith College.

TrilliumNC, http://trilliumnc.wordpress.com/ (accessed 26 July 2010).

Appendix A: A Contrast of Required and Elective Courses for the BA in Environmental Studies (2009–2010 Course Catalog) and the BA in Environmental Sustainability (2010–2011 Course Catalog) at Meredith College

For the BA in Environmental Sustainability (second column), students must take 18–19 credits of electives with at least 3 credits in each foundation. Only two courses in the new major (food and nutrition, social psychology) have introductory prerequisites. Courses that could fulfill the General Education requirement are labeled with an asterisk (*). Note that Meredith's General Education program changed prior to the 2009–2010 academic year, but stayed the same for the 2010–2011 year. If more than one course fulfilled one general education requirement, only one course is labeled so that the number of asterisks gives a representation of the quantity of requirements fulfilled by the major.

BA in Environmental Studies (2009–2010) 66 credit hours	*BA in Environmental Sustainability (2010–2011)* 36–38 credit hours
Required Courses in Math and Sciences (33 hours):	*Required Courses (18–19 hours)*
Statistics (3 hours) *	Statistics (3 hours) *
Modern Biological Concepts and lab (4 hours) *	One lab science (4 hours) *
Environmental Science and lab (4 hours)	Environmental Science (4 hours) *
Principles of Ecology and lab (4 hours)	Environmental Resources (3 hours) *
Research in Environmental Studies (3 hours)	Environmental Ethics (3 hours) *
General Chemistry I and lab (4 hours)	Environmental Politics and Policy (3 hours) *
General Chemistry II and lab (4 hours)	Environmental Economics (3 hours) *
Earth Science and lab (4 hours)	Research in discipline of choice (2–3 hours) *
Environmental Resources (3 hours) *	
	Science and Math Foundation Electives
Required Courses in Other Disciplines (12 hours):	Plant Biology and lab (4 hours)
Environmental Ethics (3 hours) *	Animal Biology and lab (4 hours)
Microeconomic Principles (3 hours) *	Aquatic Field Studies (2 hours)
Professional Writing (3 hours)	Terrestrial Field Studies (2 hours)
Environmental Politics & Policy (3 hours) *	Tropical Ecosystems (3 or 4 hours) *
	Principles of Ecology and lab (4 hours)
Biology Electives chosen from the following (6 hours):	General Chemistry I and lab (4 hours)
Plant Biology and lab (4 hours)	General Chemistry II and lab (4 hours)
Animal Biology (4 hours)	GIS (3 hours)
Aquatic Field Studies (2 hours)	Meteorology (3 hours)

(Continued)

BA in Environmental Studies (2009–2010) *66 credit hours*	*BA in Environmental Sustainability (2010–2011)* *36–38 credit hours*
Terrestrial Field Studies (2 hours) Tropical Ecosystems (3 or 4 hours) *Electives chosen from the following (15 hours):* Writing for the Media (3 hours) Public Policy Economics (3 hours) GIS (3 hours) Meteorology (3 hours) Intro to Public History (3 hours) International Politics (3 hours) State and Local Government (3 hours) Topics in Model United Nations (3 hours) Social Problems (3 hours) Population Dynamics (3 hours)	*Social Foundation Electives* Ceramics (3 hours) ★ Interior Design Materials (3 hours) Perspectives in Food and Nutrition (3 hours) World Regional Geography (3 hours) ★ Intro to Public History (3 hours) International Politics (3 hours) State and Local Government (3 hours) ★ Topics in Model United Nations (3 hours) Social Problems (3 hours) ★ Population Dynamics (3 hours) Social Psychology (3 hours) *Economics and Communication Foundation Electives* Microeconomic Principles (3 hours) ★ Macroeconomic Principles (3 hours) ★ Professional Writing (3 hours) ★ Writing for the Media (3 hours) ★ Public Speaking (3 hours) ★ Introduction to Public Relations (3 hours)

3

UNDERSTANDING STUDENT ENVIRONMENTAL INTERESTS WHEN DESIGNING MULTIDISCIPLINARY CURRICULA

Jeremy T. Bruskotter, Gregory E. Hitzhusen, Robyn S. Wilson, and Adam Zwickle

Introduction

Commitments to sustainability in higher education are gaining historic momentum. Schools of forestry and natural resources arose around the start of the twentieth century to address multiple crises of resource management; another wave of environmental programs emerged with the Earth Day era; at the start of the twenty-first century, increasing attention to climate change, biodiversity loss, energy and food security, and other issues has raised sustainability concerns to critical levels of broader engagement. Organizations such as the Association for the Advancement of Sustainability in Higher Education (AASHE), the Disciplinary Associations Network for Sustainability (DANS), and the Presidents' Climate Commitment reflect the growing consensus that sustainability must be a guiding force in education.

Investment in sustainability at The Ohio State University (OSU), one of the largest Universities in the United States, has paralleled these larger trends. The School of Environment and Natural Resources (SENR) was established in 1968 as a multidisciplinary unit to provide integrative research and education in environmental and natural resource management. SENR is associated with the College of Food, Agricultural and Environmental Sciences (CFAES), which began to address resource management issues in the early twentieth century; by 1990, CFAES adopted an "Ecological Paradigm" – a model that guides its efforts both in research and education. The ecological paradigm includes four areas of focus: environmental compatibility, social responsibility, economic viability, and production efficiency. In addition, CFAES listed Environmental Quality and Sustainability as one of its three signature program areas. In 2008, OSU's president Gordon Gee joined over 700 other college and university leaders in signing the Presidents' Climate Commitment, which pledges to make "sustainability a part of the educational experience for all students," and established a President's Council on Sustainability. Meanwhile, interest in environmental and sustainability curricula is increasing university-wide. In 2009, the description of General Education Curriculum goals for all OSU undergraduates was amended to include the goal of educating "engaged and responsible global citizens," which partially reflects these sustainability goals.[1]

Thus, to some extent, the entire university now seeks to achieve the sort of sustainability goals that occasioned the creation of SENR and units like it around the country[2], and which drove their interdisciplinary evolution particularly between biophysical and social sciences. As Ohio State and other institutions move to incorporate sustainability across their entire curriculum, including the humanities, arts, business, and other well-suited domains, insights from the microcosm of existing schools like SENR can inform these larger efforts. The integration of coursework in social and biophysical sciences has evolved through many obstacles in curricular units like SENR, and similar challenges exist for university-wide sustainable learning goals.

For decades, the main (though not only) source for environmental classes at Ohio State was SENR, but many other disciplinary units have increasingly shaped a focus around the environment. In addition to this growth, a university-mandated shift from quarters to semesters has provided the opportunity to re-design and better integrate the curriculum for all units at Ohio State. The effort to revise the curriculum during the shift to semesters occasioned the present study, developed by SENR social science faculty, to gain a better understanding of undergraduate interests in courses, programs, and careers in natural resources management and environmental sustainability, and ultimately, to modify our curriculum to provide students with the expertise they need to be successful in careers focused on environmental stewardship and natural resources management. Specifically, objectives of the study described here include:

1. determining students' environmental attitudes, environmental risk perception, and sense of responsibility and ability to address environmental issues across a variety of academic disciplines
2. determining the types of environmentally responsible behaviors in which students are engaged
3. assessing students' interest (demand for) various social and biophysical science courses focused on the environment and sustainability
4. assessing students' likelihood of taking an environmental course and pursuing an environmentally focused minor, major, and career.

The results of this survey provide valuable insight about the interdisciplinary opportunities in sustainability curricula, and provide baseline information to help deepen and clarify the conversation about "goals, objectives, learning outcomes, underpinnings and nomenclature" of education for sustainability.[3] The information contained herein will be relevant to other programs that are seeking to establish or adapt their curricula to meet the needs of the next generation of natural resource managers and environmental stewards.

Study Methods

Assessment of student environmental interests, awareness, attitudes, and values is challenging, and is not often coordinated with critical or strategic attention to sustainability curriculum design.[4] We were interested in the extent to which environmental attitudes, behavior, and concern, among other factors (i.e. sense of responsibility and efficacy), helped explain students' interests in environmental course topics, as well as program and career interests. We sought to correlate these background, interest, and disciplinary variables with environmental topic, program, and career preferences to help us to improve interdisciplinary programming for SENR students, while also expanding and re-thinking our curriculum to consider opportunities to achieve a broader integration with the humanities and to better engage students outside SENR and CFAES.

Sampling

The population of interest for this study included undergraduate students enrolled at The Ohio State University. The University registrar provided the sampling frame, which contained email addresses for all undergraduate students who registered for courses during the most recent quarter (i.e. winter 2010). Because we were interested in making comparisons between students in CFAES and those residing in other academic units, our sampling approach drew all available email addresses from students within CFAES (~2,100) and a random sample of 8,000 across other academic units (stratified by rank, i.e. freshman-sophomore, junior-senior).[5]

Method

We attempted to contact students three times via their university email accounts during the spring of 2010. Emails were sent to CFAES students on three consecutive weeks during the month of March, while students in the university-wide sample were contacted during May. Students were sent an email that explained the purpose of the study (i.e., to "…inform the development of a new environmentally focused curriculum") and provided a link to the online survey. In total, we received 306 responses from the CFAES sample and 969 responses from the university-wide sample, providing response rates of 15% and 12%, respectively. A total of 1,032 responses were complete enough to be included in these analyses.

TABLE 3.1 Measures contained within the survey, the number of items within each measure, and measure citations (where applicable)

Measure	Number of items	Source
Environmentally responsible behaviors	11	Adapted from Stern 2000
Environmental attitudes	8	New Ecological Paradigm Scale adapted from Dunlap *et al.* 2000
Risk perception	4	Adapted from Leiserowitz 2005
Perceived responsibility	1	Constructed for this survey
Perceived self-efficacy	1	Constructed for this survey
Course topics	17	Constructed for this survey
Likelihood of taking an environmental course	1	Constructed for this survey
Likelihood of pursuing a minor, major or career	1 for each	Constructed for this survey

Instrumentation

The final survey instrument contained more than 100 questions designed to assess a variety of topics (e.g., environmental attitudes, perceived environmental risks, preferences for specific classes, interest in pursuing an environmentally focused career). Wherever possible, we measured latent constructs (e.g., risk, attitudes) using previously validated measures from the peer-reviewed literature. Measurement items are summarized in Table 3.1.

Analyses

In addition to descriptive statistics (i.e., measures of central tendency, frequencies), we used one-way Analysis of Variance (ANOVA) to compare differences between students majoring in 115 different majors grouped into one of ten defined fields of study (see detail below in Table 3.2). These groups reflect both disciplinary and organizational (i.e. colleges) differences at the University. The one exception is the College of Food, Agriculture, and Environmental Sciences, which was split into two fields of study: (a) Food and Agriculture, and (b) Environment and Natural Resources (ENR). As the only College that offers undergraduate programs of study that bridge the disciplines of biological sciences, physical sciences, social and behavioral sciences, education, and business, and incorporate environmentally focused courses, it seemed appropriate to separate the College into two interdisciplinary fields of study. Additional one-way ANOVAs were conducted comparing Food and Agriculture, ENR, and the rest

TABLE 3.2 Number of subjects and the list of individual majors included in each field of study grouping. ★Indicates that major accounts for at least 10% of the subjects in that field of study

Field of study	n	Example majors
Physical Science and Math	42	Astronomy, Chemistry★, Computer and Information Science, Geography★, Geological Science, Mathematics★ and Physics
Engineering and Design	69	Architecture, City and Regional Planning, Engineering★ (Chemical, Civil, Industrial, Mechanical), Industrial Design, Interior Design, Landscape Architecture, Visual Communication Design
Biological Sciences	83	Biochemistry, Biology★, Evolution and Ecology, Microbiology★, Molecular Genetics, Zoology★
Social and Behavioral Sciences	149	Communication★, Criminology, Economics, Journalism, Marketing, Political Science★, Psychology★, Social Work★, Sociology, Speech and Hearing Science
Arts and Humanities	133	African Studies, Anthropology, Art, Comparative Studies, Dance, English★, Foreign Languages★, History★, International Studies★, Linguistics, Music, Philosophy, Theater, Women's Studies
Business and Management	105	Accounting★, Actuarial Science, Business Management, Business Administration★, Construction Management, Fashion and Retail Studies, Finance★, Health Information Management, Hospitality Management, Human Resources, Information Systems, Logistics, Medical Technology, Operations, Risk Management and Insurance
Health and Medicine	88	Athletic Training, Dental Hygiene, Dietetics★, Health Sciences★, Nutrition★, Nursing★, Pharmaceutical Sciences★, Radiologic Sciences, Respiratory Therapy
Education and Human Ecology	38	Exercise Science Education★, Family and Consumer Sciences Education, Human Development and Family Science★, Middle Childhood Education, Special Education, Sport and Leisure Studies★, Technical Education and Training
Food and Agricultural Sciences	151	Agri-Business★, Agriculture Communications, Agriculture and Extension Education★, Animal Science★, Crop Science, Food Agricultural and Biological Engineering★, Food Science and Technology★, Landscape Horticulture, Plant Pathology, Turfgrass Science
Environment and Natural Resources	104	Environmental Policy and Management★, Environmental Science★, Forestry Fisheries and Wildlife★, Parks Recreation and Tourism★

of the University (i.e., the remaining eight fields of study from Table 3.2). Chi-square tests were used to compare differences between CFAES and the rest of the University for categorical variables of interest (e.g. the percentage of students interested in a particular course topic). We report the results below, both for differences between the three College-level comparison populations (ENR, Food and Agriculture, and other) and between the ten fields of study described in Table 3.2, where appropriate.

Results

Student Characteristics

Survey respondents were 65% female and 35% male, and ranged in age from 16 to 62 years with an average age of 22 years. 50% identified their hometown as a large town or suburb with 17% coming from small towns, 16% from farms, 9% from large cities and 7% from rural areas. The majority of respondents identified as Caucasian (88%), while the remainder identified as Asian (6%), African American (2%), Native American (1%), or other (3%). Approximately 41% identified moderately or strongly as conservatives, while 49% identified moderately or strongly as liberals. Approximately 29% did not identify themselves as environmentalists, while 35% slightly identified, 21% moderately identified, and 12% strongly identified.

There were notable differences among the three comparison groups for some of the demographic characteristics of interest. Specifically, students in Food and Agriculture were significantly more likely to identify as conservative ($F = 9.213$, $p < 0.01$) and less likely to identify as liberal ($F = 14.056$, $p < 0.001$) than students in ENR and the rest of the University as a whole. Regarding identification as an environmentalist, students in ENR were more likely than all other students to identify as environmentalists ($F = 83.771$, $p = 0.000$), while students in Food and Agriculture were significantly more likely than students in the other academic units at University to identify as environmentalists ($F = 83.771$, $p = 0.040$). These results are not surprising given that CFAES students are exposed to and taught to consider the environment as it relates to their field of study. As a result, students as a whole identify more strongly as environmentalists in CFAES versus the rest of the University, even though individual political leanings vary considerably within CFAES.

Risk Perception, Environmental Attitudes, Self-Efficacy and Responsibility

Overall, students reported relatively high levels of perceived environmental risk[6] (i.e. > 4 on a 5-point scale) (see Table 3.3). However, ENR students did report significantly higher levels of perceived risk than those in both Food and

TABLE 3.3 Summary statistics for all reported survey measures split by students in Environment and Natural Resources (ENR), Food and Agriculture (Food & Ag), and students across the remaining colleges at the University (Other). Measures include the mean score and standard error in parentheses

Variable	Measure	ENR[a]	Food & Agriculture[b]	Other[c]
Environmental attitude	1 = negative to 5 = positive	3.76 (0.57)	3.33 (0.61)	3.44 (0.64)
Perceived risk	1 = low to 5 = high	4.50 (0.72)	4.22 (0.75)	4.15 (0.87)
Perceived responsibility	1 = low to 5 = high	4.59 (0.73)	4.35 (0.69)	4.25 (0.84)
Perceived ability	1 = low to 5 = high	4.38 (0.83)	4.17 (0.81)	4.09 (0.89)
Conservative identification	1 = low to 4 = high	1.85 (0.98)	2.31 (1.11)	1.96 (1.04)
Liberal identification	1 = low to 4 = high	2.69 (1.04)	2.06 (1.04)	2.49 (1.11)
Environmentalist identification	1 = low to 4 = high	3.27 (0.83)	2.20 (0.93)	2.01 (0.94)
Likelihood of taking a course	1 = low to 4 = high	3.86 (0.49)	2.78 (1.01)	2.28 (1.12)
Likelihood of pursuing a minor	1 = low to 4 = high	2.78 (1.08)	2.18 (1.03)	1.58 (0.84)
Likelihood of pursuing a major	1 = low to 4 = high	3.89 (0.31)	2.03 (1.13)	1.31 (0.73)
Likelihood of pursuing a career	1 = low to 4 = high	3.83 (0.49)	2.22 (1.14)	1.54 (0.84)
Social science interest score	0 = low to 9 = high	4.46 (2.10)	3.34 (1.95)	3.44 (2.46)
Natural science interest score	0 = low to 8 = high	4.99 (1.95)	3.56 (2.08)	2.89 (2.29)
Number of reported behaviors	0 = low to 11 = high	9.50 (1.71)	7.60 (2.08)	8.91 (1.86)

[a] Valid N (listwise) equals 93
[b] Valid N (listwise) equals 166
[c] Valid N (listwise) equals 757

Agriculture, and the rest of the University ($F = 7.749$, $p = 0.000$). Students generally agreed that protecting the environment was their responsibility (i.e. perceived responsibility, > 4 on a 5-point scale) and that they had the ability to do so (i.e. perceived self-efficacy, > 4 on a 5-point scale) (see Table 3.3). However, students in ENR along with those in Food and Agriculture perceived a greater responsibility and a greater ability to protect the environment when compared to students across the remaining disciplines at the University ($F_{responsibility} = 8.452$, $p = 0.000$, $F_{self\text{-}efficacy} = 5.514$, $p = 0.004$). These results provide some support for the idea that knowledge and training can empower individual students to take action on behalf of the environment.

Overall, students reported a slightly positive attitude toward the environment (i.e., just less than 4 on a 5-point scale, see Table 3.3). However, students in ENR reported a significantly more positive attitude than those in Food and Agriculture and those across the rest of the University ($F = 15.304$, $p = 0.000$). Comparing these results across the University in the ten fields of study, students in the biological sciences and humanities reported the next most positive attitudes after those in ENR. In addition, their attitudes were significantly more positive than students in Engineering, Business, and Food and Agriculture ($p < 0.015$). These results generate some support for the idea that a positive attitude toward or concern for the environment is not necessary to feel responsible or perceive the ability to do something to protect the environment. Perhaps some students will be drawn to a particular field of study due to their positive environmental ethic and concern (e.g., ENR, Biology, Humanities), while others will be drawn to a particular field of study due to their interest in addressing environmental problems despite lower individual concern (e.g., Food and Agriculture, Engineering).

Environmentally Responsible Behavior

Overall, students reported participating in the majority of the environmentally responsible behaviors (8.75 out of 11) we inquired about in the survey. Consistent with the findings about positive attitudes toward the environment, students in ENR, the humanities and biological sciences reported the greatest number of behaviors, 9.50, 9.25, and 9.12, respectively. Interestingly, despite indicating fairly high levels of responsibility and self-efficacy, students in Food and Agriculture reported significantly fewer environmentally responsible behaviors (7.60) than students in ENR (9.50) and the rest of the University as a whole (8.91) ($F = 43.632$, $p < 0.000$). Students in ENR also reported significantly more environmentally responsible behaviors than students across the rest of the University ($F = 43.632$, $p < 0.01$, see Table 3.3). Again, these results provide support for the idea that positive attitudes, high perceived risk, and the adoption of environmentally responsible behaviors are connected, and students with these characteristics are drawn to particular fields of study (e.g. ENR, Biology, Humanities).

Accounting for Differences in Perceived Risk, Attitudes, and Environmentally Responsible Behavior

The fact that students majoring in ENR reported higher perceived risk, more positive attitudes, and more frequent environmentally responsible behaviors than students from other disciplines was not unexpected, given their choice of majors. However, these results left us wondering if these differences were the result of students' exposure to SENR's curriculum, or a selection bias on the part of the students – that is, were ENR students' heightened scores on these environmentally relevant variables a function of their coursework, or were these students majoring in ENR because they *already had* heightened risk perception and more positive attitudes toward the environment when they entered the program? To answer this question we conducted a series of one-way ANOVAs using perceived risk, environmental attitude, and environmentally responsible behavior as the dependent variables, and student's rank (i.e. freshman, sophomore, junior, senior) as the grouping variable. Only one of the F-tests was significant; subsequent post hoc tests revealed that freshmen in ENR exhibited more positive environmental attitudes than juniors (means were 4.09 and 3.47, respectively, $F = 0.391$, $p = 0.011$). Overall, the results of these tests support the idea that students are pre-selecting into those majors focused on environmental sustainability, and not necessarily becoming more responsible and aware due to exposure to the curriculum.

Interest in Specific Environmental Course Topics

The promotion of sustainability at the university level can be improved by understanding the preferences of students for various course topics. Understanding such preferences allows educators to tailor course offerings and market existing courses to appeal to a broader audience of students – beyond that traditionally served by resource management programs. In our survey, students were given a list of nine biophysical and eight social science courses, each focused on the environment or environmental issues, and asked to indicate which courses they were interested in taking. While the most popular course, chosen by nearly 53% of students, was a social science course (i.e. Environment and Society), seven of the ten most popular courses were natural science courses. The most popular social science classes were: Environment and Society (53%), Environmental Psychology (42%), Environmental Education (38%), Parks and Recreation (36%), and Environmental Ethics and Religion (34%); the most popular natural science courses were: Wildlife Ecology and Management (52%), Environmental Science (49%), Aquatic Ecosystems (48%), Sustainable Agriculture (47%), and Restoration Ecology (45%). These results indicate that students, as a whole, prefer natural science courses to social science courses when focusing on the environment and environmental issues.

We also examined differences between students in CFAES (i.e. those already enrolled in interdisciplinary programs with a purposeful focus on the environment) and students from outside CFAES (i.e. the rest of the University). CFAES students were significantly more interested in Soil Conservation and Management, Sustainable Agriculture, Fisheries Ecology and Management, and Wildlife Ecology and Management, while non-CFAES students are significantly more interested in Environmental Psychology, Environmental Economics, Environmental Ethics and Religion, Environmental Law, Environmental Policy, and Environment and Society (see Table 3.4). It is notable that interest in

TABLE 3.4 Interest in course topics and Chi-square analyses by interdisciplinary college (CFAES) and other disciplinary units across the University (non-CFAES)

		% Interested in topic			
		CFAES	*Non-CFAES*		
Course topic	*Course type*	*n = 329*	*n = 747*	*Difference*	*Chi-square*
Wildlife ecology and management	Biophysical	**62.0**%	52.7%	9.3%	7.94★★
Sustainable agriculture	Ambiguous	**61.4**%	46.1%	15.3%	21.52★★★
Environmental science	Ambiguous	54.1%	51.4%	2.7%	0.67ns
Aquatic ecosystems	Biophysical	51.4%	50.9%	0.5%	0.23ns
Environment and society	Social	51.1%	**58.1**%	−7.0%	4.59★
Restoration ecology	Biophysical	48.6%	49.0%	−0.4%	0.12ns
Water quality and management	Biophysical	47.7%	44.3%	3.4%	1.07ns
Environmental education	Social	42.6%	40.6%	2.0%	0.37ns
Forest ecology and management	Biophysical	41.6%	38.2%	3.5%	1.17ns
Parks and recreation	Ambiguous	41.0%	38.0%	3.0%	0.87ns
Soil conservation and management	Biophysical	**38.6**%	20.5%	18.1%	38.96★★★
Environmental psychology	Social	33.7%	**48.7**%	−15.0%	20.81★★★
Environmental law	Social	30.4%	**37.9**%	−7.5%	5.59★
Environmental policy	Social	30.4%	**37.6**%	−7.2%	5.21★
Environmental ethics and religion	Social	28.9%	**39.2**%	−10.3%	10.61★★★
Environmental economics	Social	28.0%	**40.2**%	−12.2%	14.67★★★
Fisheries ecology and management	Biophysical	**27.7**%	15.5%	12.1%	21.63★★★

★ $p < 0.05$, ★★ $p < 0.01$, ★★★$p < 0.001$

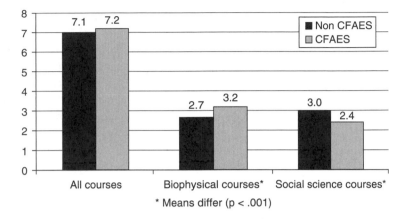

FIGURE 3.1 Mean number of course topics in which students expressed an interest.

environmentally focused courses was high both among CFAES students as well as students from outside the college. In fact, a post hoc *t*-test revealed no significant differences between the number of courses that CFAES students were interested in (7.2) compared with non-CFAES students (7.1) (Figure 3.1). Rather, CFAES students exhibited greater interest in biophysical courses, while non-CFAES students exhibited greater interest in courses grounded in the social sciences and humanities (Figure 3.1).

Comparing Social Science with Biophysical Science Interests

The course topics were also separated by discipline (biophysical and social science/humanities) and the student responses were summed to produce a biophysical interest score and a social science interest score for each student. A one-way ANOVA was then run for each interest score, comparing them across the three groups. ENR students reported significantly higher interest in biophysical courses (4.99) than those in Food and Agriculture (3.56) ($F = 44.733$, $p < 0.001$), and those in Food and Agriculture reported significantly higher interest than those across the rest of the University as a whole (2.89) ($F = 44.733$, $p < 0.01$). Other high biophysical interest scores by specific fields of study were biology and ecology (3.76), physical science and math (3.64), and engineering and design (3.53). All other fields reported scores below the overall mean of 3.45. Similarly, ENR students reported the highest social science interest score with a mean of 4.46, significantly greater than students in Food and Agriculture and across the University as a whole ($F = 9.305$, $p=0.000$). The other fields showing interest levels above the overall mean of 3.84 were arts and humanities (4.30) and social science (4.08).

Comparing the interest in biophysical and social science based environmental courses showed a logical division across the field of study. Students who have already committed to studying the environment reported the highest levels of interest in both the biophysical and social science categories. Traditionally, biophysical science fields reported above-average interest in biophysical science environmental courses, and social science fields reported above average interest in social science environmental courses. These findings suggest that an interdisciplinary program should focus recruitment efforts initially on disciplinary interests, while including interdisciplinary coursework in the program to broaden student understanding of sustainability across human and natural systems. Of particular interest were strong correlations between a discipline's interest score and courses from the other field. The strongest correlations between a student's biophysical science score and specific social science courses were Environmental Education ($r = .46$) and Environment and Society ($r = .44$). The highest correlations between the social science score and biophysical science courses were Restoration Ecology ($r = .51$) and Environmental Science ($r = .50$). These results indicate that interdisciplinary programs that address these multiple elements of education, society, ecology and basic science should be particularly appealing to students.

Finally, we asked students to list the first three environmental issues that came to mind. Student responses were coded to identify major themes of interest; such themes should be of particular interest to those designing courses focused on the environment and sustainability due to their broad appeal. Student responses reflected 11 common themes including (in rank order from most often mentioned to least often mentioned): climate change, water (quality, access, scarcity), pollution and waste management, ecosystems (habitat and wetland loss), plant and animal biodiversity, soil (quality and conservation), energy and resource issues, overpopulation, land use (development), agriculture and world hunger, and air quality.

Likelihood of Taking an Environmental Course and Pursuing an Environmentally Focused Minor, Major, or Career

Students were also asked about their likelihood of pursuing an environmentally focused course, minor, major, or career, using a scale of 1 ("Not likely") to 4 ("Very likely"). Using the three-group comparison, all scores were significantly different ($p < 0.05$) across all four pursuits (see Table 3.3). Specifically, ENR students were more likely than both Food and Agriculture and other students across the University to take an environmentally focused course ($F = 107.987$, $p = 0.000$), and pursue a minor ($F = 99.143$, $p = 0.000$), major ($F = 519.470$, $p = 0.000$) or career ($F = 330.199$, $p = 0.000$).

If we break down the results further to look at likelihood across the ten defined fields of study (see Table 3.5) we find considerable variation in these four items. Specifically, following students in ENR and Food and Agriculture, students in

TABLE 3.5 Mean likelihood of taking an environmental course, or pursuing an environmental minor, major, or career by ten defined fields of study

Discipline	n	Environmental course	Environmental minor	Environmental major	Environmental career
Physical science and Math	42	2.38	1.57	1.52	1.80
Engineering and Design	142	2.53	1.81	1.33	1.76
Biology and Ecology	81	2.56	1.70	1.51	1.70
Social Science	149	2.14	1.44	1.11	1.44
Arts and Humanities	132	2.37	1.51	1.17	1.39
Business and Management	103	2.12	1.63	1.31	1.58
Health and Medicine	88	1.95	1.51	1.26	1.37
Education and Human Ecology	38	1.87	1.13	1.00	1.05
Food and Agricultural Science	145	2.78	2.18	2.03	2.22
Environment and Natural Resources	101	3.86	2.78	3.89	3.83

engineering and biology report the next highest interest in taking an environmental course. For an environmental minor, students in engineering and biology again show the highest interest. For an environmental major, students in physical science and biology show the highest interest. And for an environmental career, students in physical science, engineering and biology show the highest interest. These results indicate an opportunity to offer more environmentally focused options in these fields where they would be met with great interest and appreciation, or to market such opportunities to students with these dominant interests. In addition, some of the students who indicated lower interest in general (e.g. humanities and social sciences), were also some of the students outside of CFAES who indicated the most positive attitudes and reported the greatest number of environmentally responsible behaviors. In such cases, there exists great opportunity to incorporate courses and curricula in these fields where perhaps there is interest, but students do not perceive the opportunity to pursue those interests in their department or even in their future career.

Discussion and Conclusions

Not surprisingly, students who display the greatest environmental awareness, interest, concern, behavior, and career intentions tend to already be enrolled in environmental programs, specifically in the School of Environment and Natural Resources. Beyond these environmentally focused students, however, the majority of students are interested in a range of sustainability-related courses, and as reported above, a wide range of course topics appeal to students across disciplines. University-wide at Ohio State, the goal for sustainability across the curriculum is not to simply multiply ENR programs so that all students prioritize environmental careers and foci, but rather to foster engaged global citizenship with higher levels of environmental awareness, concern, and responsible behavior. Interestingly, there are students in several fields of study, including the humanities and social science, which demonstrate fairly high levels of concern and responsible behavior, but report a lower likelihood of pursuing environmental interests during their academic tenure. We believe that the disciplinary silos and existing curricular boundaries tend to discourage more significant crossover between students of different colleges. Given the interest that clearly exists across much of the University, future efforts at integrating sustainability in the curriculum should include both the opportunity to pursue coursework and minor fields of study across disciplines, as well as to integrate the idea of environmental sustainability into existing courses and curricula offered within disciplinary areas of study.

At Ohio State, the School of Environment and Natural Resources is a microcosm of environmental interdisciplinarity and sustainability, and although lessons can be drawn from the experiences within SENR over the past 40 years, the University may need to think more broadly regarding their integration of sustainability across the curriculum. The focus and interest in SENR over time have been more in the biophysical science courses rather than the social sciences. Although interest and investment in the social sciences have recently increased, the School has only made minor headway in incorporating the humanities. This trajectory parallels that of environmental science in many ways, where the focus was historically on understanding the natural system at the expense of understanding how social systems play a role. Currently, increasing calls are being made to understand the human dimensions of environmental issues in order to achieve a truly sustainable world (Mascia et al. 2003; Phillipson et al. 2009). If efforts to better incorporate the human dimensions into research and decision-making are to succeed, future scientists and resource managers must receive a strong grounding in the social sciences. Moreover, some have suggested that understanding the history of environmental problems is essential to addressing these problems, thereby necessitating at least some grounding in the humanities (Meine 1999). We might suggest a balance in any new or emerging efforts to give students a good environmental perspective of 50% biophysical, 40% social science, and 10% humanities.

The Ohio State University has prioritized a "one university" goal that invites greater integration and connection in all fields while also prioritizing sustainability goals that invite interdisciplinary collaboration. SENR has built an integration of natural and social science environmental course offerings and programs over the last 40 years that attracts and serves students with high levels of environmental engagement and responsibility. It has worked particularly hard over the last decade to strengthen its social science programs, courses, and faculty to support student interests and training for related careers and further study. Seen from the rest of the University, SENR courses and programs can help meet the environmental interests of students outside CFAES, with opportunities to engage in both social and/or natural science foci. At the same time, as units in the humanities continue to increase their environmentally focused offerings, opportunities are created for students in environmentally focused programs to broaden their academic environmental training beyond traditional social and natural science approaches. As individual colleges each approach the issue of sustainability from their own unique perspectives, the foundations of the interdisciplinary connections needed to achieve Ohio State's "one university" goal are being built.

In sum, this chapter is a first attempt to apply the results of this survey to the practical development of the curriculum at the university level. More data is available that we have yet to examine and that invites many other interesting questions to explore. We hope that as we move forward we can continue to gain additional insights from this study, and provide empirical support to those hoping to engage in building curricula to foster environmental stewardship in college undergraduates. Promotion of sustainability across society must begin with the training of individuals in our education system to promote greater awareness and understanding.

Notes

1   For more information about the programs and initiatives mentioned above, see: http://www.ag.ohio-state.edu/ cfaes/paradigm.html#; http://cfaes.osu.edu/about-us/cfaes-strategic-plan-2009-2013; http://www.presidentsclimatecommitment.org/; http://president.osu.edu/sustainability/; http://ucat.osu.edu/read/sustainability/index.html; http://oaa.osu.edu/assets/files/caa/CurricularEducation21_2_031910pdf_000.pdf.

2   For example, the Institute of Natural and Environmental Resources (INER) at the University of New Hampshire as described in Abner *et al.* (2009).

3   This goal is identified as a critical action in AASHE's *Sustainability Curriculum in Higher Education: A Call to Action* (2010).

4   This concern was discussed in a 2009 AASHE Campus Surveys online forum: (http://www.aashe.org/forums/campus-surveys)

5   Note: Our sampling approach anticipated low response rates due to (a) method of contact, (b) the population of interest (i.e. students), and (c) length of the survey instrument (see Dillman 2007), necessitating the large sample size.

6 Perceived environmental risk was measured as holistic concern for the environment as well as the perception of negative environmental impacts being felt locally, nationally, and around the world.

References

AASHE. Sustainability Curriculum in Higher Education: A Call to Action. Publication. Association for the Advancement of Sustainability in Higher Education, 2010. Print.

Carroll, J. (2009). "Teaching and Learning Sustainability: Curriculum and Pedagogy." In Abner, J., Kelly, T., & Mallory, B. (Eds.) *The Sustainable Learning Community: One University's Journey to the Future* (Durham, NH: University of New Hampshire Press, pp. 54–55).

Dillman, D. A. 2007. *Mail and internet surveys : the tailored design method.* 2nd edition. John Wiley & Sons, New York.

Dunlap, R. E., K. D. Van Liere, A. G. Mertig, and R. E. Jones. 2000. Measuring endorsement of the New Ecological Paradigm: A revised NEP scale. *Journal of Social Issues* **56**:425–442.

Leiserowitz, A. A. 2005. American risk perceptions: Is climate change dangerous? *Risk Analysis* **25**:1433–1442.

Meine, C. 1999. It's about Time: Conservation Biology and History. *Conservation Biology* **13**:1–3.

Mascia, M. B., J. P. Brosius, T. A. Dobson, B. C. Forbes, L. Horowitz, M. A. McKean, and N. J. Turner. 2003. Conservation and the social sciences. *Conservation Biology* **17**:649–650.

Phillipson, J., P. Lowe, and J. M. Bullock. 2009. Navigating the social sciences: interdisciplinarity and ecology. *Journal of Applied Ecology* **46**:261–264.

4

LEARNING OUTCOMES

An International Comparison of Countries and Declarations

Debra Rowe and Lucas F. Johnston

Introduction

The global population is growing at an exponential rate. Ecosystems are stressed and humans are consuming resources in ways that are unsustainable. Opportunities to create sustainable abundance and higher quality of life for present and future generations exist, but they will not be realized unless humans are educated about both sustainability challenges and opportunities, and are able and willing to engage in solutions at both the personal and systemic levels. Agenda 21, which derived from the first "Earth Summit" (World Conference on Environment and Development, Rio de Janeiro, 1992) included materials and conceptual frameworks focused on education. But while several European nations, Japan, Australia and a number of other regions' and countries' educational institutions and governments adopted that document's emphasis on education for a sustainable future and its provisions, the United States government has been much slower to respond. A national trend is now occurring regarding educating for a sustainable future (ESF) in the educational institutions in the United States. Thousands of individuals in a variety of institutional roles, and dozens of national academic disciplinary associations and national educational associations have taken on leadership roles.

In what follows, learning outcomes as well as some specific benchmarks related to education are discussed. Specific examples are provided of learning outcomes from Mexico, the United States, and Sweden in the context of international declarations and conferences. Common elements of these various approaches are highlighted. What will become clear is that education for sustainability does require and can help to produce a transformation toward systemic, interdisciplinary thinking and actions for a sustainable future. Committing to and utilizing concrete learning outcomes and creating curricular and co-curricular programming that achieves them is one of the first and most important steps in this transformation.

Background: What Are LOs and Where Do They Come From?

In simplest terms, learning outcomes (LOs) are the specific skills, capacities, attitudes, and knowledge that a student ought to possess as a result of a particular educational activity. The Council for Higher Education Accreditation states that "Student learning outcomes are properly defined in terms of the knowledge, skills, and abilities that a student has attained at the end (or as a result) of his or her engagement in a particular set of higher education experiences." LOs are important both for teachers and for students. For educators, LOs provide an organizing concept (or set of ideas) which anchor academic instruction. In addition, student learning is enhanced when LOs are made explicit, and students can perceive the connection between learning activities and the proposed outcomes. This is a sort of frame alignment process – what Lindy Biggs has called "constructive alignment" (Biggs 1999) – that occurs between instructor and students, where checks built in to the curriculum ensure that LOs are achieved. These are valuable tools for achieving any set of educational goals. When it comes to education for sustainable development, however, there is an additional normative presupposition: that higher education institutions have an obligation to ensure that their graduates attain a set of LOs that enhance not only their professional lives, but also their life roles as family member, community member, consumer, and investor.

Education in this instance is not merely an intellectual exercise, but is a process through which learners become effective change agents who have the skills, persistence, and the resilience to catalyze the emergence of healthy ecosystems, social systems, and economies (the triple bottom line of sustainability). It is education with a purpose: it aims to create a higher quality of life for present day humans and for future generations, and fosters the health of the ecosystems we depend upon for survival. Progress toward such goals requires a way to assess and improve the attainment of these outcomes that are central to moving toward sustainability. This is where specific, sustainability-focused LOs, learning activities, assessments, and continuous improvement processes are necessary.

Such LOs have long been part of an international conversation, with perhaps the first focused international attention paid to education for sustainability occurring at the First Intergovernmental Conference on Environmental Education in 1977. Hosted by the United Nations Educational, Scientific and Cultural Organization (UNESCO) and the United Nations Environment Program (UNEP) in Tbilisi, Georgia (14–26 October), this conference addressed education at all levels and was the first attempt to formulate sustainability-oriented LOs. At this time, the idea that sustainable development should be an international policy goal had only recently emerged into international public discourse (for instance at the Stockholm Conference on the Human Environment, 1972). Most references to education, however, used the trope of "environmental education" and focused on education for loosely defined holistic perspectives. The Tbilisi Declaration also emphasized the social and economic spheres of sustainability, and moreover emphasized the interconnectedness between the different dimensions of sustainable development.[1] The categories of *objectives* of environmental education in the document were:

1. Awareness – to help social groups and individuals acquire an awareness and sensitivity to the total environment and its allied problems.
2. Knowledge – to help social groups and individuals gain a variety of experience in, and acquire a basic understanding of, the environment and its associated problems.
3. Attitudes – to help social groups and individuals acquire a set of values and feelings of concern for the environment, and the motivation for actively participating in environmental improvement and protection.
4. Skills – to help social groups and individuals acquire the skills for identifying and solving environmental problems.
5. Participation – to provide social groups and individuals with an opportunity to be actively involved at all levels in working toward the resolution of environmental problems.

These educational objectives emphasize the capacity of learners to serve a positive function within the social group, to be engaged, invested, and sensitive citizens.

This language provided insight into the educational challenges of educating for sustainability. The goals for sustainability education and the means of achieving them were formulated more than 30 years ago, and yet few educational institutions have managed to completely implement the sort of transformational learning that the Tbilisi Declaration recommended for all of its students as the institutional norm. UNESCO and UNEP continue to be the lead UN agencies in these attempts to create behavior change to promote a more sustainable future.

The United Nations declared 2005–2014 the Decade of Education for Sustainable Development (DESD), with the goal of integrating the principles, values and practices of sustainable development into all aspects of education and learning.[2] Alluding to the language included in the Tbilisi Declaration, "The DESD at a Glance" document suggests that it is necessary to move beyond "environmental education" to "education for sustainable development." Citizen change agents prepared by the DESD are expected to be able to: "a) have acquired various skills (critical and creative thinking, communication, conflict management and problem solving strategies, project assessment) to take an active part in and contribute to the life of society, b) be respectful of the Earth and life in all its diversity, and c) be committed to promoting democracy in a society without exclusion and where peace prevails."[3]

At the halfway mark of the DESD, UNESCO, and the German Federal Ministry of Education and Research hosted a World Conference on Education for Sustainable Development in Bonn, Germany. During this conference, and in the Declaration which resulted from it, the delegates created an agenda they called "Education for All," which focused on making improvements in preschool and rural education, and adult literacy. The Declaration further noted the complicity of the now global economic system and its narrow focus on short-term financial gains in the generation of unsustainable societies, and highlighted the impacts of biocultural simplification and increasingly scarce resources on the world's poorest citizens. As with previous documents and declarations, this document called for re-orienting educational institutions for more systemic and holistic learning, providing problem-based education, and promoting education as a means to break the cycle of poverty.[4]

All of these examples illustrate that education is one of the keys to truly sustainable development. Education, especially of rural populations and of women, is an investment in peace-building and improvement in quality of life. It is crucial, however, to develop adequate monitoring tools to assess whether these important goals are being approached in the DESD. Among the examples of meaningful steps toward education for sustainable development, the Bonn Declaration noted that a global monitoring and evaluation framework had been designed.[5] Their call to action, however, also noted that further improvements were needed to strengthen these evaluation tools, and to generate better national monitoring programs. This work to re-orient systems to educate for a sustainable future has grown and become a substantial trend in many areas of the world. Some comparisons of the learning outcomes in use are instructive to understanding the common core of these efforts.

Example Sets of Learning Outcomes

In 2001, the Instituto Tecnológico y de Estudios Superiores de Monterrey, Monterrey Institute of Technology and Higher Education (ITESM) initiated their Sustainable Campus Program. The Program attempted to integrate sustainability into campus operations, but also sought to integrate a systems perspective into coursework by making sustainable development the "golden thread" that tied courses and curricula together (Lozano et al. 2006; see also Svanström et al. 2008). While these efforts began at the main campus in Monterrey, by 2005 ITESM had generated vision and mission statements for the other 32 satellite campuses.[6] These statements had a clear mandate to bring sustainability into most curricula. By 2006 sustainable development concepts had been incorporated into classes across the curriculum, and new mandatory courses (in ethics and citizenship formation, and socio-political perspectives) were created to foster the vision and mission statements.

As ITESM began to investigate the possibilities for external accreditation, it became clear that LOs for sustainability were needed to assess progress toward education for sustainable development. LOs focused on two levels: "Broad education and learning" was intended to assess the capacity to reason and solve problems from a systems perspective; "Disciplinary education and learning" was meant to focus more specifically on relevant material from a particular academic discipline. Table 4.1 provides the LOs that are currently being tested at ITESM (for elaboration see Svanström *et al.* 2008).

In addition to the LOs in Table 4.1, it was further suggested that the following are also crucially important outcomes: (1) an understanding of the social impacts

TABLE 4.1 ITESM learning outcomes

Broad education and learning

A. An understanding of the ethical responsibility, toward present and future generations.
B. A knowledge of contemporary issues.
C. An understanding of the carrying capacity of ecosystems, in order to provide services to humankind.
D. An understanding of the social responsibility as a future professional, and as a citizen.
E. An understanding of the impact that human activities have on the Planet, regarding sustainable and unsustainable resources appropriation.
F. Knowledge of global trends that impact the life quality of present and future generations.

Discipline education and learning

A. An ability to establish the connections to the triple bottom line (TBL) and other sustainable development (SD) dimensions that influence their own knowledge discipline.
B. An ability to apply assessment criteria or sets of principles or available tools related to sustainability in their own discipline.
C. The systemic education needed to understand the impact of their discipline solutions or actions in a TBL context.
D. For disciplines that prepare engineering professionals: An ability to design processes, products and components taking into account the life cycle analysis using the appropriate SD dimensions constraints.
E. For disciplines that prepare professionals that provide or design services: An ability to design services that take into account the connectedness and implications for those services as related to the SD dimensions constraints.
F. An ability to implement the needed actions to foster sustainability in their professional and personal life.

of human activities, especially the causes of human suffering; and (2) a capacity for systems thinking and the ability to motivate behavior change. Although the LOs in Table 4.1 focus on the triple bottom line (that is, maximizing economic, social, and ecological values), it is clear that sustainable development should be considered to have multiple additional dimensions, including normative, political, and legal dimensions.

The second example provides a perspective from the United States. The Disciplinary Associations Network for Sustainability (or DANS)[7] was formed after the US Partnership for Education for Sustainable Development convened the leaders of over 20 academic disciplinary associations to discuss each discipline's potential contributions to a more sustainable future.[8] These meetings included national associations for psychology, sociology, philosophy, religion, biology, chemistry, engineering, anthropology, political science, math, broadcasting, architecture, women's studies, and others. DANS focuses on infusing sustainability into curricula in all academic disciplines; providing professional development for faculty; creating standards (including tenure, promotion, and accreditation criteria) that value sustainability research, applied scholarship and action; initiating cross-disciplinary projects; informing policy makers; and educating the public about how to help to create a sustainable future. The network now includes 39 participating associations.

Another national network, the Higher Education Associations Sustainability Consortium, or HEASC, was formed to catalyze education for a sustainable future in the programs and operations of mainstream higher education associations and their members.[9] The HEASC includes the professional organizations for most of the, approximately 4,000, US college and university presidents, and the majority of facilities directors, business officers, college and university planners, purchasers, and residential and student affairs staff. These associations recognize that LOs are valuable for both academic and co-curricular experiences on campus, and are helping higher education institutions develop academic assignments that focus on real-world sustainability challenges on campus and in the surrounding communities, nationally and globally. HEASC also supports the efforts of the American College and University Presidents' Climate Commitment and called for the Sustainability Tracking and Rating System (STARS) assessment for higher education, which has been developed and deployed by AASHE.[10]

Some of the DANS and HEASC members have worked together on LOs. College Students Educators International (or the American College Personnel Association [ACPA]) took a lead role and has created a list of LOs being used by members of the associations in both networks (see Table 4.2). Note that these learning outcomes move from understanding societal and ecosystem sustainability challenges toward development and implementation of solutions. In addition, the outcomes hold students accountable for understanding the impacts of their personal choices on living systems and highlight the need for effective systemic transformations, including one outcome devoted to learning change agent skills.

TABLE 4.2 ACPA learning outcomes

In order to develop and maintain sustainable communities:

1. Each student will be able to define sustainability.
2. Each student will be able to explain how sustainability relates to their lives and their values, and how their actions impact issues of sustainability.
3. Each student will be able to utilize their knowledge of sustainability to change their daily habits and consumer mentality.
4. Each student will be able to explain how systems are interrelated.
5. Each student will learn change agent skills.
6. Each student will learn how to apply concepts of sustainability to their campus and community by engaging in the challenges and solutions of sustainability on their campus.
7. Each student will learn how to apply concepts of sustainability globally by engaging in the challenges and the solutions of sustainability in a world context.

The ACPA recognizes that these LOs can be promoted outside the classroom as well, and has published lists of competencies and possible development strategies to attain these LOs in a co-curricular context.[11]

Within the United States, there is increasing recognition of this need to move beyond critical thinking to be able to be effective at solving systemic problems. Accordingly, ACPA has delineated the skills required to be an effective change agent (see Table 4.3 below).[12]

TABLE 4.3 ACPA change agent skills

Change Agent Abilities Required to Help to Create a Sustainable Future

In order to be a successful sustainability change agent, an individual must have the following:
1. Knowledge of the environmental, economic, and social issues related to sustainability (understanding);
2. A value system and self-concept to support and under gird the actions of a change agent (motivation); and
3. Change agent abilities (skills).

Change agents are:

Resilient	Optimistic	Tenacious	Committed
Passionate	Patient	Emotionally intelligent	Assertive
Persuasive	Empathetic	Authentic	Ethical
Self-aware	Competent	Curious	

They can:
- Communicate ideas clearly, concisely, and precisely both orally and in writing
- Listen to others and incorporate their ideas and perspectives
- Accommodate individual differences (cultural, socioeconomic, global, etc.) in their decisions and actions and be able to negotiate across these differences

- Engage in self-assessment, self-reflection, and analysis
- Reflect on what is happening to make meaning, gain perspective and understanding
- Engage in civil discourse and debate
- Mediate and resolve conflicts
- Analyze power, structures of inequality, and social systems that govern individual and communal life
- Recognize the global implications of their actions
- Span boundaries
- Challenge the status quo effectively when appropriate
- Creatively and collaboratively solve problems using critical thinking skills; search for "families" of solutions for complex multi-faceted issues
- Collaborate, network, develop alliances and coalitions, build teams
- Involve others, inspire and excite participants, engender support and commitment
- See the big picture and the larger goal and understand the need for systemic change
- Adjust to the diverse and changing needs of both individuals and society as a whole
- Set realistic and clearly-defined goals and objectives
- Be both a leader and a follower, as necessary
- Analyze and influence group dynamics
- Make ethical decisions which incorporate responsibility to self, community, and society
- Help envision, articulate, and create positive scenarios for the future of society
- See the paths, small steps, for changes needed for a more sustainable future, convert it into a tasklist and timeline, and follow through effectively
- Tolerate ambiguity and cope effectively with change

They have:

- Insights into the functioning and interconnectedness of systems
- A commitment to finding solutions to societal problems
- Political efficacy, a belief that what they think and do civically and politically matters
- Integrity
- Courage
- An understanding of "organic" change

Hundreds of colleges and universities in the United States have instituted initiatives to include some sustainability learning outcomes into the general education core requirements for all degrees, into new minors in sustainability, or throughout the institution's curricular and co-curricular activities (Rowe 2002).[13,14] Each academic discipline brings unique and important perspectives and knowledge to solving societal sustainability challenges, so the participation of every academic discipline in educating for a sustainable future is important. Opportunities to problem solve and apply these solutions are increasingly recognized as essential by disciplinary societies and educational administrators as well as faculty involved with education for sustainability.[15] The US Department of Education and the National Science Foundation have funded a variety of sustainability oriented grants that are part of this national trend. Faculty in many disciplines are recognizing the importance of such problem solving and change agent skill building both within their disciplinary courses and in interdisciplinary assignments. Revived attention to applied scholarship, action research, civic engagement, project-based learning and service learning suggests some promising trends.

Some other sets of LOs available in English may provide additional input for higher education institutions that are in the process of formulating or developing their student sustainability LOs. Most of them exhibit some of the commonalities discussed below, and they have in some cases provided input to this analysis. These include the LOs provided by The Washington Center for Improving the Quality of Undergraduate Education's "Curriculum for the Bioregion" initiative.[16] Or, as an example from Canada, the Learning for a Sustainable Future organization initiated a program to integrate education for sustainable development into the curricula at all grade levels, and has vetted its set of LOs online.[17] An education for sustainable development initiative in Manitoba, Canada (connected to the UNESCO DESD) lists sustainability LOs from kindergarten through grade 10 which are specific to three disciplinary areas: social studies, science, and physical/health education.[18] The US Partnership for Education for Sustainable Development has developed a set of sustainability standards for K-12 education that has been utilized to help inform and formulate knowledge and skills statements and performance elements for national career and technical education, STEM education, and the curricula of specific school districts throughout the country.[19]

Globally, there are many other initiatives that are presently described only in languages other than English. Examples providing LOs which are similar to those detailed above include the network Higher Education for Sustainable Development (HU2) in Sweden.[20] At Chalmers University of Technology in Göteborg, Sweden, one of those leading the charge toward sustainability education, LOs for education for sustainable development are under development in a process involving teachers, program directors, students and other stakeholders in the educational system. The on-going workshop discussions that are part of this process provide a model for other higher education entities.[21] Chalmers provides innovative programming which attempts to create partnerships with companies and corporations in Sweden which are developing green technologies, chemistries, and other industrial systems and consumer products. They are helping to create new types of educational structures, and such developments can inspire other countries and institutions of higher learning to reevaluate traditional educational arrangements.

The Tbilisi and DESD initiatives discussed above address educational efforts in society as a whole (including, for instance, on-going adult education), but there are also many initiatives that target higher education or specific professions. One example is the Declaration of Barcelona, formulated during the Engineering Education for Sustainable Development conference in 2004, which specifically dealt with education for sustainability among engineers.[22] Another example of an organization which has provided input and strategic pressure on higher education over the last 15 years is the World Business Council for Sustainable Development (WBCSD), a set of concerned businesses who recognize that the adoption of sustainable business models and a sustainable consumer base are important for their own financial futures.[23]

These examples of learning outcomes and institutional commitment to education for sustainable development, though drawn from very different associations and from different socio-cultural-political contexts, do exhibit some similarities. While ideas about what sustainable development *is* and the means to achieve it vary somewhat among these various nations, their institutions, and their educational partners, there is a remarkable convergence in their vision of the desired learning outcomes that create the effective change agents who can make sustainable societies a reality. Descriptions of some of these commonalities may be instructive.

Common Elements, Transformational Learning

For education for SD, LOs typically focus on what Wals and Corcoran (2006) have termed "transformative learning." Transformative learning includes the ability to integrate, connect, confront, and reconcile multiple ways of looking at the world. Additional competencies that students require include the ability of students to cope with uncertainty, poorly defined situations, and conflicting or at least diverging norms, values, interests, and reality constructions. Transformative learning, in other words, does not focus on mastering clearly defined sets of text-based competencies. Rather, it emphasizes students' dynamic qualities and competencies, attitudes, and self-concepts. Crucially important to navigating an increasingly complex and dynamic world, students must be able to empathetically engage the perspectives of cultural others, to think across disciplinary boundaries, and to recognize the influences of geographical and temporal constraints. This means that they must develop the capacity to integrate local and global analyses, as well as short-term and long-term planning considerations. Transformative learning goes beyond fact-based, instrumental learning to promote critical reflection on a students' own knowledge, experiences, beliefs, and values, ensuring that personal and professional decisions reflect this enhanced self-awareness. Common attributes of education for sustainability strategies, which aim to produce this type of student, typically include the following:

- systems thinking or holistic perspectives
- integrating different perspectives or viewpoints

- change agent skill sets
- analysis of attitudes and values
- efficacy in creating positive change

Analytical thinking is about breaking things into their constituent parts, while *systemic or holistic* thinking is about connecting the dots between them. It is clear that all things interact in complex ways with other entities and with their environments. This complex web of relationships often exhibits properties or patterns that are not apparent in constituent parts. Systems thinking is concerned with discerning these larger patterns, being able to conceptually model such a system, and being able to pinpoint cause and effect within it to identify leverage points and strategies for systemic change. The Tbilisi Declaration, for instance, stated that both individuals and communities must "understand the complex nature of the natural and the built environments resulting from the interaction of their biological, physical, social, economic and cultural aspects."[24] The Declaration of Barcelona also cited holistic thinking as a major goal of education, and stated that future professionals "should be able to use their expertise not only in a scientific or technological context, but equally for broader social, political and environmental needs," and that they should be able to "move beyond the tradition of breaking reality down into disconnected parts."[25]

Related to systems thinking is the importance of obtaining an *inter- or multidisciplinary perspective*, another of the common outcomes specified by these diverse constituencies. The Tbilisi Declaration stated that "environmental education should be interdisciplinary in its approach, drawing on the specific content of each discipline in making possible a holistic and balanced perspective." Likewise, the Barcelona Declaration specified that "today's engineers must be able to work in multidisciplinary teams," and that social sciences and humanities should be incorporated in teaching for engineers. Gaining an interdisciplinary perspective also requires being aware of time and space. The importance of spatial perspective appears in the Tbilisi Declaration when it suggests that learners ought to possess "insights into environmental conditions in other geographical areas," and should "understand the necessity of local, national and international cooperation." The Declaration of Barcelona suggests that engineers "must be able to understand how their work interacts with society and the environment, locally and globally." The importance of time, of a proper historical perspective, appears when the Tbilisi declaration talks about a "focus on current and potential environmental situations while taking into account the historical perspective" and when the Declaration of Barcelona mentions a "long-term approach to decision-making." These are important correctives to societies that tend to make decisions which maximize short-term benefits and discount the needs of future generations.

Each academic discipline has unique and important contributions to make to a sustainable future, but those contributions will be more grounded in reality and of higher quality when generated from a multidisciplinary understanding.

To be credible change agents, however, learners need more than merely technical know-how and awareness of historical context. They also need skill sets related to forming and sustaining interpersonal relationships as well as effective leadership training.

Some of the most commonly cited change agent skill sets include creative problem-solving, critical thinking and reflection, the importance of self-motivated learning, persistence and resilience, and effective interpersonal skills, including conflict resolution and teamwork. Interestingly, the development of these skills also depends on awareness of personal attitudes and values and those of other people, and the ability to accurately articulate them in sensitive situations. For instance, the Declaration of Barcelona suggested that education should include an "*integrated approach* to knowledge, attitudes, skills and values," and argued that we need to address "the whole educational process in a more holistic way." Addressing attitudes and values is normally seen as a means to create commitment and concern that motivates active participation to achieve lifelong learning and self-discipline with the aim of changing behaviour. In addition, the Declaration of Barcelona specifically called on engineers to "help redirect society" toward a more responsible and sustainable direction, and suggested that they "must be able to apply professional knowledge according to deontological principles and universal values and ethics." Going far beyond the traditional boundaries of engineering education, the Declaration further suggested that engineers should promote *participatory decision-making* based on *democratic principles,* they "must be able to listen closely to the demands of citizens and other stakeholders and let them have a say in the development of new technologies and infrastructures." The Tbilisi Declaration articulated the importance of "a set of values and feelings of concern for the environment," and mentioned a "sense of responsibility and solidarity among countries and regions." Moreover, it advanced the claim that "environmental education should encourage those ethical, economic and aesthetic values which will further the development of conduct compatible with the preservation and improvement of the environment." These are decidedly normative claims and aims. But they are not overly prescriptive. In fact, as the preceding discussion has shown, these goals and desired outcomes have cross-cultural relevance, and if anything represent a convergence on visions of desired learning outcomes, even if the associations, nations and institutions discussed are widely divergent in context and focus. Although this analysis focused only on a few examples, the similarities to other sets of LOs found in the literature are clear, regardless of level and type of education.

Once the outcomes of sustainability education have been agreed upon, to be attainable teachers must also be provided with the appropriate resources and incentives, which may challenge traditional educational structures and reward systems. Curricula, syllabi, and teaching and learning activities have to be shared to facilitate the attainment of the LOs. Along with the commonalities among the LOs reviewed above, there are also common pedagogical strategies designed to emphasize active learning, real-world and problem-based learning, and the creation of reflective learning communities. Teaching methodologies must move beyond content to help construct the self-concept of a student as a lifelong learner and change agent for sustainable development. As the Tbilisi Declaration described it, the most desirable educational approaches exemplify "diversity in learning environments and educational approaches," "stress on practical activities and first-hand experience," a "closer link between educational processes and real life," and a focus on "problems that are faced by particular communities."

Conclusions

Our aim here has been to explore and compare the importance of learning outcomes for education for sustainability. Certainly, further and more in-depth work on clarifying the desired outcomes for specific geographical and cultural contexts is needed. But this discussion has illustrated that there already exist significant and potentially productive commonalities across countries and cultures. The convergence among these learning outcomes includes knowledge about ecosystems, basic understandings of social scientific analyses of human cultures, systemic thinking, inter- and intrapersonal skills, and the development of change agent skills, strategies and self-concepts. Of course, each association or institution must take further steps to integrate these broad learning outcomes into their own contexts, but it is clear that this type of transformative education must go beyond consideration of the triple bottom line, to actually educate students in ways that move them from thinking to effective action. It will require shifting away from the traditionally siloed disciplines of most higher education institutions to create what David Orr once called the next generation of renaissance men and women – learners who are effective professionals and leaders in their own disciplines, but who also have an awareness of deeper connections and obligations to others in the broader society. In short, it requires the development of a sort of careful empathy combined with enlightened self-interest that can aid in the education of well-rounded and pragmatic problem-solvers who have a desire, both personally and professionally, to help create a more sustainable world.

Notes

1 See http://www.gdrc.org/uem/ee/tbilisi.html for the full text (accessed 19 October 2011). All of the quotes attributed to the Tbilisi Declaration are drawn from this online document.
2 See http://www.unesco.org/new/en/education/themes/leading-the-international-agenda/education-for-sustainable-development/about-us/ (accessed 17 October 2011).
3 Link to the PDF available at http://www.unesco.org/new/en/education/themes/leading-the-international-agenda/education-for-sustainable-development/about-us/ (accessed 17 October 2011).

4 For the full text of the declaration, see http://www.esd-world-conference-2009.org/en/whats-new/news-detail/item/conference-proceedings-published.html (accessed 16 November 2011).

5 See http://www.esd-world-conference-2009.org/ (accessed 19 October 2011).

6 The ITESM 2005, Vision and Mission is available at http://www.itesm.mx/2015/english/index.html (accessed 19 October 2011).

7 See DANS (Disciplinary Association Network for Sustainability), at http://www.aashe.org/dans (accessed 19 October 2011).

8 For the US Partnership for Education for Sustainable Development, see http://www.uspartnership.org (accessed 21 October 2011).

9 See http://www.aashe.org/heasc (accessed 21 October 2011).

10 See https://stars.aashe.org/ (accessed 16 November 2011).

11 See http://www.myacpa.org/task-force/sustainability/docs/Learning_Outcomes_Sustainability_Map.pdf (accessed 21 October 2011).

12 See http://www.myacpa.org/task-force/sustainability/docs/Change_Agent_Skills_and_Resources.pdf (accessed 21 October 2011).

13 See also a reprint from the National Science Council for Science and Environment at http://www.ncseonline.org/EFS/DebraRowe.pdf (accessed 21 October 2011).

14 Education for Climate Neutrality and Sustainability, see http://www.presidentsclimatecommitment.org/resources/publications#guidance (accessed 21 October 2011).

15 http://www.aacu.org/pkal/disciplinarysocietypartnerships/mobilizing/index.cfm (accessed 21 October 2011).

16 See http://www.evergreen.edu/washcenter/resources/upload/Sustainability_Learning_Outcomes_2008.doc (accessed 21 October 2011).

17 See http://www.lsf-lst.ca/en/teachers/learning_outcomes.php (accessed 21 October 2011).

18 See http://www.edu.gov.mb.ca/k12/esd/correlations/index.html (accessed 21 October 2011).

19 See http://www.uspartnership.org/main/show_passage/33 (accessed 16 November 2011).

20 See http://www.hu2.se/nlhu2.htm (accessed 21 October 2011).

21 See http://www.chalmers.se/gmv/EN/ (accessed 21 October 2011).

22 See http://www.upc.edu/eesd-observatory/who/declaration-of-barcelona for the full text (accessed 21 October 2011).

23 See http://www.wbcsd.org (accessed 21 October 2011).

24 See http://www.gdrc.org/uem/ee/tbilisi.html. All quotes from the Tbilisi Declaration in this and the following paragraphs are from this website unless otherwise noted.

25 See http://www.upc.edu/eesd-observatory/who/declaration-of-barcelona. All quotes from the Barcelona Declaration in this and the following paragraphs are from this website unless otherwise noted.

References

Biggs, J., 1999. *Teaching for Quality Learning at University*. Society for Research into Higher Education & Open University Press.

Lozano, F.J., Huisingh, D., and Delgado, M., 2006. An integrated, interconnected, multi-disciplinary approach for fostering SD at the Monterrey Institute of Technology, Monterrey Campus. In J. Holmberg and B.E. Samuelson (eds), *Drivers and Barriers for Learning for Sustainable Development in Higher Education*, UNESCO, Education for Sustainable Development in Action, Technical Paper No. 3, pp. 37–47.

Rowe, D., 2002. Environmental literacy and sustainability as core requirements: success stories and models. In Walter Leal Filho (ed.), *Teaching Sustainability at Universities: Toward curriculum greening.* New York: Peter Lang.

Svanström, M., Lozano, F.J., and Rowe, D., 2008. Learning outcomes for sustainable development in higher education. *International Journal of Sustainability in Higher Education*, **9** (3).

Wals, A. and Blaze Corcoran, P., 2006. Sustainability as an outcome of transformative learning. In J. Holmberg and B.E. Samuelsson (eds), *Drivers and Barriers for Implementing Sustainable Development in Higher Education*, UNESCO, Education for Sustainable Development in Action, Technical Paper No. 3.

SECTION 2

Sustainability Across the Curriculum

Strategies and Tactics

5

SYSTEMS STUDY OF AN INTERNATIONAL MASTER'S PROGRAM

A Case from Sweden

Sanaz Karim, Nadarajah Sriskandarajah, and Åsa Heiter

Introduction

Among the few fundamental suppositions that modern civilization is built on, and for which multiple ways of articulating the meaning exist, we can mention the concepts of liberty, social justice, democracy, and the contested concept of sustainable development (SD). Michael Jacobs has argued that the ambiguity of this concept does not necessarily make it ineffective or counterproductive, but rather the very nature of these concepts is to be ambiguous at one level of meaning while facilitating the integration of a set of core ideas at a second level of meaning (Jacobs 1999). He summarized the core ideas of SD into six categories, namely, environment–economy integration, care for future generations, environmental protection, equity, quality of life, and participation.

In fact our everyday political and academic language has been influenced largely by these core ideas since the introduction of SD as a term in the Brundtland report (WCED 1987), but on the other hand some sections of the academic community continue to strive for a definition of what SD is, and what it is not.

In proposing the alternative concept of "systemic development" as a way of enhancing the SD concept, systems thinkers (Bawden 2005; Ison *et al.* 2009) set some rules to help us get past arguments over diverse definitions of SD. These scholars accepted that intellectual and conceptual diversity could be productive and purposive, if it initiated an on-going process of mutual learning. Taking part in such a process of mutual learning, however, called for new mental models and for critical questions about the old ones. In conventional positivistic science education, presentation of the objective knowledge or the "universal truth" takes priority over acceptance of any subjective purpose while exploring aspects of social reality. If that social reality is taken not as a given but one that is "continuously socially constructed" then subjectivity would be impossible to avoid, and critical reflection on the effect of our norms and values on perceptions becomes a necessity. Reflective learning as described by Churchman (1971) is "the thinking about thinking, doubting about doubting, learning about learning and (hopefully) knowing about knowing."

In theorizing education for sustainable development (ESD), the ambiguity surrounding the concept of SD remains with the definition of ESD too. But in the same way that a systemic understanding of development could help to clarify the confusion, it could help to give a better description for ESD. In an ESD program, students need to learn within a wide array of disciplines and about technical and scientific tools. It might not be important to choose the most appropriate definitions of SD, but there must be an agreement on how to select among the most urgent areas of concern and the appropriate forms of science for the classroom. According to the rules set by systems thinkers for these situations, we would agree that diversity of interpretations is an opportunity for innovation rather than a problem to be solved. Going a step further, the question would be to see how diversity could be increased through, for example, inclusion of all the parties in order to embrace what might have been ignored previously. In systems language, this requires increasing our mental flexibility and willingness to redraw the boundaries (Meadows 2009).[1] In contrast, in the disciplinary tradition of scientific research, the borders of a system of interest are given, and the researchers work within a fixed boundary without necessarily questioning the boundary itself.

We believe that this is the exact place where ESD could play a role: on the borders between different disciplines and between different interests, by examining the boundaries critically and, if necessary, by redrawing them. In what follows, we offer details about the Master's program in SD (MSD) available at Uppsala University and the Swedish University of Agricultural Sciences (*Sverigeslantbruksuniversitet* [SLU]), where the students come in with their own disciplinary knowledge, and with the aim of reshaping it by exposing it to other disciplines. The MSD clearly states in its description that it has an interdisciplinary basis and applied holistic perspective using economic, social, and ecological dimensions (Uppsala University n.d.). The initiators of the MSD wished it to be an exemplary and practice-oriented program which created more opportunities for cooperation between the two universities as well as knowledge transmission between the different departments working with sustainability issues. In practice, however, interpretation and implementation of the initial proposal ran into some difficulties that were expressed as everyday problems by the first cohort of students in 2007, of which the first author of this chapter was a member. It was also clear that many of these challenges were not unique to the MSD but applied to ESD in general and indeed to any interdisciplinary program of education. We conducted a systemic inquiry aimed at identifying, expressing, and handling those challenges. In this chapter, a brief history of education for SD in Sweden, an outline of the MSD program, a description of the specific systemic inquiry used for the study, and the main outcomes of the inquiry are presented.

Education for Sustainable Development in Sweden and at Uppsala

Being close to nature has always been valued highly in Swedish society. Sweden has nearly 100 years of history in environmental education. According to Hansson (1993), formal environmental education in Sweden began in the early twentieth century, when the National School Plan (*Normalplanenförfolkskolan*) was initiated in 1919. This initiative is regarded as a forerunner to modern environmental education in Sweden, as it stressed the need for education in nature conservation and animal protection in accordance with the social needs of the rural, agrarian society of that time (Breiting and Wickenberg 2010). Nevertheless, serious concern about environmental degradation among scientists and in the public appeared in the mid-1960s. Although the phrase SD had not been coined yet, the sustainability discourse in the Swedish media existed by presenting two opposing arguments: one defending the development of the welfare state project (which characterizes social development and security in Sweden), and the other resisting further exploitation of the landscape and nature. Putting the two arguments together, however, took some time, and the Green Welfare State (*GrönaFolkhemmet*) was introduced by the Social Democrats in 1996 as a response to the need for both. At the same time, the phrase "education for SD" entered the environmental education discourse with considerable emphasis on the importance of social sciences and global issues (Breiting and Wickenberg 2010).

Although this account is too brief to analyze the whole spectrum of ESD in Sweden, it shows some evidence that ESD belongs to the category of "environmental problem-solving" sustainability discourse, as depicted by Dryzek (1997). Dryzek characterized this discourse as

> taking the political-economic status quo as given but in need of adjustment to cope with environmental problems especially via public policy. Such adjustment might take the form of extension of the pragmatic problem-solving capacities of liberal democratic governments by institutionalizing environmental concern and expertise in its "operating procedures".
>
> *(Dryzek 1997)*

Education is obviously one of these operating procedures that had been subject to extension of the pragmatic problem-solving capacities of the Swedish democracy.

Although the establishment of the MSD program was not a direct result of any political initiatives, since it was planned by an independent council of interested teachers from the two universities in 2005, it is apparent from the program's description that the dominant discourse was projected in the structure of it. In the basic description of the program there was a clear emphasis on obtaining the skills required to apply qualitative and quantitative methods in managing natural resources, and on the ability to pursue a career in different sectors of society as stipulated by the Swedish Ministry of Education and Research (Uppsala University n.d.).

The program was intended to move the learner from a wide general knowledge of sustainability toward a narrower case-specific practice. In this approach, critical and more radical views are not ignored, but rather are engaged as important pieces of data (Figure 5.1). If the students pass the first year (see Figure 5.1), then they will be able to orient themselves and apply their knowledge in their original field of expertise in the second year of their study.

A program in SD was first proposed by Bo Sundqvist, a physicist and the former rector of Uppsala University (Karim 2009); the Faculty of Science and Technology (TEKNAT) officially launched it in 2007. At the time of writing, the MSD program has been running for four years with the enrollment going up remarkably from 20 in 2007 to 100 in the fourth year of admission (2010). The Department of Earth Sciences at Uppsala University was its home, but many of the administrative tasks took place at another location, the Evolutionary Biology Centre (EBC). The collaborating university, SLU, assigned responsibility for the program to its Faculty of Natural Resources and Agricultural Sciences; within the Faculty, the Department of Economics and the Department of Urban and Rural Development (SOL) played important roles in the MSD. Although there was a strong natural science thrust within the program, the long established Faculty of Social Sciences at Uppsala University had little contribution to the program.

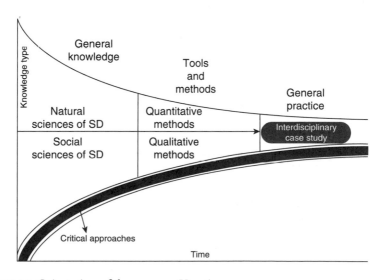

FIGURE 5.1 Orientation of the program Year 1.

It seemed that the decision about the right academic home for SD, and its position as a subject of scientific research was a hard one, so running it jointly and cooperatively was proposed by the initiators as the immediate solution. Yet the pattern of cooperation was a matter of debate at administrative and scientific levels.

In addition to the discipline-based departments, there were a number of interdisciplinary centers active in different areas of SD at both universities, such as the Uppsala Center for Sustainable Development (CSD), the Centre for Environment and Development Studies (CEMUS), the Baltic Sea University Program, and the Swedish Environmental Impact Assessment Center at SLU (EIA). Though these centers played a part in running the MSD program, a systematic coordination of these many actors was beyond the normal responsibilities of the program head. The variety of the actors as well as their relative importance is illustrated in Figure 5.2.

The Approach Used

The complexity of the concept of SD in conjunction with the multiplicity of the institutional structure in the MSD program created a problematic situation or a "mess" in the systems language. In a messy situation, the problems and the opportunities interlock with each other and produce an indefinable sense of unease (Ison 2008). Peter Checkland from the University of Lancaster developed an

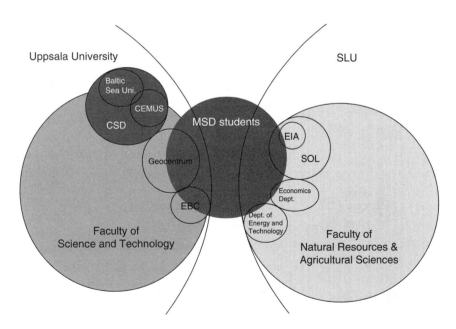

FIGURE 5.2 Main actors in the MSD.

approach called Soft Systems Methodology (SSM) in the 1970s to clarify and formulate the problems and opportunities arising from messy human situations (Checkland 1981). This was an approach for combining and optimizing different mental models over a problematic situation. Systems thinkers would argue that everything we know about the world is just a model. Our models have a strong congruence with the world but fall far short of representing the real world fully (Meadows 2009). SSM proposed a way to make a pragmatic model which ideally results in beneficiary action for most of the people involved in the problematic situation, recognizing that there would be beneficiaries and in some situations even victims among the key players. According to soft systems thinking, in such situations there are no final solutions to a *problem*, but rather there could be improvements in the *problematic situation*.

Checkland (1981) arranged the methodology in seven stages for use by practitioners who wanted to facilitate this learning process to enable the stakeholders to come up with the most feasible and desirable plan for changes (Figure 5.3). At the first stage, the situation would be unstructured and described by as many different accounts as possible as a way of comprehending its complexity. At stage two, the facilitator would be able to help participants to assimilate these accounts, express the problem situation in more explicit terms, and select the most important themes of concern for further work. These themes of concern are elaborated

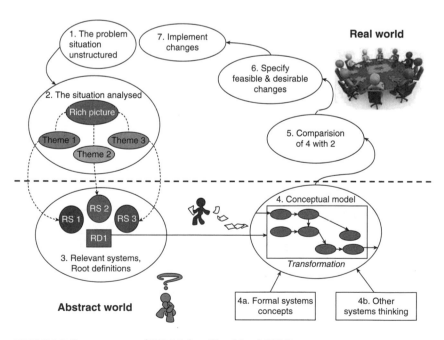

FIGURE 5.3 Seven stages of SSM (after Checkland 1981).

in systemic terms by developing a root definition, which forms a basis for modeling. Drawing on the root definition, the facilitator at stage four would be able to assist in the design of human activity systems and model them for an improved future. By discussing the root definitions with the stakeholders, the facilitator finds out what is desired by them as potential improvements and what core transformation processes should be the focus. Once a vision of an improved situation is shaped, and the transformation processes identified, the task is to build conceptual models of the activities that must be carried out to realize each of those transformation processes. At the next stage, the team returns to the real world to see which of the proposed activities were being carried out and how, and which were missing and why. Discussing the activities proposed in terms of their systemic desirability and their cultural feasibility at stage six, the changes are then implemented at stage seven, leading to a new improved situation and the likelihood of passage through the entire cycle again and again. This iterative process of experiencing real-world issues and their conceptualization in systemic terms, coupled with the accompanying flux between reflective observations at the abstract level and testing actions at the concrete level, amount to a cyclic learning process for all actors in the situation (Sriskandarajah *et al.* 1991; Checkland and Scholes 1990).

The launch of the MSD program was a success in terms of bringing the idea of SD up to the level of an integrated Master's degree and giving it an academic credibility equal to other well-established programs, instead of running individual and unconnected courses. After the intake of the first cohort in 2007, however, many sensed a need for improvement but no one was able to formulate clear-cut problems to be solved. Thus, the SSM was employed to unpack the challenges and opportunities existing in the MSD. As a prelude to obtaining a rich picture of the situation, the first author of this chapter reviewed all official literature on the program and conducted interviews with a number of participants. Interviewees included one or two representatives from each of the groups named in Figure 5.2, some of the initiators, present and previous leaders of the program, the coordinators of the courses, and 20 students from three different cohorts. Brainstorming was used as a group creativity technique in order to include as many perspectives as possible. Then the facilitator (also the primary researcher and the first author) drew the rich picture of the situation and extracted relevant themes out of it to be discussed by the program council, which consisted of the current heads of the program, the coordinators of each of the courses, and two student representatives. After agreeing upon the most relevant themes to be explored further, the desired ideal situation was pictured for each theme, and a system of interest was modeled as a set of human activities that would help to realize that system (Checkland 1981).

Some of the activities derived from this process were not welcomed by the program council, and thus were dropped. A few were modified and approved to be implemented within the bounds of existing rules of the two universities, which in fact do not allow for structural changes in a Master's program to be made within a single academic year. Thus, a major part of the plan for changes proposed for the academic year 2010–2011 have not been implemented, and therefore the true impact of this study cannot be deduced; yet the overall application of the SSM in this study, however, and some of the outcomes are reported in the next section.

Challenges and Opportunities

Taking the first step of the inquiry gave the participants an opportunity to express their opinions about the program freely. Consequently, about 40 different items of concerns were revealed. The following five relevant themes were selected for further discussion, as presented in the composite mind map in Figure 5.4: (1) the variety of the academic traditions present in the program; (2) the variety of the cultural and academic backgrounds of the students; (3) the difficulties of coordinating a large program; (4) the lack of coherence in the framework; and (5) the absence of a link with the real-life issues.

Variety and Coherence

In order to analyze and make sense out of this mind map, we started with the term, *variety*, which appeared in many branches of the mind map such as in variety of disciplines, academic departments, teachers' views on SD, and students' cultural backgrounds. *Coherence*, on the other hand, appeared to be lacking in some of the same areas. Therefore, it seemed possible to establish a cause–effect relationship between the two concepts and conclude that *the program suffers from lack of coherence resulting from the diversity in its different parts.* Taking this argument further one could, in a reductionist sense, reach an immediate solution to the issues arising from diversity by breaking them down into parts and solving each part separately. In this case, some obvious solutions might include limiting the number of students admitted, restricting the range of acceptable academic backgrounds, or reducing the number of disciplines and departments involved. Such solutions would amount to focusing on one specific area within SD at a time and even offering the MSD as a set of divided sub-programs, as proposed by one participant. This option, however, was not welcomed by most of the actors in the program. The majority thought that the pluralism resulting from diverse worldviews and different interpretations of SD was an important feature of the MSD – an inherent advantage that should be appreciated and coordinated rather than eliminated (Karim 2009).

Taking the opposite view, one can argue that variety and diversity are not the causes of incoherence, even though they increased the risk of it. In many debates over ESD, it is considered that differences must be explicated rather than be concealed (Corcoran and Wals 2004). In line with the propositions of systemic

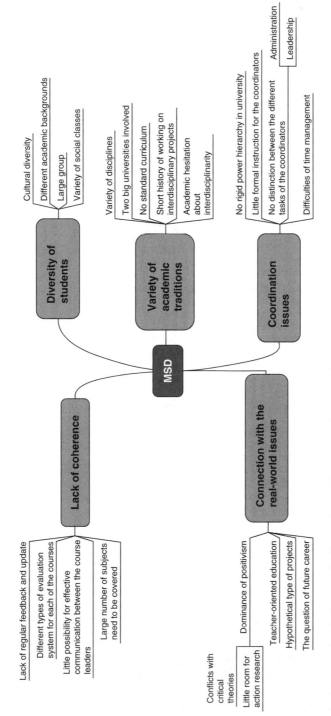

FIGURE 5.4 The challenges of offering the MSD, presented as a mind map.

development, ESD – unlike many classic disciplines – is not about specialization in one specific area of knowledge. In other words, the goal of ESD in higher education is not to train "*sustainabilists*" in the way that we train physicists, chemists, managers, and so on, but rather to fill the gap between the capabilities of a chemist and those of a manager when they come together to address a sustainability issue. But the question is how these learners could gain enough knowledge in every area relevant to SD, while acknowledging that any individual has a limited capacity for the knowledge s/he can accumulate. Even if comprehensiveness was achievable, would it not just result in shallow and scattered knowledge in several areas that has no actual effect and value, as seen in Figure 5.4, expressed as one of the concerns of the actors in the MSD program? The answer to this question very much depends on our definition of what knowledge is and how we come to know. In other words it depends on our ontologic and epistomologic positions. If we are just to discover and describe the mechanisms of social and natural phenomena, then knowledge could be seen as building a more and more accurate picture of reality. But philosophers such as Midgley (2000) believe that the question of *purpose*, for which we are building a picture from reality, is of crucial importance in defining this form of knowledge. According to Midgley:

> Knowledge cannot be seen as cumulative (building into a more and more accurate picture of reality) in any absolute sense; so the theories should be seen as more or less useful in terms of the purposes of the intervention being pursued; there is always an agent making choices (variously defined) amongst a plurality of options and we should talk in terms of locally relevant rather than universal standards for choice.
>
> *(Midgley 2000)*

Being Purposeful

Purpose is the driving force that makes us move from one point to another. It is the driving force that transforms our knowledge from one level to a higher one. Both the departure point and the destination matter in shaping this transformation. The departure point is not only the quantum of information and skills that we have in the beginning, but it is also interwoven with the worldview and the culture that have shaped it. Positivism requires that these two are kept as far apart as possible in order to extract an objective and "purely scientific" viewpoint. That is why dealing with individual purposes is not a subject in positivistic education, and the destination is wherever the value-free research will take us. Different pieces of value-free science are constantly being developed in academia and their subsequent utilization is usually determined by the needs of the market. In a program like the MSD, which deals with different types of knowledge, the desire to be holistic and coherent are not compatible with a purely positivist stance.

In critical systems thinking it is proposed that instead of putting our values away or ignoring that we necessarily carry them, we have to be aware of the sources of those values, observe their role in shaping the context of our knowledge, and be flexible enough to reform them when needed. Therefore, being purposeful as a quality in learning should be accompanied by an awareness of values, with sufficient space and opportunities in the education process for learners to embrace new kinds of knowledge and new ways of knowing. Acknowledging different worldviews is an indispensable condition that must come along with purposive learning. In the MSD program the opportunity for encountering different ways of knowing was available both for students and educators. Embracing differences also occurred but randomly and without any planned facilitation, and thus slowly and not purposefully. Therefore, we propose three transformative processes that would draw on the pluralism inherent in the program and orient the MSD toward a certain purpose.

Three Transformations

These three transformation processes are *collaborative learning among the educators*, *collaborative learning among the students*, and *action learning as an overall principle*. Our claim here is that such transformations would enable learners to pursue common and coherent pathways within the program, but with the freedom of choice with regard to their direction. Such a shift would still be in line with the goals of MSD whilst not eliminating its inherent pluralism.

The human activity systems that can facilitate and systematize these processes in order to bring them explicitly onto the agenda of education would have different structures depending on the organization of the educational institution and their past experiences and progress. In the current structure of the MSD program, three subsystems were identified, together with their specific actors, inputs, outputs, and measurements to enact the transformation processes.

Transformation 1: Collaborative Learning Among the Educators

The educators within the MSD were mostly well-qualified teachers in the Swedish university system. Almost all of them, besides their responsibility in the program, held a high position in their own disciplinary department, some of them with experience with working on interdisciplinary projects relevant to SD, but none with a specific degree directly relevant to ESD.

Communication among them took place mostly at the administrative level on the practical issues of the program. Knowing about each other's views on SD was not one of those issues, and the chance of communicating at the epistemic level was not supported. Therefore, although the educators had some experience with interdisciplinary teaching and integrating some aspects of SD into coursework, there was little possibility for them to gain shared experiences teaching in the program. In other words, the educators were not learning collaboratively about the MSD and they were teaching their separate units in an unconnected way. Collaborative learning is a specific process that begins with a comprehensive discussion of ideas and views (Daniels and Walker 2001) and leads to agreement and production of collaborative knowledge about a specific situation. At the individual level it also has the potential to transform the learning attitudes of the participants, since it provides them with a rich experience of examining and refining their own views, thereby offering the chance to transform experience into meaningful knowledge, the essence of experiential learning according to Kolb (1984). Such an attitude among the teachers can also help to shift the burden of interdisciplinarity from the students, as at present, to the teachers.

The activities proposed as necessary mechanisms of the collaborative learning system, partly inspired by the propositions of Wals *et al.* (2009), were: regular communication; investing in process facilitation; documentation of the knowledge produced during the communication sessions; revising past experiences; commitment to active participation; collective analysis of course evaluation; and reporting the challenges and progresses of each of the courses to the other course leaders. The output of such a system would be a group of coordinated and collaborative educators who were aware of each other's position and had enough flexibility to revise their educational plan when needed according to the inputs they gained from other colleagues.

Transformation 2: Collaborative Learning Among the Students

The educators who have gone through collaborative learning cycles themselves have a better ability to facilitate collaboration among their students and to transmit the correct mechanisms of collaboration to them. Although teamwork and class discussions were part of most of the courses in the MSD, students were selected randomly into groups to work together, and they regulated their communication on their own without ample guidance for managing conflicts or promoting active participation.

The same activities proposed for collaborative learning among the educators are applicable for the students, but building productive teams out of the different possible combinations of students needs to be done more carefully in order to enhance team efficiency. Therefore, in addition to teaching, the educators became responsible for building efficient, effective and contextual knowledge acquisition among groups of learners, thus assuming a facilitator's role.

Transformation 3: Action Learning

While collaborative learning was a way to glue together the different pieces of our current knowledge surrounding SD, exploring and constructing new knowledge to meet the demands of SD calls for another ability which cannot be detached from real-life contexts. Returning to the discussion about the importance of purpose, the destination in the learning process matters as much as the departure point. The students must have the ability to figure out their destination based on the context in which they are working. Acting and reflecting recursively in a real-life context creates a feedback loop that enables the learners to measure the distance between their ideals and their current knowledge, and then to retrieve new knowledge in connection with the context that they are trying to change. This transformative potential of action learning shares the same philosophical ground with experiential learning (Zuber-Skerritt 2002).

The outline of the program shown in Figure 5.1, however, does not highlight the limited but real links between experiential elements of the program and learning, which are offered at two points in the program. First, there is a specific course at the end of the first year of studies designed with practice in mind, and second, there is an opportunity to take an internship in the second year. These two courses come after the phase of knowledge accumulation which, therefore, only serves to reinforce the existing separation between the academic world inside the classroom and the real world outside the university. A system designed for pursuing action learning more purposefully would connect parts of the classroom to the real world, requiring the MSD program to take on a different shape in which practice is incorporated within critical thinking and knowledge development.

Educational Leadership

The actors of the systems proposed above, i.e., the students and the educators, welcomed the overall purpose of collaborative learning and making a comprehensive plan for it, yet the process needed a facilitator to initiate, lead, maintain, and record progress. Educational leadership here refers to a system that should be put in place to enable the above transformations, and more importantly to emphasize the distinction between the two tasks of the program heads, namely, management and leadership. The mission statement of the MSD program did not recognize this distinction and the large administrative load of the program heads left little room for educational leadership tasks.

In organizational terms, leaders are the initiators and motivators of change while managers are the administrators and regulators of change (Burke 2008). Leaders create opportunities for innovation, they persuade their followers to question assumptions and to be critical about the current situation, while managers try to keep stability and persuade the followers to be pragmatic and cooperative to get the job done (Scott et al. 2008). Both roles are needed to maintain the functionality of an organization, and to modify its structure when it needs to be adaptive to a highly dynamic environment. As we have maintained, SD is a dynamic concept and the MSD would benefit from the setting up of a few systems of human activity to deal with this dynamic nature of higher educational institutions. Accordingly, without appropriate leadership, the dynamic nature of SD could not be institutionalized in the MSD program.

Actions Taken

Following the conclusion of the study, and after agreeing upon the importance of collaborative learning, the communication sessions of the program council were held more regularly. The transformation processes proposed in Karim's study (2009) were put on the agenda as a basis for discussion. The outcome of the regular communication sessions was the recognition of the need for minor changes in the orientation of the program. As a result, a framework course has been inserted into the curriculum to offer the basic capabilities for collaborative learning, such as the ability to build and work in interdisciplinary and intercultural teams, to gain multi-cultural awareness and to identify the role of values and ethics in research. This course was placed at the beginning of the academic year in order to get the students involved in experiencing the practice of SD in a local context as early as possible. For example, a visit to a nearby location, well known for its attempts to include sustainability into community planning, was arranged as part of the framework course. The examination of this course was designed to evaluate the experiential learning competencies of the students and the educators were responsible for giving comprehensive feedback to the students in order to help them to identify these competences.

Educational leadership, as described above, was not recognized as a distinct position by the program council. Nevertheless, the program heads, out of their personal commitment, offered more time and resources to employ the necessary structural changes within the program, encouraged the communication between the different parts of the program, assisted the transmission of knowledge and experience between them, involved the senior student cohorts in designing the transformation processes, and acknowledged that taking part in a learning process for improving the MSD was also a necessary step in transferring the lessons to the higher authorities of the two universities.

Conclusion

The nature of the MSD program at Uppsala University and SLU is highly pluralistic, despite being based in natural science faculties which interpreted SD as a problem-solving enterprise. The diversity of students and teachers, as well as the presence of a variety of sometimes contradictory views on SD, is evidence of this. Although diversification, interdisciplinarity, and pluralism are appreciated by systems thinkers and many other advocates of ESD, this diversity turns out to be a serious challenge when institutionalized at disciplined universities like Uppsala and SLU. Collaborative learning enriched by action learning among the students and the educators is proposed as the transformation process that can give a coherent framework to the program while also preserving the inherent pluralism.

We have argued for a reorientation of education for SD which implies a new kind of mental capability to comprehend complex systems. We presented systems thinking, which essentially deals with appreciating wholes in terms of an interrelated complex, as an aspect of that capability, and introduced the concept of systemic development as a reinterpretation of sustainable development or as an improvement on it. The main feature of systemic development is its proposal to utilize abstract systems ideas to help inform actions when dealing with messy issues in the real world. In doing so, learning capabilities are developed through a formal scrutiny of how we learn, and are enhanced by a greater awareness of our worldviews and our epistemic position. Learning about learning is well served when a specific platform provides the opportunity for coming across different worldviews and different epistemologies, and for checking one's own position against reality. Experiential learning, taken in conjunction with systems thinking, offers both the platform and the theory to support the meta-learning demanded by SD, and the complex, messy uncertainties that come with it (Sriskandarajah *et al.* 2010). We believe the combination of the processes of collaborative and action learning proposed here for improving the MSD program could well offer the required epistemic development amongst the learners. Nevertheless, these processes, which take sustainability to the next level, cannot begin without an epistemically aware leadership and educators who are concerned with learning for change.

Note

1   The boundary of a system does not exist in reality; it is defined by the observers who want to determine the particular area of their interest and/or responsibility (Ison 2008).

References

Bawden, R., 2005. Systemic development at Hawkesbury: Some Personal Lessons from Experience. *Systems Research and Behavioral Science*, 22:151–164.

Breiting, S. and Wickenberg, P., 2010. The Progressive Development of Environmental Education in Sweden and Denmark. *Environmental Education Research*, **16**: 9–37.

Burke, W., 2008. *Organization Change, Theory and Practice*. Sage Publications Inc.

Checkland, P., 1981. *Systems Thinking, Systems Practice*. Chichester: John Wiley & Sons.

Checkland, P. and Scholes, J., 1990. *Soft Systems Methodology in Action*. Chichester: John Wiley & Sons.

Churchman, C.W., 1971. *The Way of Inquiring Systems: The Design of Inquiring Systems*. New York: Basic Books.

Corcoran, B.C. and Wals, A., 2004. The Promise of Sustainability in Higher Education. In C. Blaze and A. Wals (eds), *Higher Education and the Challenges of Sustainability* Dordrecht: Kluwer Academic, pp. 223–225.

Daniels, S.E. and Walker, B.G., 2001. *Working through Environmental Policy Conflict: The Collaborative Learning Approach*. Westport, CT: Praeger.

Dryzek, J.S., 1997. *The Politics of the Earth: Environmental Discourses*. Oxford: Oxford University Press.

Jacobs, M., 1999. Sustainable development as a contested concept. In A. Dobson (ed.), *Fairness and Futurity: Essays on environmental sustainability and social justice*. Oxford: Oxford University Press, pp. 21–47.

Hansson, B., 1993. Miljöfrågornas Framväxt i Läroplanerna. In *Skolverkets rapport. No. 34, Skolan och miljöundervisningen. Ett referensmaterial*. Stockholm: Skolverket.

Ison, R.L., 2008. Systems Thinking and Practice for Action Research. In P.W. Reason and H. Bradbury (eds), *The Sage Handbook of Action Research Participative Inquiry and Practice*, 2nd edn. London: Sage Publications.

Ison, R.L., Bawden, R.J., McKenzie, B., Packham, R.G., Sriskandarajah, N. and Armson, R., 2009. From Sustainable to Systemic Development: An Inquiry into Transformations in Discourse and Praxis. In J. Sheffield (ed.), *Systemic Development: Local solutions in a global environment*. Mansfield: ISCE Publishing.

Karim, S., 2009. Applying Systems Approach to Educational-Organizational Change Improvement of the Interdisciplinary Program. MSc in Sustainable Development. Unpublished Master Thesis, Uppsala University.

Kolb, D., 1984. *Experiential Learning: Experience as the Source of Learning and Development*. Englewood Cliffs, NJ: Prentice Hall.

Meadows, D.H., 2009. *Thinking in Systems*. London: Earth Scan.

Midgley, G., 2000. *Systemic Intervention: Philosophy, Methodology and Practice*. New York: Kluwer Academic.

Scott, G., Coates, H. and Anderson, M., 2008. *Learning Leaders in Times of Change, Academic Leadership Capabilities for Australian Higher Education*. University of Western Sydney and Australian Council for Educational Research, Strawberry Hills, NSW.

Sriskandarajah, N., Bawden, R.J. and Packham, R.G., 1991. Systems agriculture: a paradigm for sustainability. *Association for Farming Systems Research-Extension Newsletter*, **2**(3): 1–5.

Sriskandarajah, N., Bawden, R. J., Blackmore, C., Tidbal, K., and Wals, A.E.J., 2010. Resilience in Learning Systems: Case Studies in University Education. *Environmental Education Research*, 16: **5**, 311–324.

Uppsala University. n.d. Master Programme in Sustainable Development 2010/2011. http://www.uu.se/en/node605?pKod=THU2M&lasar=10%2F11 (accessed 25 August 2010).

Wals A. E.J., van der Hoeven, N. and Blanken, H., 2009. *The Acoustics of Social Learning; Designing Learning Processes that Contribute to a More Sustainable World*. Wageningen: Academic Publishers.

World Commission on Environment and Development (1987). *Report of the world commission on environment and development: Our common future*. Published as Annex to General Assembly document A/42/427, Development and International Cooperation: Environment.

Zuber-Skerrit, O., 2002. The concept of action learning, *The Learning Organization*, **9**(3), 114–124.

6

KEYS TO BREAKING DISCIPLINARY BARRIERS THAT LIMIT SUSTAINABLE DEVELOPMENT COURSES

William Van Lopik

Introduction

A nagging question plagues university and college administrators as they seek to respond to the rising demand to offer courses on sustainable development: "in what discipline do we place these new courses?" The topical area of sustainable development is a challenge to the fourteenth-century tradition of dividing higher education academics into distinct disciplines. Sustainability is a very inclusive area of study that encompasses elements of many disciplines. It is difficult to deconstruct and categorize it given our present structure of higher education. This chapter looks at the unique response of one college institution to this challenge.

The Undisciplined Nature of Sustainability

The frustration of trying to place and compartmentalize the fluid concept of sustainability into a rigid academic structure is addressed by several prominent authors. David Orr of Oberlin College says that

> Sustainability is about the terms and conditions of human survival, and yet we still educate at all levels as if no such crisis existed. The content of our curriculum and the process of education, with a few notable exceptions have not changed, the crisis [of sustainability] cannot be solved by the same kind of education that helped create the problems.
>
> *(Orr 1991: 83)*

Orr puts much for the blame of our present environmental crisis directly on higher education, which has emphasized a robust economy at the expense of environmental pillage. Anthony Cortese, Executive Director of the non-profit organization Second Nature, also gives a stinging critique of our institutions for higher education:

> Learning is fragmented, and faculty, responding to long-established incentives (e.g., tenure, research) and professional practices, are often discouraged from extending their work into other disciplines or inviting interdisciplinary collaboration. Higher education institutions bear a profound, moral responsibility to increase the awareness, knowledge, skills, and values needed to create a just and sustainable future.
>
> *(Cortese 2003: 16)*

In 1987 when the term "sustainable development" was first coming to the fore of mainstream dialogue, the World Commission on Environment and Development published an important book called *Our Common Future*. It made the point that the paths toward sustainable development cut across the divides of national sovereignty, of limited strategies for economic gain, and of separated scientific disciplines. The book highlighted the realization that environmental degradation, global poverty, inequality, and cultural disintegration are problems that cannot be addressed in a simplistic, monodisciplinary manner (World Commission on Environment and Development 1987).

The United Nations Educational, Scientific and Cultural Organization (UNESCO) program of the United Nations reiterated this understanding in 2002 during the World Summit on Sustainable Development when they stated that the current educational system falls far short of what is required to sustain the earth, and education for sustainable development must be among society's most important priorities (UNESCO 2002). This concern led to the 2005 declaration of the United Nations Decade of Education for Sustainable Development. Their directives were to break down the traditional educational schemes and promote a system that was based on:

- interdisciplinary and holistic learning rather than subject-based learning
- values-based learning
- critical thinking rather than memorizing
- multi-method approaches: word, art, drama, debate, etc.
- participatory decision-making
- locally relevant, rather than nationally relevant, information (UNESCO 2003).

These calls to change are the pretext by which college and universities across the United States are now re-examining their curriculum and designing creative and relevant ways of infusing sustainability into their traditional disciplinary structures. It is rare indeed, however, to find a college campus that has effectively exposed all of their graduating students to the foundational principles of sustainable development.

Sustainability and the Curriculum

The Association for the Advancement of Sustainability in Higher Education (AASHE) is an association of colleges and universities that is working to create a sustainable future. AASHE does this by providing resources, professional development, and a network of support to enable institutions of higher education to model and advance sustainability in everything they do, from governance and operations to education and research. AASHE interprets sustainability in a holistic and inclusive way, encompassing human and ecological health, social justice, secure livelihoods, and a better world for all generations. AASHE recently released a *Call to Action* document that was produced as a result of their *Summit on Sustainability in the Curriculum* held in San Diego, CA on 25–27 February 2010. The document pointedly stated that

> what is needed is a curriculum that prepares learners for living sustainably, both professionally and personally, and that explicitly helps the learner deeply understand the interactions, inter-connections, and the consequences of actions and decisions. Regardless of the subject of the curriculum, students must learn and practice holistic systems thinking and be able to apply such thinking to real world situations.
>
> *(AASHE 2010)*

Their website contains a list of colleges and universities across the country that have submitted "campus sustainability profiles." These profiles highlight the governance and administration, operations, research and curriculum, community service/outreach, and campus culture as they all relate to sustainability. The focus of interest for this chapter is to look at how these academic institutions have integrated sustainable development into their curriculum.

There were a total of 70 colleges and universities across North America, including a mixture of 2-year and 4-year academic institutions, on the profiles list. Particular emphasis was placed on examining how sustainability is being integrated into their curriculum development. Of the 70 institutions examined, 90% of them had infused some aspect of sustainability into the courses that they currently offer. Examples include an entire course devoted to sustainability or a module added to a pre-existing course. The courses were housed in a variety of different academic departments such as environmental studies, biology, English, business, and sociology. They were offered to all students and many students were required to take at least one course on sustainability for their academic program.

A total of 63% of the surveyed institutions had established degree programs by which a student could choose to get a major or minor in sustainability (AASHE 2009). Most institutions equated sustainable development with environmental studies and offered a degree in this pre-existing program. Impressively, much effort has been expended attempting to infuse sustainability into the traditional college structure of disciplines.

However, out of the 70 academic institutions that were surveyed, only one currently has courses in sustainable development, offers a degree in the subject, *and* requires all graduating students to take a semester course of Introduction to Sustainable Development. Although some institutions are moving in this direction, only the College of Menominee Nation (CMN) in Keshena, Wisconsin, has made sustainability a general education requirement for all students. Additionally, this has been their policy for the past five years. CMN's uniqueness in its approach to integrating sustainability can best be understood by looking at the fundamental values of the college.

The Reasons Why

Academic institutions in the United States have a well entrenched system of how departments and courses are divided up and classified. Sustainable development does not neatly fit into the present structure because it is transdisciplinary in its thinking. In universities, new ideas only slowly diffuse into practice, and the orientation toward historically entrenched concepts plays a much stronger role. Universities are known to follow path-dependency in their higher education. Their pace of change is considerably slower at the institutional-structural level than it is at the discursive level. The point is that institutional change is not transformed merely by the creation of representatives and offices (Krucken 2003). The College of Menominee Nation was established in 1993 and therefore does not have a deeply entrenched structure of departments and disciplines. Its youth has prevented it from resorting to the limitations of path dependency, although there remained significant obstacles to incorporating the principles of sustainability into CMN's courses. Specifically, CMN overcame significant barriers related to politics, diverse motives, and consensual knowledge, and these experiences help explain the successful infusion of sustainability into the curriculum in a manner unparalleled in most other academic institutions. The following is a brief description of how CMN surmounted these barriers.

Politics

When this tribal college was chartered in 1993 by the people of the Menominee Indian Tribe it was mandated that there should be a Sustainable Development Institute (SDI) tied to the college. The SDI shared tandem purposes of reflecting upon and disseminating Menominee expertise in sustainable development, and forwarding that expertise into other sectors of community life locally, regionally, nationally, and globally. The SDI has accomplished these goals by looking at sustainable development through the lens of Menominee efforts to sustain their forest and society for the last century or so in the face of steadily increasing assimilation pressures by both the United States economy and society. Author Tom Davis writes in his book *Sustaining the Forest, the People, and the Spirit* that the Menominee example of sustainable development is so significant that it holds "the promise of providing a series of lessons about how we might create a sustainable world that can prosper into the future" (Davis 2000: 5). This vision for sustainable development that Davis describes is exemplified by Dr. Verna Fowler, who is an enrolled Menominee tribal member and founding president of CMN. She was instrumental in bringing sustainable development to the fore of the college's identity and mission some 16 years ago when integrating sustainability across the curriculum was still a nascent concept. That Dr. Fowler is still the current president of the college has been important in assuring that sustainability remains a constant value of the institution.

Motives

Sustainability takes on a whole new meaning amongst people who have been pushed to the point of losing their land, culture, language, and sovereignty. The term basically becomes synonymous with survivability. It is not a difficult concept for a Native American nation to understand and embrace. The land base of the Menominee Indian Nation used to encompass most of the state of Wisconsin and much of the Upper Peninsula of Michigan. They are now left with 236,000 acres in northeast Wisconsin, a remnant of what was once theirs. They have cared and nurtured this remnant of forest in such a way that it is now more healthy and robust than it was 140 years ago. This accomplishment has warranted the Menominee's special recognition by the United Nations and the United States Presidents for their sustainable land management practices. There is no lack of motive for teaching sustainability at the campus because history has shown them that sustainable livelihoods can easily be lost. There is an intuitive realization that the same can be true at the planetary level.

Consensual Knowledge

There is cohesion and shared values amongst the staff and faculty in regards to the value of requiring that all students be exposed to sustainable development. Some of this cohesion is a result of the small number of full-time faculty members (21) who regularly interact, meet, and discuss. Another factor is the influence and prestige that the SDI brought to the college. They sponsor international guests, offer campus-wide workshops, provide student internships, initiate sustainability projects, present at national conferences, and raise funds. The institute is instrumental in branding the college as a leader in sustainable development. A third factor contributing to consensual knowledge is the motivation of the students.

Their study of sustainable development in the introductory course is a significant catalyst for them to integrate this knowledge into their other classes. They come to realize the connections between sustainability and economics, business, biology, English, anthropology, nursing, and education. They begin to expect that these concepts be addressed in their other classes.

Course Content

The Introduction to Sustainable Development course at CMN is offered in at least two sections every semester. Because it is a 100 level course, most of the students are freshmen. Course learning objectives for the course are as follows:

1. To introduce students to some of the past, present, and future initiatives in sustainable development.
2. To acquire an understanding of the Menominee model of sustainable development, as demonstrated in their history of sustainable forestry, institutional development, and cultural preservation.
3. To develop an understanding of how sustainable development concepts can be used to systematically analyze problems and think critically.
4. To raise an awareness of career options in sustainable development.
5. To motivate students to develop a sense of social and ethical responsibility as global citizens.
6. Think critically and analyze problems systematically.
7. Acquire computer and technology skills and integrate this knowledge with course work across the curriculum.

The course puts much emphasis on what Andres Edwards calls the 3 Es of sustainability. These are Equity, Environment, and Economics; additional focus is placed on the importance of the fourth "E," Education, since sustainable development requires behavioral change which comes through education (Edwards 2005).

The class is structured around a framework (logo) that is referred to as the "Menominee Model of Sustainable Development" (see Figure 6.1). This model is depicted in a hexagon that contains six components. These components are the environment, technology, institutions, economics, sovereignty, and human behavior/perceptions. The Sustainable Development Institute logo also serves as its research and extension theoretical model. This theoretical model conceptualizes sustainable development as the process of maintaining the balance and reconciling the inherent tensions between the various dimensions of sustainability. Each dimension is understood to be dynamic, both in terms of its internal organization, and its relationship to each of the other five dimensions of the sustainable development process. The model takes as its point of departure the idea that change within one dimension will impact other dimensions in an ever-unfolding

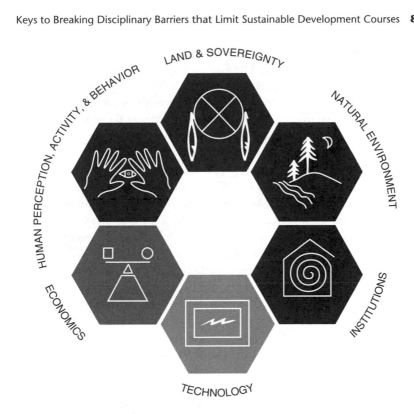

FIGURE 6.1 Menominee model of sustainable development.

diffusion of responses to change, whether externally driven or inherent to the dynamism of a specific dimension. It is this interactive process which guides the research agenda and the academic programming of the college.

The course examines each component in the model and provides examples of how each component relates to the other five. The model itself demonstrates the difficulty of trying to categorize sustainable development. As Cedric Cullingford says, "sustainability is both a subject in itself and covers subject boundaries" (Cullingford 2004). The pedagogy used in the course is based on the analyses of both local and international case studies. The most powerful example of how these components interact to form a sustainable system is the Menominee Nation itself.

The land on the Menominee Indian reservation is controlled by the sovereign Menominee Indian Nation. It is a contiguous piece of communal trust land that has not been fragmented into private ownership like so many other Indian reservations throughout the country. Community control is written into the Menominee constitution and was decided by the tribe years ago. Menominee Tribal Enterprises (MTE) is in charge of the tribal sawmill and all forest management decisions. This institution is vigilant in maintaining the health and integrity of the natural environment. They understand that the wealth of the forest is not solely based on financial capital. The forest is important for recreational, spiritual, fishing, hunting, and cultural gathering purposes. MTE's main goal is to maintain a healthy forest ecosystem. They do this by utilizing the most advanced scientific technology available to monitor, inventory, and manage the forest. The sawmill provides jobs to the community and also distributes a portion of its profits to the community at the end of the year. The mill plays a very important economic role in the reservation. Each component is vital to maintaining the environmental and socio-economic sustainability of the Menominee Nation.

Each component of the model is obviously tied to a traditional academic discipline; the approach however is unique in that they are each examined in the context of the whole. The pedagogical approach is learner-centered rather than teacher-centered. It is also praxis-oriented learning, linking theory and experience, rather than allowing learning to be dominated by theory (Van de Bor *et al.* 2000).

Not Without Challenges

There were certainly challenges to the route that CMN has taken in approaching sustainability in its curriculum. Four principal challenges were confronted and continue to be issues for the future.

First, there was initially pushback from faculty in creating a new general education course. This was a difficult period of adaptation because it required a new way of thinking and an understanding that sustainable development is not synonymous with environmental studies. The college President and Dean of Instruction were instrumental in making the change happen because of their clear understanding of the fundamental differences between the topical areas and their rejection of maintaining a curriculum that had no place for instruction on sustainable development.

Second, the transferability of credits was another significant challenge. The question was always "do the credits from the sustainable development class transfer to other colleges and institutions?" This was resolved by communicating with all the other public institutions of higher education in Wisconsin and explaining the purpose and rigor of the course. They all responded in a positive fashion that they would accept the course for credit.

Third, there was the challenge of what type of faculty was actually qualified to teach such a broad topical area, since initially there were no upper level degrees being offered in sustainable development. The constraints of this challenge are being eased now that other universities are offering graduate degrees in sustainability.

A fourth challenge is the comprehensive nature of sustainable development. It encompasses so many issues and topical areas, a breadth that is difficult to cover in a single course. We have addressed this challenge by explaining to students and faculty that the course is designed to initially introduce students to sustainability concepts and to demonstrate the relevancy of sustainability to the subsequent courses they take in nursing, business, natural science, English, etc.

Factors Crucial to Success

The AASHE *Call to Action* lists a number of recommendations that are vital to integrating sustainability into college and university curricula (AASHE 2010). Many of these recommendations reinforce the decisions that the College of Menominee Nation previously made in its transformation of the academic curriculum. The following factors are supportive of the on-going process of integrating sustainability across the curriculum.

Relevant Stakeholders Were Brought Together to Collaborate on Sustainability

During the winter months of 2009 a comprehensive survey was conducted on the SDI at CMN. The purpose of the survey was to provide evaluative insights and perspectives on the sustainability activities of the Institute. Qualitative and quantitative data were gathered over a 3-day period from 60 external and internal stakeholders using the Appreciative Inquiry (AI) process. This is an organizational survey process that seeks to find out the positive aspects of an organization, it basically asks participants "what is working well?" This information can then lead the organization into thinking about "what is possible in the future?" It is an inquiry into the positive rather than dwelling on the negative of organizational performance (Johnson and Ludema 1997: 20). A key result of the survey was that stakeholders want the staff of the SDI to serve as resources in support of faculty research and curriculum development related to sustainability. The survey confirmed the importance of bringing together campus and community leaders to work together and collaboratively seek funding. It also affirmed the value of SDI in its role of enabling the college to become more sustainable in all aspects of its operations.

Commitment of Campus Leadership to Address Climate Change

Dr. Verna Fowler, President of CMN, signed the American College and University Presidents Climate Commitment (ACUPCC) in 2007. She was one of the first signatories of this document and currently serves on the ACUPCC's Steering Committee. Her commitment to sustainability has affected the campus environment in a myriad of ways, from operations management and procurement to curricular transformation. She is adamant in her goal of moving the whole heart, mind, body, and soul of the campus into exemplary actions of sustainability.

Funding Proposals Are Designed to Complement Sustainable Development

The SDI makes it a regular practice to write grant proposals that support curriculum development and research pertaining to sustainability. These proposals are vital to advancing sustainability on the campus. Grants have allowed faculty to attend national conferences to present research papers on sustainability and have paid for student interns to conduct waste stream analysis both on and off the campus. They have also allowed for the purchase of campus composters, energy efficiency monitors, permaculture workshops, and the hosting of community sustainability fairs. Most importantly, the grants have enabled the SDI to hire a full-time campus Sustainability Coordinator. The staffing of this position has allowed the campus to delve much deeper into honoring Dr. Fowler's commitment to the ACUPCC goals. CMN has established itself as one of the leaders in the country on sustainability initiatives, and this reputation is very helpful in terms of name recognition and credibility of leadership. Potential funders know that the concept is not a fad at CMN, but has been practiced since the college's beginning. The sponsored program office at CMN has developed a rich portfolio of governmental and non-governmental funding agencies that are receptive to funding sustainability programs.

Sustainability Criteria Is Integrated into Hiring Policy

The Academic Program Director for Sustainable Development was asked to take an active role in hiring several new faculty members at the college. During the interview process, the faculty candidates were questioned on their views and perspectives on sustainability. They were asked to define it, give their opinions, and commit to supporting campus sustainability efforts while integrating it into the classroom setting. It is hoped that the same line of questioning may soon permeate the interview process of all potential staff and faculty hires, regardless of their academic discipline.

The Impact of Sustainability Efforts Are Evident Outside of the Classroom

CMN faculty are actively involved in melding the concepts of sustainability from the classroom with applications in project-based learning and the development of interdisciplinary connections.

There are two concrete examples of this occurring in the past year. The Campus Grind Coffee Shop is an indigenous business created by two student organizations at CMN: Strategies for Environmental Education, Development and Sustainability (SEEDS) and the American Indian Business Leaders (AIBL). To begin, the SEEDS club fostered a collaborative relationship with a fair trade coffee distributor to learn about and understand ecologically, socially, economically, and politically sustainable aspects of the coffee industry. This connection led to selling the coffee products on the CMN campus. It also created an opportunity for students to participate in two different delegations to Chiapas, Mexico, to meet with the indigenous farmers to better understand the coffee industry. While SEEDS grasped the environmental sustainability component, the business expertise was missing from the coffee sales efforts. SEEDS contacted AIBL for assistance with the business plan and implementation, forming a partnership between the two groups. The result of the SEEDS/AIBL alliance melded the interests of the two campus organizations and created an exemplary case study for the practice of sustainability and indigenous entrepreneurship. The coffee shop is now used as a case study of sustainability in all the business courses offered at the college.

The second example comes out of the "Indian Student Renewable Energy Challenge," an intercollegiate competition sponsored by the US Department of the Interior. This was a pilot project intended to create interest and expertise in building a wind power generator. Argonne National Laboratory, in partnership with the Department of the Interior's Bureau of Indian Education and the Office of Indian Energy and Economic Development, announced the challenge in the fall of 2009 to all Native American tribal colleges and high schools. They requested designs for small wind turbine systems that would harness wind energy, store it mechanically or electrically, and then use the stored energy to power an array of light-emitting diode lights (LEDs). A group of five faculty members and ten students from CMN entered the challenge. They ultimately placed first in this national competition and were awarded a trip to Washington, DC in April 2010 to meet with the US Secretary of the Interior. This project helped create momentum on the campus to initiate additional alternative energy projects both on the operational level and on the community education level. Sustainability is now a common theme in the technical education classes that the college offers.

Sustainability Is Integrated into Strategic Learning Objectives

Concepts of sustainability are now part of the overall learning objectives of all students at the college. Our first objective is for students to learn how to reflect upon the relevance of sustainability to their lives and their values, and how their actions impact issues of sustainability in other parts of the world. The second objective is to equip students to recognize the historical parallels between their cultural history in the United States and the cultural history of other indigenous peoples in other parts of the world. These objectives are assessed through various writing assignment given in the class, the creation of a group poster, short quizzes, and a final reflection paper, which students present to the entire class. In addition, achievement of these objectives is being assessed through an instrument that was pilot tested in the sustainable development class. Last year, I utilized the Global Perspectives Inventory (GPI), an online test that measures college students' degree of understanding and awareness of various cultures and their impact on our global society. It also looks at the students' degree of engagement with others who are different than themselves, and degree of cultural sensitivity in living in a pluralistic society. The inventory was administered at the beginning and end of the semester to see whether the intercultural awareness and attitudes of the students changed as a result of the course. The initial results of the pretest indicated that the students in our first year course tested at the same level as the other 15,000 freshman and sophomores from across the United States who previously took the GPI. The GPI[1] was then given to the same students in my class at the end of the semester. This time the test results indicated that the students scored at the same level as senior level students from across the country (Van Lopik 2010). The "global awareness" of the students in the class had essentially increased in three months to a level that usually requires 4 years of instruction with students from other colleges and universities. The results were a positive indication that the course is indeed effective at changing the attitudes and perspectives of students in regard to their views on being global citizens.

Sustainability Knowledge Base Is Shared with a Broader Audience

The SDI is a valuable resource for CMN faculty and staff. SDI has sponsored two international conferences in the past six years. The underlying premise for both conferences was the belief that indigenous peoples from all over the world are steadily confronted with outside pressures of having both their land and cultures assimilated into the dominant cultural context. There is currently an acute need to explore successful models of sustainable development that allow for the preservation of indigenous lands, sovereignty, and culture, while also allowing for the integration of economic development, institutional capacity-building, and technological advancement.

The Menominee believe their model of sustainable development provides clues to the kind of values, economic system, and social order that might be necessary in a sustainable world. As the state of the world's environment becomes more critical, it is believed that this model as well as other principles derived from indigenous wisdom might offer clues from which the modern world can learn as it desperately seeks development alternatives.

The 2007 Sharing Indigenous Wisdom: An International Dialogue on Sustainable Development Conference[2] was held on the Oneida Indian Reservation and had over 120 persons in attendance. There were representatives from throughout the world including Central and South America, New Zealand, Finland, the Philippines, India, Nigeria, Nepal, Australia, Canada, Mexico, and the United States. Indigenous nations represented included: Anishnabe, Awajun, Dineí, Karuk, Mauri, Metis, Oneida, Okanagan, Pikangikum, Pueblo of Pojoaque, Potawatomi, Pueblo Miskitu, Sac and Fox, Salish-Kootenai, Seminole, Tingguian, Yakama, and the hosts, the Menominee. In attendance were scholars, academics, foresters and forest managers, institutional and governmental policy makers, planners and implementers, undergraduate and graduate students from both local and foreign colleges and universities. The conference was an excellent forum for sharing sustainability efforts, particularly among indigenous practitioners, from around the world.

Faculty and staff who are linked to the SDI are asked to provide leadership on issues of sustainable development both on and off the campus. In 2008, two half-day workshops were conducted for 30 regional Wal-mart managers to explore ways that they could integrate sustainability practices into their stores. A half-day in-service was also conducted with all CMN faculty members to help them to strategize how sustainability could be integrated into their individual courses across the curriculum. Faculty members have presented the model of sustainability at national and international conferences and have been asked by other tribal colleges to serve as outside consultants as they try to replicate some of CMN's efforts. CMN's accomplishments have been recognized through national awards and citations in numerous books and periodicals. As Ted Bernard pointed out in his book *Hope and Hard Times*, written about the college and its sustainability efforts: "Every student must take a course on sustainable development that focuses on the Menominee model of sustainability, [it is] woven throughout the college's curriculum, research, outreach, and service activities" (Bernard 2010: 128). It is important for an institution to develop and market their expertise in an area of study and research. The more they are recognized for their leadership, the more they will continuously develop their expertise. Recognition breeds leadership.

Summary

We at the College of Menominee Nation strongly advocate that all students need to be exposed to the concepts and values of sustainable development. Sustaining our world is not an option that some can choose to ignore and others can respond too. The aforementioned strategy is the method that we have adopted. We understand that this method would not necessarily work in other institutions, but somehow all institutions must get the message. We applaud the efforts that all the AASHE members have undertaken in transforming their curricula and exposing their students to a rapidly changing world. The urgency of our challenge can best be summarized from a quote from Janice Woodhouse in the journal *Thresholds in Education*:

> the sustainability across the curriculum movement is part of a new sustainability world view. …the consequences of not finding the space and time for this education are unacceptable – they threaten the very ecological, cultural, and economic systems that support our existence.
>
> *(Woodhouse 2009: 6)*

Notes

1 For more information on the Global Perspectives Inventory, please visit the website http://gpi.central.edu.
2 For more information on the Sharing Indigenous Wisdom Conference, go to www. sharingindigenouswisdom.org

References

Association for the Advancement of Sustainability in Higher Education (AASHE) *Campus Sustainability Profiles*, http://www.aashe.org/resources/profiles/profiles.php (accessed 10 August 2009).
Association for the Advancement of Sustainability in Higher Education (AASHE), 2010. *Sustainability Curriculum in Higher Education: A Call to Action*. Denver, CO: AASHE.
Bernard, T., 2010. *Hope and Hard Times: Communities, collaboration and sustainability*. Gabriola Island, British Columbia: New Society Publishers.
Cortese, A., 2003. The critical role of higher education in creating a sustainable future. *Planning for Higher Education*, **31**(3): 15–22.
Cullingford, C. 2004. Conclusion: The Future – Is Sustainability Sustainable? In C. Cullingford and J. Blewitt (eds), *The Sustainability Curriculum*. Earthscan: London, pp. 251–252.
Davis, T., 2000. *Sustaining the Forest, the People, and the Spirit*, Albany, NY: SUNY Press.
Edwards, A., 2005. *The Sustainability Revolution: Portrait of a Paradigm Shift*, Gabriola Island, British Columbia: New Society Publishers, p. 20.
Johnson, S. and Ludema, J.D., 1997. *Partnering to Build and Measure Organizational Capacity: Lessons from NGOs around the world*. Grand Rapids, MI: CRC Publications.
Krucken, G., 2003. 'New, new thing': on the role of path dependency in university structures. *Higher Education*, **46**(3), 315–339.
Orr, D., 1991. *Ecological Literacy: Education and the Transition to a Postmodern World*. Albany, NY: SUNY Press, p. 83.
UNESCO, 2002. *Education for Sustainability*. Paris: United Nations Commission on Sustainable Development.
UNESCO, 2003. *The Decade of Education for Sustainable Development*. New York: United Nations.
Van de Bor, W., Holen, P., Wals, A., and Filho, W., 2000. *Integrating Concepts of Sustainability into Education for Agriculture and Rural Development*. Frankfurt: Peter Lang, p. 309.
Van Lopik, W., 2010. Success at Achieving Intercultural Awareness. *Midwest Connection*, p. 5.
Woodhouse, J., 2009. The place of education for sustainability in higher education. *Thresholds in Education*, vol. XXXV, p. 6.
World Commission on Environment and Development, 1987. *Our Common Future*. Geneva: Oxford University Press.

SECTION 3
Educating the Professional

7

STRATEGIES FOR TRANSFORMING HEALTHCARE CURRICULA

A Call for Collaboration Between Academia and Practitioners

Carrie Rich and Seema Wadhwa

What Is Healthcare Sustainability Management?

What is sustainable healthcare and how does academia teach sustainable health-care management? When this question was asked of faculty in the School of Nursing and Health Studies at Georgetown University, colleagues mentioned public health, ecological health, and environmental health sciences curricula as educational tools. But within the Department of Health Systems Administration, where healthcare managers are grown, the answer to this question remained unclear. Public health and ecological health programs teach different, though equally necessary, skills as compared to the business management and health policy focuses of healthcare administration programs.

Healthcare sustainability management at Georgetown University meant examination of the social trends and drivers of sustainable health systems with a special focus on hospitals. The purpose of the management sustainability curriculum was to explore fiscally responsible approaches for healthcare providers and systems to become better stewards of the environment (Rich 2010). The most effective method of integrating sustainability in healthcare management education was to nurture partnerships between students and healthcare administrators who practiced sustainable management. Collaboration between academia and healthcare delivery systems provided students with purposeful, practical experience uniquely focused on the business management perspective of sustainability. Industry partners gained fresh student ideas and opportunities to mold academic requirements to be more in concert with desired leader skill sets. Viewed in tandem, Georgetown University's informal collaboration with industry leaders helped bridge the gap between academia and sustainable management in the medical field (Kohn *et al.* 2000).

This chapter provides the case for interdisciplinary healthcare sustainability curricula. The featured case study explains how to improve healthcare management sustainability education through collaboration between academia and healthcare.

Faculty Awareness

Sustainability education is not traditionally part of healthcare administration training. Nonetheless, Georgetown University offered a broadly focused graduate-level elective course, Environmental Healthcare Sustainability, to Health Systems Administration students housed within the School of Nursing and Health Studies. The Environmental Healthcare Sustainability course raised awareness about the role healthcare leaders play in environmental stewardship. In order to reach a larger audience than feasible with the elective course, components of course content will be integrated into nursing, managerial ethics and healthcare quality courses through focused discussions and guest lectures. The Department of Health Systems Administration at Georgetown University ultimately concluded that sustainability is not a core element of educational strategy, though lecturers without previous sustainability awareness are seeking methods of integrating components with sustainability content.

Healthcare Sustainability: A Fusion of Disciplines

There were key distinctions between efforts to integrate sustainability into the existing curriculum as opposed to offering a more comprehensive healthcare sustainability learning tract. The comprehensive approach attracted a diverse student body to cooperate with the multidisciplinary professional teams of students engaged upon entering the workforce (Kaplan *et al.* 2009). The Environmental Healthcare Sustainability course at Georgetown University included undergraduate, medical, and graduate students with educational and professional backgrounds/interests in nursing, public health, global health, law, health information technology, rural health, long-term care, and zoology. The student body of the Environmental Healthcare Sustainability class demonstrated that sustainability education must be interdisciplinary, requiring adaptation of best practices from other industries to the healthcare sector. What is more, healthcare professionals external to Georgetown University, including military leadership, made requests for participation in the class, recognizing the uniqueness of Georgetown University's interdisciplinary offering and relevance of course content to their work.

A primary goal and highlight of the curriculum was cooperation between academics and practitioners internal and external to the Georgetown University campuses. Collaborations facilitated multidisciplinary learning that leveraged existing competencies and resources pertinent to healthcare sustainability.

Cooperation between local hospitals and the academic campus is a promising strategy, and should be considered in future healthcare curricula development and dissemination. Administrators at Georgetown University believed that partnership between academia and professionals engaged in healthcare practice created the platform for a more sustainable, holistic, healing healthcare industry.

Unsustainable Healthcare Spending

The most significant challenge for healthcare sustainability is answering the question, how should healthcare educators define a cohesive, consistent approach to sustainability that subscribes to broad principles while focusing implementation efforts on specific processes? Deloitte (2010) asked a similar question when surveying sustainability executives from leading companies as part of a study on Sustainability in Business Today: A cross-industry view. Deloitte (2010) targeted leaders from five major industry sectors selected to draw a portrait of sustainability in business: automotive, consumer products, process and industrial, technology, and telecommunications. The critical success factor in aligning sustainability with business strategies, according to the survey, was executive leadership commitment in driving a sustainability vision throughout organizational culture (Deloitte 2010; Berns *et al.* 2009). How can these findings be translated to the healthcare industry? How has academia prepared healthcare leaders to prioritize sustainability objectives in alignment with business objectives? In large part, we have not.

According to the most recent Centers for Medicare and Medicaid Services (CMS) data, national healthcare expenditures (NHEs) are projected to have reached 2.5 trillion dollars in 2009 at a growth rate of 5.7%, up from 4.4% in 2008, while the overall economy is anticipated to have fallen 1.1%. In 2010, NHE growth is expected to decelerate to 3.9% while GDP is anticipated to rebound to 4.0% growth. Much of the projected slowdown in NHE growth is attributable to a reduction in Medicare physician payment rates called for under Sustainable Growth Rate (SGR) provisions. Looking forward over the projection period of 2009 to 2019, CMS anticipates average annual health spending to grow by 6.1%, outpacing average annual growth in the overall economy, which is projected to occur at 4.4%. If these projections are accurate, NHEs are expected to reach 4.5 trillion dollars by 2019, which will comprise 19.3% of gross domestic product (GDP) (CMS 2009). Based on the financial bottom line alone – excluding, for a moment, the environmental and social drivers of sustainability – one might reasonably ask why healthcare sustainability leadership was excluded from the Deloitte study (Deloitte 2010). The more appropriate concern of this chapter is what higher education will do about the unsustainable healthcare problem faced by society. How can we – multidisciplinary educators, eventual patients, industry leaders, and current witnesses of unsustainable healthcare practices – capitalize on our responsibility to educate healthcare sustainability managers?

First, Do No Harm

Environmental Healthcare Sustainability

CMS uses the term "Medicare Sustainable Growth Rate," which underscores the otherwise unsustainable financial practices our healthcare system employs (CMS 2009). Financial implications are driven by management practices. Thus, curriculum transformation in healthcare management needs to be a key concern for sustainability educators.

Returning to the concern of how healthcare educators define a cohesive, consistent approach to sustainability, Georgetown University colleagues renamed the Healthcare Sustainability course "Environmental Healthcare Sustainability" to emphasize the environmental component of sustainability. This decision was made despite an awareness of the triple bottom line, which focuses on social, environmental, and economic performance drivers, also known as people, planet, profit (Savitz and Weber 2006). For the sake of expediting the administrative process, educators agreed to insert the term "environmental" into the healthcare sustainability course title because of an overall familiarity with existing "green" practices on campus. More importantly, environmental stewardship is one starting point for fiscally sustainable healthcare management, which is also often socially responsible in practice (Institute for Innovation in Large Organizations 2008; Global Health and Safety Initiative 2009).

Georgetown University's School of Nursing and Health Studies supported the Environmental Healthcare Sustainability course housed and funded within the Department of Health Systems Administration. At the completion of the course, students were held accountable for being able to:

(1) apply the operational and theoretical definitions of "sustainability";
(2) describe best practices of environmental sustainability in healthcare systems;
(3) critique sustainability initiatives in contemporary health systems;
(4) discuss the elements of a business case for sustainable health systems;
(5) critique the state of evidence-based hospital design;
(6) analyze the impact of the built environment on clinical, financial, and human resource indicators;
(7) discuss leadership and managerial strategies for improving sustainability indicators in healthcare systems;
(8) analyze the implications of environmentally sustainable delivery systems on both private and social costs.

To achieve these objectives, students researched the following environmental strategies framed in a healthcare management context:

(A) corporate social responsibility and social entrepreneurship: a call to governance (CERES 2002);

(B) how to make sustainability a competitive advantage (Institute for Innovation in Large Organizations 2008);

(C) strategy development for baseline performance and systems checklist (Green Team Checklist 2009);

(D) waste management: analysis methodology and risk assessment (Washington State Department of Ecology 2005);

(E) energy management: transparency and self-assessment (Green Guide for Health Care 2007);

(F) evidence-based facility design: tools and decision making (Sadler *et al.* 2009);

(G) sustainable buildings: metrics navigation and business incentives (Guenther 2009);

(H) supply chain management meets environmentally preferable purchasing: sustainable sourcing, cleaning, and vendor partnerships (Chase Wilding *et al.* 2009);

(I) sustainable food sourcing, preparation and nutrition: incentive strategies (Healthcare Without Harm 2008);

(J) sustainable health information technology (Messervy 2010);

(K) policy implications: community impact and industry-nonprofit partnerships (Global Environmental Management Initiative and the Environmental Defense Fund 2008);

(L) future outlook: strategic partnerships;

(M) public speaking and networking in a sustainable environment (Rich 2010).

Students additionally conducted interviews with the Sustainability Officer at Inova Health System, a healthcare delivery system leading the path toward healthcare sustainability. The Environmental Healthcare Sustainability curriculum incorporated and merged the triple bottom line of people, planet, and profit in a manner that benefitted both healthcare managers and healthcare administration education (Practice Greenhealth 2009).

Connections with Undergraduate Education

The School of Nursing and Health Studies awards the Bachelor of Science degrees in Nursing and in Health Studies with concentrations in Human Science, Health Systems Administration, and International Health Science. These programs offer an interdisciplinary perspective and prepare Georgetown University undergraduate students for careers in nursing, international public health, the biomedical field, or healthcare administration. The Environmental Healthcare Sustainability curriculum further built on interpersonal communication to prepare students for working as team members with clinicians, managers, scientists, engineers, regulators, technicians, and public stakeholders (Brown 2008). For instance, students developed marketing strategies for how to promote sustainable food sourcing in hospitals (Health Care Without Harm 2008) and employee engagement campaigns for surgical blue wrap recycling, which built on marketing and human resources classes at the undergraduate and graduate levels (Chase Wilding *et al.* 2009). Undergraduate students who participated in the graduate-level course required special permission to participate. All Environmental Healthcare Sustainability students interacted with healthcare design professionals from Perkins+Will to discuss contracting strategies for Leadership in Energy and Environmental Design (LEED) certified buildings and spoke with vendor representatives about contracting with materials suppliers that promote sustainable products and services (Global Environmental Management Initiative 2004b; Moore 2010).

Practitioner–Academic Partnership

A hallmark of the Environmental Healthcare Sustainability curriculum was access to current industry data, presented by guest lecturers in healthcare sustainability management positions as well as the course instructor – a member of the adjunct faculty at Georgetown University. Throughout the Environmental Healthcare Sustainability course, students accessed Practice Greenhealth webinars, developed by and for healthcare sustainability management professionals (Practice Greenhealth webinar 2009) and were prompted to participate in revising the Green Guide for Healthcare (GGHC) in partnership with practicing healthcare sustainability professionals (Green Guide for Health Care 2008).

Case Study: Inova Health System

Improved healthcare management results from moving beyond "green" to the social and fiscal sustainability issues that help healthcare organizations better serve patients and communities. Inova Health System is one example of a partner that demonstrates the positive fiscal possibilities of corporate responsibility in sustainable healthcare management. Inova Health System is a not-for-profit comprehensive network of hospitals, outpatient services, assisted and long-term care facilities, and healthcare centers located throughout Northern Virginia. Inova has over 1,700 licensed hospital beds and over 16,000 employees, equating to a significant impact on the surrounding community. The Inova Health System mission relates to improving the health of the community, and with this mission in mind, Inova realized the importance of being a sustainable member of its community.

Similar to Georgetown University, leaders at Inova asked: What does environmentally sustainable healthcare look like? Followed by: What are the financial implications of operating according to environmental stewardship principles? When looking to industry, there was not a clearly defined, evidence-based model to answer these questions. Rather, the answers emerged with the evolution of the healthcare sustainability industry.

Inova's initial efforts to address the aforementioned questions in practice were limited. Limitations stemmed from a lack of resources and a lack of qualified, dedicated management to direct the initiatives. These outcomes were incongruous with Inova's commitment to being a sustainable member of its community.

Inova's sustainability program flourished with positive fiscal, social, and environmental outcomes only after fiscal and human capital was allocated. Similarly, only after Georgetown dedicated resources to strategically develop a curriculum in Environmental Healthcare Sustainability did students in higher education learn about the benefits of sustainable healthcare management.

In 2008, Inova contracted with a sustainability consulting firm to develop the sustainability program. The goals were clear from the start: create a program that would engage employees, produce positive effects on the community and create fiscal savings – all while positively effecting the environment. In short, Inova aimed to put into practice the tenets of the triple bottom line: people, planet, and profit.

Inova was committed to creating a baseline culture of sustainability. This objective was founded on a comprehensive program including both operational and strategic goals tied to values-based initiatives. Table 7.1 displays the triple bottom line benefits of Inova's sustainability program (see Table 7.1).

Upon learning about Inova's sustainability management strategies, the question for Georgetown University became: How should higher education use Inova's results to inform curricula? Sustainability is here to stay (Berns *et al.* 2009) and the healthcare industry is only growing (CMS 2009). The disciplines of sustainability and healthcare are on intersecting paths. How will higher education prepare healthcare leaders to manage this interdisciplinary but foreseeable future? The Georgetown University informal partnership with Inova is one model by which sustainable healthcare managers were trained. The success of the model is predicated on the positive outcomes generated by Inova. The underlying assumption is that the healthcare industry would benefit socially, environmentally, and fiscally if more administrators behaved according to sustainability management principles. Georgetown University's curricular goals were to produce graduates with the skill sets needed to generate outcomes reflective of Inova's success. Industry partnerships with academic institutions helped mold a sustainable future from a pragmatic viewpoint, allowing healthcare to be part of the academic solution.

Transforming Student Learning

When asked through an informal survey whether Environmental Healthcare Sustainability should be part of a healthcare management curriculum in the future, one student responded, "Yes. We continue to need a class that focuses exclusively on sustainable practices." Another student wrote, "The topic of sustainable healthcare management will only become more increasingly relevant."

TABLE 7.1 Triple bottom line benefits of Inova's sustainability program

Area of focus	Example strategy	Environmental benefit	Social benefit	Fiscal benefit
Energy management	Demand load response shedding	Curtailing energy use on high energy demand days	Reduction in carbon footprint	Over $15,000 for a hospital
Water usage reduction	Sterilization equipment	1.2 million gallons annually	Water conservation	Over $60,000 annually
Waste management	Waste segregation through education	Over 750 tons recycled in 2009 (that's more than 90 elephants)	Avoided use of landfills	Over $100,000 saved annually though recycling efforts
Alternative transportation	Employee fringe benefits	Reduction in carbon emissions from transportation	Reduction in carbon footprint and traffic impacts	Up to $2,200 pre-tax spending annually for employees partaking ir the program
Sustainable foods	Community supported agriculture	Reduction in carbon emissions from transportation	Supporting the local economy	Over $13,000 directly, supporting a local farm from one hospital
Environmentally preferable purchasing	Changed 35 of the top 150 used office supply products to environmentally preferable alternatives	Reduction in virgin material content use	Over 3,500 trees saved through recycled content paper	$27,000 saved in 2009
Green construction	Lighting retrofits	Reduction in energy demand	Reduction carbon footprint	Pending savings of $12,000 at a facility

Followed by, "Having spoken to other students in the [Health Systems Administration] program, there is much interest expressed by students to take the elective course in the future. As future leaders, I think it is very important for my classmates to take a course about sustainability in healthcare. Perhaps course content could even be intertwined with other classes in addition to standing on its own" (Georgetown University, School of Nursing and Health Studies 2010a).

Environmental Healthcare Sustainability was taught by a graduate of the Health Systems Administration program, providing opportunity for student feedback to inform course development. The course's interdisciplinary approach was tailored to suit the existing framework of Georgetown University's Health Systems Administration program. In short, the course was taught by an emerging practitioner for emerging practitioners. Furthermore, several of the guest lecturers were early and mid-level careerists from not-for-profit healthcare delivery systems as well as for-profit consultants who responded directly to the challenges of incorporating sustainability in the emerging career path of sustainable healthcare management.

When asked through an informal survey about the strengths of Environmental Healthcare Sustainability, students said, "I think healthcare sustainability is an emerging field, making this class truly unique. I would have never thought about these concepts if it was not for this class." Another student wrote, "The relevant and informative content complimented by practical work and realistic projects made me feel like I was making a difference." Another student said, "I was able to incorporate the issues from Environmental Healthcare Sustainability into my other courses. I feel I will be significantly more prepared for considering the implications of topics discussed in my other courses and will be better prepared for entering the workforce" (Georgetown University, School of Nursing and Health Studies 2010a).

Employment Opportunities and Generational Expectations

For graduates of higher education, there is an expectation that sustainability principles will be incorporated into the fabric of business practices. Students of healthcare are no exception (Georgetown University, School of Nursing and Health Studies 2010). Yet, for graduating students to obtain employment, practical field experience is often considered as a prerequisite, and many healthcare delivery systems do not currently incorporate sustainability in practice. The curriculum's mid-term and final project engagement with current healthcare sustainability managers provided on-the-job learning that buttressed classroom learning, making students increasingly competitive in the growing healthcare sustainability market (Bureau of Labor Statistics 2008–2009).

A front page *Washington Post* article reported that a recent survey by the Association of American Colleges and Universities found that 16% of institutions offer majors or minors in public health (Brown 2008). In the 2007–2008 academic year, graduate student enrollment in environmental health science programs increased 13% in eight graduate programs polled in an annual survey. These statistics highlight increased public and environmental health interests. Students in these fields as well as Environmental Healthcare Sustainability monitor and interpret the implications of human actions on environmental ecosystems. Additionally, students have an opportunity to be engaged in the strategic development of systems to reduce the human footprint (Centers for Disease Control and Prevention 2009). Given the relationships between public health, environmental health sciences, and Environmental Healthcare Sustainability, statistics highlight an increasing opportunity to engage students.

Differentiation of Environmental Healthcare Sustainability from Existing Courses

Environmental Healthcare Sustainability, as taught within the Department of Health Systems Administration, School of Nursing and Health Studies at Georgetown University, was not public health and was not environmental health sciences. Rather than focus on in-depth expertise in a specific area of environmental health, for instance, the Environmental Healthcare Sustainability curriculum allowed students to gain a broader, interdisciplinary perspective. Students qualified for a wide array of job opportunities because they were exposed to a combination of healthcare management training with training from other disciplines, such as consulting, design, business, law, and engineering. Students were additionally exposed to the complimentary fields of risk management, public health, occupational health, ecological health, and environmental health.

Graduates of the Environmental Healthcare Sustainability course might pursue careers in the public sectors as program managers, environmental and occupational health coordinators, risk managers, project managers, regulators, or researchers. Academia, the private sector, trade associations and local, state, and federal governmental agencies will also provide potential career paths for graduates, as will international and multinational entities (Global Environmental Management Initiative 2009). First and foremost, however, the course prepared students to be business managers of sustainable healthcare delivery systems. Course graduates are positioned to be professionals to whom the healthcare community will turn to understand what sustainability means in a healthcare business context (Global Environmental Management Initiative 2004a). Georgetown University students witnessed the significance of their healthcare sustainability work when they presented at a conference titled First Do No Harm: Partnerships for Patient Safety through Sustainability and Evidence Based Design at the Georgetown University Earth Day. This conference was designed as a dissemination and implementation forum where research findings and evidence-based information were summarized, communicated, and used by organizations and individuals capable of improving outcomes, quality, and the utilization of healthcare services (Georgetown University 2010).

Future Outlook

Demand for sustainability training in healthcare administration education will result from the need to comply with complex environmental laws and regulations as the Environmental Protection Agency (EPA) and The Joint Commission (JC) continue to develop and hold healthcare delivery systems accountable to environmental sustainability regulations (The Joint Commission 2008; Environmental Protection Agency 2009). The United States healthcare system requires multidisciplinary approaches to address the dynamic field of environmental healthcare sustainability (Rich 2010). Healthcare administrators with an understanding of sustainable practices share a unique vantage point to address challenges and foster solutions that cut across all aspects of business. They are positioned to identify problems and opportunities, and to broker information effectively.

If higher education institutions are to offer similar classes in environmental healthcare sustainability or topics related to sustainability in healthcare management, it is likely that the Association of University Programs in Health Administration (AUPHA) will play an important role in disseminating knowledge and supporting faculty development within the emerging field of healthcare sustainability (Olden and Friedman 2010). The American College of Healthcare Executives (ACHE) will also be a crucial participant in the continuing education of sustainability executives positioned to educate staff, clinicians, boards of directors, and communities about the implications of ignoring healthcare sustainability. Georgetown University's proximity to healthcare policymakers, research institutes, and specialty healthcare organizations provides prime opportunity to further collaborate with the aforementioned organizations (Clancy 2010). The Environmental Healthcare Sustainability course taught at Georgetown University has the opportunity to set a model for the rest of the country. Working in partnership with professional organizations, such as the National Capital Region Sustainable Healthcare Alliance (NCRSHA), an alliance of professionals in the greater DC area, will benefit the field of healthcare sustainability. Georgetown University and other local universities could encourage students to participate in professional organizations by hosting healthcare sustainability education, professional development and networking events.

It is the responsibility of healthcare administration education to use interdisciplinary teaching and practical, problem-oriented learning to enable students to be effective healthcare managers. Educators must be proactive in melding disciplines that reflect the healthcare environment and the diverse student populations/interests. The sustainability of healthcare and the broader community is at risk, should strategies for adaptation across the sustainability fail to be implemented.

References

Berns, M., Townend, A., Khayat, Z., Reeves, M., Hopkins, M., and Kruschwitz, N., 2009. The Business of Sustainability: Findings and Insights From the First Annual Business of Sustainability Survey and the Global Thought Leaders' Research Project. MIT Sloan Management Review.

Brown, D., 2008. For a Global Generation, Public Health is a Hot Field. *Washington Post*, 19 September 2008, p. 1.

Bureau of Labor Statistics, 2008–2009. US Department of Labor, Occupational Outlook 2008–2009 edition. *Handbook, Environmental Scientists and Hydrologists*. http://www.bls.gov/oco/ocos050.htm (accessed 24 August 2010).

Centers for Disease Control and Prevention, 2009. Keeping track, promoting health, connecting the dots. Centers for Disease Control and Prevention, National Environmental Public Health Tracking Program. Atlanta, GA, USA.

Centers for Medicare and Medicaid Services (CMS) 2009. United States Department of Health and Human Services. National health expenditure projections 2009–2019. http://www.cms.gov/NationalHealthExpendData/downloads/proj2009.pdf http://www.cms.gov/NationalHealthExpendData/03_NationalHealthAccountsProjected.asp#TopOfPage

CERES, 2002. Value at Risk: Climate Change and the Future of Governance. April 2002. CERES Sustainable Governance Project Report.

Chase Wilding, B., Curtis, K., and Welker-Hood, K., 2009. Hazardous Chemicals in Health Care: A Snapshot of Chemicals in Doctors and Nurses. Physicians for Social Responsibility.

Clancy, C., 2010. State of the Science: Perspectives from AHRQ. First Do No Harm: Partnerships for Patient Safety Through Sustainability and Evidence Based Design. Washington, DC. http://nhs.georgetown.edu/news/2010/04evidencebased_presentations.html

Deloitte, 2010. Sustainability in Business Today: A Cross-Industry View. http://www.deloitte.com/view/en_US/us/Services/additional-services/sustainability-climate-change/f0dc9cb025ee8210VgnVCM200000bb42f00aRCRD.htm

Environmental Protection Agency, 2009. Standards of performance for new stationary sources and emissions guidelines for existing sources: hospital/medical/infectious waste incinerators; final rule. 6 October 2009. http://www.epa.gov/ttn/atw/129/hmiwi/fr06oc09.pdf

Georgetown University, School of Nursing and Health Studies, 2010a. Course Evaluation, HESY 470. Healthcare Environmental Sustainability: Issues and Challenges. Georgetown University School of Nursing and Health Studies, Department of Health Systems Administration.

Georgetown University, School of Nursing and Health Studies, Department of Health Systems Administration, 2010b. First Do No Harm: Partnerships for Patient Safety Through Sustainability and Evidence Based Design. Washington, DC. http://nhs.georgetown.edu/news/2010/04evidencebased_events.html

Global Environmental Management Initiative, 2004a. Environment: Value to the Investor. Global Environmental Management Initiative, Washington, DC, USA.

Global Environmental Management Initiative, 2004b. Forging New Links: Enhancing Supply Chain Through Environmental Excellence. Global Environmental Management Initiative, Washington, DC, USA.

Global Environmental Management Initiative, 2009. Fostering Environmental Prosperity: Multinationals in Developing Countries. Global Environmental Management Initiative. Washington, DC, USA.

Global Environmental Management Initiative and the Environmental Defense Fund, 2008. Guide to successful corporate-NGO Partnerships. http://edf.org/documents/8818_GEMI-EDF%20Guide%20Final.pdf

Global Health and Safety Initiative, 2009. The Eco-Health Footprint Guide: Measuring Your Organization's Impact on Public Health and the Environment, Version 1.2. May 2009.

Green Guide for Health Care, 2007. A prescriptive path to energy efficiency improvements for hospitals. 19 December 2007. Development of a prescriptive package of energy efficiency measures to obtain energy savings and earn points under the green guide for health care version 2.2. Green Guide for Health Care, Austin, TX, USA.

Green Guide for Health Care: Best Practices for Creating High Performing Healing Environments. Version 2.2 Operations Section. December 2008. Revision.

Green Team Checklist, 2009. Energy Star, United States Environmental Protection Agency.

Guenther, R., 2009. Demystifying first-cost green building premiums in healthcare. *Health Environments Research & Design Journal*, **2**(4): 10–45.

Health Care Without Harm, 2008. Menu of Change: Healthy Food in Health Care. Survey of Healthy Food in Health Care Pledge Hospitals. 12 May 2008. Health Care Without Harm.

Joint Commission, The, 2008. Environment of Care: Hazardous Materials. 24 November 2008. The Joint Commission. http://www.jointcommission.org/Accreditation Programs/HomeCare/Standards/09_FAQs/EC/Hazardous_Material.htm

Kaplan, S., Orris, P., and Machi, R., 2009. A Research Agenda for Advancing Patient, Worker and Environmental Health and Safety in the Healthcare Sector. Global Health and Safety Initiative.

Kohn, L.T., Corrigan, J., Donaldson, M.S., Institute of Medicine, 2000. *To Err is Human: Building a Safer Health System*. Washington, DC: National Academy Press.

Messervy, B., 2010. Green Infrastructure Optimization: Sustainable Health Information Technology. First Do No Harm: Partnerships for Patient Safety Through Sustainability and Evidence Based Design. Washington, DC. http://nhs.georgetown.edu/news/2010/04evidencebased_presentations.html

Moore, D., 2010. Valley Health: Winchester Medical Center Campus Expansion. Presentation, Georgetown University, Washington, DC, USA.

Olden, P.C. and Friedman, L.H., 2010. Preparing Today's Students to Lead Tomorrow's Green Healthcare Organizations. *Journal of Health Administration Education*, **27**(2).

Practice Greenhealth and the Institute for Innovation in Large Organizations, 2008. The Business Case for Greening the Health Care Sector. 10 January 2008.

Practice Greenhealth, 2009. Eco-Checklist for Operations: How Green is Your Healthcare Organization? Version 1.0. April 2009.

Practice Greenhealth webinar, 2009. Introduction to the Revised Green Guide for Health Care Operations Section. http://www.practicegreenhealth.org/tools/webinars/archive/archive/439

Rich, C., 2010. Healthcare Environmental Sustainability: Issues and Challenges. Syllabus. Georgetown University School of Nursing and Health Studies, Department of Health Systems Administration.

Sadler, B.L., Joseph, A., Keller, A., and Rostenberg, B., 2009. *Using Evidence-Based Environmental Design to Enhance Safety and Quality*. IHI Innovation Series white paper. Cambridge, MA: Institute for Healthcare Improvement.

Savitz, A.W. and Weber, K., 2006. *The Triple Bottom Line: How Today's Best-Run Companies are Achieving Economic, Social And Environmental Success – and How You Can Too*. San Francisco, CA: John Wiley & Sons.

Washington State Department of Ecology, 2005. Best Management Practices for Hospital Waste. October 2005. Washington State Department of Ecology, Hazardous Waste and Toxics Reduction Program.

8

SUSTAINABILITY AND PROFESSIONAL IDENTITY IN ENGINEERING EDUCATION

Mark Minster, Patricia D. Brackin, Rebecca DeVasher, Erik Z. Hayes, Richard House, and Corey Taylor

> Why, Hal, 'tis my vocation, Hal; 'tis no sin for a man to labour in his vocation.
>
> Sir John Falstaff, *1 Henry IV*, I.ii

Consider three students at an engineering school: Emily, Morton, and Douglas. The three are completing end-of-term evaluations for a junior-level course called RH330: Technical & Professional Communication, which is required by their majors – civil engineering, software engineering, and mechanical engineering – and which also meets one of the school's liberal arts requirements. The course culminated with a seven-week, project-based unit that taught research, audience and context analysis, project management, and a variety of professional genres from needs analysis and feasibility study to grant proposal and Gantt chart. The project asked student groups to identify, on their own campus, a practice or technology that is unsustainable, and to propose a sustainable solution.

Here is what Emily, the civil engineering student, writes on her evaluation of the project:

> Good idea/content for the environmental RFP [Request for Proposals]. It was a little more real than most projects, which made it easier to do and a more useful experience.

Morton is a software engineer. Here are his comments about the class:

> Using a required course to force us to examine environmental sustainability and watch films such as "An Inconvenient Truth" seems inappropriate to me.

It would be better if RH330 were divided into sections by major.... If I am to spend weeks doing research, writing papers, and giving presentations, at least let it be related to my field of study.

Hippy-izing any talk about conservation or sustainability automatically turns off a good portion [of the] population. Conservation and sustainability should stick to the facts, deal in reality, and stay away from politics.

And here are the comments of Douglas, the mechanical engineering major:

I am sick of sustainability and green. It has been pushed onto me to the point of overload. It has lost all meaning. But somehow my career path…is going down a very green road, perhaps to make it so I don't have to hear sustainability ever again.

Nevertheless, the sustainability project allowed me to see the process for a proposal. It showed me the work that goes into it and the best way to do it. Working with my group gave me responsibility and through them I learned a lot, too.

The names have been changed here, course evaluations being anonymous, but these comments come from students in a course that three of us teach at a highly regarded undergraduate engineering school of about 1800 students in Terre Haute, Indiana. These comments are representative of three typical categories of student feedback we have received since introducing the campus sustainability project into our course on technical and professional communication (see Anderson *et al.* 2008).[1] Not all comments fall into these categories, of course, but the categories are instructive.

Emily's assessment of the sustainability RFP project as "more real than most projects" and therefore "easier" and "more useful" represents comments by students who see sustainability as a professional concern. It would be easy to read too much into her comment, attributing her sense of the project's utility and authenticity to her discipline (Civil Engineering at Rose-Hulman houses the Environmental Engineering minor) or to the assumptions she appears to hold about professionalism and/or sustainability. Nevertheless, the logic of Emily's comment is that the project was useful to her *because* it struck her as real, which suggests an area of significant overlap between the environmental aspects of what she has learned and how she intends to apply it. Her professional identity and her understanding of sustainability coincide.

Morton's response, by contrast, is typical of those whose disciplinary identification is at odds with their definition of sustainability. In addition to the common feeling of resignation about projects and courses that are mandatory ("a required course"; "if I am to spend weeks…at least…"), there is a protest against courses that are interdisciplinary: "it would be better if RH330 were divided into sections by major." As importantly, Morton objects to sustainability itself, singling out cultural, political, and contextual aspects of sustainability as "inappropriate" and alienating: "using a required course to force us to examine environmental sustainability…seems inappropriate"; "hippy-izing…automatically turns off" students. As someone with a clear sense of what is "related to my field of study," Morton identifies sustainability as unpalatably political, unrelated to his major and chosen profession.

Like Morton, Douglas views discussion of sustainability as an intrusion, something "pushed onto me to the point of overload." Instead of critiquing the politicization of environmental issues, however, Douglas is bothered by the ubiquity of talk, linking sustainability with the word "green," seeing both as one entity and observing that "it has lost all meaning." Ironically, he is surprised to find that, whatever its definition, sustainability is an important part of his professional identity: "somehow my career path…is going down a very green road." Douglas ends by pinpointing aspects of the project that seem relevant to his profession – writing process, hard work, responsibility, and teamwork – *without* mentioning sustainability at all. It is as if he is having trouble understanding the relationship between what sustainability means and who he intends to become. Whereas Emily and Morton have strong conceptions of their own professional identity but disagree about whether sustainability constitutes part of that identity, Douglas is in a muddle, believing sustainability and professionalism each to have some value, but remaining mystified by how the two relate.[2]

These students' responses represent three of the most common understandings of the relationship between education for sustainability in higher education and the processes of professionalization and disciplinary identification that are central to college students' academic experience. Unlike most liberal arts students, engineering students' disciplinary identity commonly emerges from a committed identification with the profession they know they will enter upon graduation. They thus provide a useful test case for how interdisciplinary education for sustainability might be taken to the next level. In particular, as we revise this course – and others – to ensure that engineering students emerge with a clear sense that sustainability is an integral part of who they are as professionals, how should we proceed? Are the challenges we face in this junior-level course endemic to the course itself, or, if there are larger dynamics at work, what are they, and how ought they be addressed?

Professionalism and Sustainability in Engineering Codes of Ethics

While Emily, Morton, and Douglas all perceive different relationships of sustainability to the profession with which they identify, one official self-definition of their field – the codes of ethics defining professional expectations for engineers – has evolved over the last decade to include sustainability as an imperative. The National Society of Professional Engineers defines environmental protection as a necessary condition for the obligation that "engineers shall at all times serve the interest of the public." The codes of ethics specific to individual engineering disciplines have also incorporated sustainability. See, for example, the websites for the National Society of Professional Engineers (NSPE, http://www.nspe.org/index. html), American Society of Mechanical Engineers (ASME, http://www.asme. org/kb/topics/sustainability), American Society of Civil Engineers (ASCE, http:// www.asce.org/sustainability/), and the Association for Computing Machinery, http://www.acm.edu/index.html). Traditionally, codes of ethics of disciplinary professional societies repeat and interpret the NSPE's Fundamental Canons. It is thus surprising to see that those societies have actually promoted sustainability to a place of prominence well beyond the NSPE's own code. For the NSPE, the Professional Obligations section, amended in 2007 to include sustainability, is tertiary, following both the Fundamental Canons and the Rules of Practice. The disciplinary societies have instead tended to add environmental considerations to their versions of the First Fundamental Canon – treating it as a dimension of "safety, health, and welfare of the public" – which signals an increasing perception that sustainability is central to the engineers' mission.

In educating future engineers, though, the imperative to sustainability is more frequently encountered in the relatively pedestrian form of accreditation criteria administered by ABET, Inc. (formerly the Accreditation Board of Engineering and Technology), the body responsible for certifying engineering programs in US colleges and universities. ABET requires that students exhibit "an ability to design a system, component, or process to meet desired needs within realistic constraints such as economic, environmental, social, political, ethical, health and safety, manufacturability, and sustainability." The environmental impact of a design here is abstracted into a hypothetical "constraint" alongside so many other generalized perspectives that its impact is diluted. The ABET criteria provide no metrics to guide a judgment as to whether a student design is sufficiently benign to the natural environment (or, for that matter, to human safety or to the economic means of a client). They merely indicate that programs should provide a "realistic" range of constraints. Most importantly, the sheer breadth of these criteria – and his list is only item 3(c) of the Engineering Accreditation Criteria – encourages a balkanized curricular approach. These various constraints are farmed out to specific lessons or assignments within courses whose larger focus is on "harder" technical subject matter. It is no wonder that students and faculty can perceive these aspects of an engineering education as secondary and even ephemeral.

When engineering institutions consider sustainability, then, there is no single vantage point to define their professional view. Engineers are likely to believe that rational, technical, specialized means can mitigate harms to the environment, and may even recall that sustainability is included in the formalized ethical demands of the profession (see Rowden and Striebig 2004). At the same time, though, the identity of the individual engineer, department, or workplace is dominated by expertise in particular technologies, whether products or processes.

Environmental responsibilities are likely regarded as the purview of the select few who have pursued arcane specialties such as geotechnical or water resource engineering. Many engineering educators already believe that environmental problems must become instead the common property of the engineering profession as a whole, and that future professionals must see those problems as urgent, exigent matters in the workplace and the wider world (Vanasupa and Splitt 2004). If this transition is to be realized, though, institutions teaching engineers must programmatically devise new ways to confront engineering students with issues related to sustainability.

Professionalization, not Disciplinarity

A common theme in the literature on sustainability in higher education is that disciplinarity presents an impediment to progress. In the humanities, social sciences, and natural sciences, the argument goes, each discipline provides concepts and methods that may be useful for comprehending those problems that lie within its own provinces but that are less helpful for problems that arise across the borders (or down the hall), or that transcend boundaries altogether (Norgaard 2004; Fenner *et al.* 2005). Economics does best with economic problems, sociology with sociological matters, psychology with the psyche – and this is more than just the truism that lenses discover what they were ground and polished to see.

In the last several decades, there have been frequent calls for interdisciplinary education.[3] In the engineering context, "the competence for interdisciplinary cooperation appears to be central" (Barth *et al.* 2007; see also Thomas 2004). Project Kaleidoscope (2006), which advocates for strong undergraduate science, technology, engineering, and mathematics (STEM) programs, lists several "barriers and challenges to changing the system" including "organizational barriers that create competitive instead of cooperative environments among departments and organizations; cultural differences between disciplines and agencies; lack of innovative approaches in education; scientific disciplines [which] are too compartmentalized and tend to focus research on disciplinary interests." Case studies have shown that faculty can be "ideologically resistant to curriculum changes that emanate from outside the bounds of their discipline" (Alabaster and Blair 1996). "Significant institutional and intellectual barriers for the emergence of integrated systems thinking...remain major problems in both research and education" (Ashford 2004).

In engineering departments, as in other pre-professional programs, however, disciplinary differences are secondary to the processes of professionalization and identity formation, which are not as well understood. Majors in the humanities, social sciences, and even the natural sciences are primarily classified by the terminology and methodologies they use, whereas pre-professional majors are classed by the jobs they will have. One *studies* history and psychology, in other words, but one *becomes* a teacher or a nurse. A student can pursue many careers with a degree in English – writing, education, business, and law are four common options – but she cannot become "an English." Presumably she sees her education, and its goals, somewhat differently than a student studying accounting, architecture, or engineering. According to PayScale, which tracks college graduate employment, the four most common options for those who graduate with a bachelor's degree in mechanical engineering are Mechanical Engineer, Mechanical Design Engineer, Manufacturing Engineer, and Project Engineer (2010–2011 College Salary Report). An engineer is not just learning a discipline; she is training for a vocation.

This is not to say that disciplinary differences do not matter in pre-professional programs. Peak oil and soil and water pollution remain just as overdetermined and transdisciplinary, and engineering students need literacy in the humanities and social sciences as much as students at a liberal arts college. In engineering programs, however, what matters more to sustainability is the more troubling issue of professionalization, which can be summarized in three questions.

(1) How does college prepare future engineers for the sustainability challenges they will face in the careers they are likely to pursue? How, in other words, do college students become pre-professionals, and how do pre-professionals become professionals?

(2) To what extent do these processes of professionalization necessitate and invite, or inhibit and prevent those dynamic pedagogies of identity formation that might challenge, enrich, or recontextualize what it means to become a "professional"?

(3) In practice, how does education for sustainability fit with these processes of professionalization and identity formation? That is, if sustainability is seen as an extracurricular collection of personal preferences and feelings, consumer decisions, and lifestyle choices, is it also seen as a professional matter, a problem to be addressed at the workplace, on the job, with the practices and principles one has trained for in the curriculum itself? Is sustainability taught as an extracurricular set of issues, or as a curricular necessity or desideratum, or as both – and if both, how?

These questions matter greatly for those who want to incorporate sustainability into and/or across the curriculum. As we ask where and how education for sustainability ought to be incorporated into the curriculum, we must also ask about the pedagogical processes it participates in, those it forestalls, and those it transforms.

What we are proposing is that careful attention to the patterns by which students form professional identities allows for a more thorough integration of sustainability than the "sustainability across the curriculum" movement has promoted. The problem that needs to be solved, in other words, is not that sustainability needs to be included in the curriculum, nor that the curriculum needs to be expanded by the addition of sustainability as a constraint on design or even as a technique or principle of design (see Lourdel *et al.* 2005; contrast with Ashford 2004). The problem is that the definition of a "professional," the very concept of professional identity, needs to be reformulated with sustainability at its root, stem, and blossom.

Our main problems with professional identity as it is most commonly conceived and approached – and as all three of our students above seem to understand it – are threefold. (1) It misconstrues the recursive relationship between theory, technique, and praxis, seeing it as a sequence of stages; (2) it strips problems from their contexts, reducing useful knowledge to that which can be practiced on the job; and (3) its understanding of sustainability is therefore atrophied by being unnecessarily bifurcated into the personal and the vocational. Morton and Douglas's comments are paradigmatic. Both are troubled by the creep of the personal and the social into vocational and professional realms, and by the muddying of proper academic concerns with the messy world. Even Emily, however, may see herself as a professional in much the same way, seeing sustainability as merely a practical application (praxis) of the hard scientific principles (theory) and technological processes (technique) that are truly foundational to her profession. This, we believe, is not enough.

What Does It Mean to Be a Professional?

In order to trace how students come to identify themselves as professionals, we have to know what they believe "professional" means, even if this definition varies over time or is more idealized than real. In the 1970 volume *Professional Education*, Edgar H. Schein presents a landmark assessment of what it means to become a professional. The traits Schein identifies can be grouped into several categories, and ordered by the chronology in which one attains them. First, one masters a clearly defined body of knowledge which is specialized and autonomous. Second, one is authorized to practice in one's area of expertise by a professional organization, a code of ethics, and/or by established standards. And finally, one serves clients towards whom one is responsive and responsible, though the professional remains "objective" or "detached" about their needs. A would-be doctor, for example, may begin by wanting to help people or by wanting to make money. In either case, however, he must master the concepts, skills, and discourse relevant and unique to his profession. Having attained this mastery, he must be licensed to practice by a professional organization, governed and guided by its procedures and ethical codes. With this guidance and knowledge, his personal aspiration becomes a professional vocation to serve patients *as patients*: neither as neighbors, nor as objects. He may, voluntarily, go above and beyond this calling, but can only do so and remain a professional if he remains within his field, its body of knowledge, its organizational strictures.

Most importantly, Schein explains that as professionals learn their bodies of knowledge, they follow a pattern of education. Early in their careers they are taught "an underlying discipline or basic science component." Next, they learn "an applied science or 'engineering' component," and finally, atop this base, they learn "a skills and attitudinal component" (Schein 1970: 43). In the building that is the engineering curriculum, basic science is the foundation, applied science and problem-solving are the ground floor, and decision-making and professional ethos are the top floor.

Donald Schön, perhaps more than anyone else, has excavated the pedagogical assumptions and consequences of this floor plan, which he calls "Technical Rationality – the view of professional knowledge which has most powerfully shaped both our thinking about the professions and the institutional relations of research, education, and practice." "According to this view," Schön writes in *The Reflective Practitioner*, "professional activity consists in instrumental problem-solving made rigorous by the application of scientific theory and technique" (Schön 1983: 21). Technical rationality comprises both a definition of the professional and a sequence for becoming one: first, theory; then, technique; then, application and problem-solving.

It is worth noting here that technical rationality itself constitutes a root cause of sustainability crises. Schön traces its rise back through positivism to the industrial revolution, concurrent with the rise of the German ideal of the university. He quotes Edward Shils on the shaping of Johns Hopkins University:

> knowledge could be accepted as knowledge only if it rested on empirical evidence, rigorously criticized and rationally analyzed...The knowledge which was appreciated was secular knowledge which continued the mission of sacred knowledge, complemented it, led to it, or replaced it; fundamental, systematically acquired knowledge was thought in some way to be a step toward redemption. This kind of knowledge held out the prospect of the transfiguration of life by improving man's control over the resources of nature and over the powers that weaken his body....
>
> *(Shils 1978: 171)*

If becoming a professional requires "improving...control over the resources of nature," we can see a possible basis for Morton's resistance to seeing sustainability as a professional concern, and for Douglas's cognitive dissonance. Fundamental convictions of sustainability – namely, that the natural world poses practical and ethical limits to human control – pose a threat to this model of professionalism.

Indeed, the pedagogical problem that Schön has described sounds like a problem identified by sustainability experts as well:

> With this emphasis on problem *solving*, we ignore problem *setting*, the process by which we define the decision to be made, the ends to be achieved, the means which may be chosen. In real-world practice, problems do not present themselves to the practitioner as givens. They must be

constructed from the materials of problematic situations which are puzzling, troubling, and uncertain.

(Schön 1983: 40)

Technical rationality, in other words, promotes a professionalism that begins by uprooting problems from contexts and ends by dividing researchers from practitioners. "In the varied topography of professional practice, there is a high, hard ground where practitioners can make effective use of research-based theory and technique, and there is a swampy lowland where situations are confusing 'messes' incapable of technical solution" (Schön 1983: 42).

Instead, Schön proposes "reflection-in-action," which inverts the architecture, putting context and practice at the ground floor. Schön's proposal has been repeated – and practiced – in a number of contexts. Dall'Alba and Sandberg (2006), for instance, note that the interplay between theory and practice cannot be taught in a simple sequence, yet this is how professional education often operates. "Aspiring professionals are expected first to acquire basic knowledge and skills relevant to their chosen profession, and, later, more advanced knowledge and skills. In the workplace they are expected to accumulate additional knowledge and skills" (Dall'Alba and Sandberg 2006: 386). And yet "a fundamental dimension of professional skill development – namely, *understanding of, and in, practice* – is overlooked in stage models" (Dall'Alba and Sandberg 2006: 388). Instead of teaching abstract science as the foundation for students who will only eventually become professionals, Dall'Alba and Sandberg see "patterns of professional development as arising from the relation between practitioner (with a particular history located in local and broader practice contexts) and professional practice, which is dynamic, intersubjective, and pluralistic" (Dall'Alba and Sandberg 2006: 396).

Revising the definition of the professional affects the beginning of students' education, resituating professional knowledge in its social and environmental contexts of practice as foundational. Challenging the model of technical rationality all affects the *end* of students' education, its aims and trajectories. The key figure here is William M. Sullivan, whose book *Work and Integrity* argues for broadening and restructuring the common notion of professionalism

in ways that suffuse technical competence with civic awareness. Thanks in part to the challenges unrelentingly posed by the new global society and its host of attendant problems, specialists find themselves increasingly having to learn the principles of each other's specialties. They must also learn to relate their expertise to publics concerned and affected by change....Emerging forms of practice recognize that there is finally no successful separation between the skills of problem solving and those of deliberation and judgment, no viable pursuit of technical excellence without participation in those civic enterprises through which expertise discovers its human meaning.

(Sullivan 2005: xix)

In the early twentieth century, Sullivan argues

> professionals were in the main aware that their lives had to respond to two pulls. On the one hand there were the claims of conscience, identification with the values of vocational integrity and a justly ordered polity. On the other, there was essential concern for technical competence and practical efficiency, the components of successful modern enterprise.
>
> *(Sullivan 2005: 70)*

Sullivan traces the continued separation of these two values, and makes a Deweyan case for a necessary reintegration, with civic purpose as the aim of all education, professional education not least of all:

> professionalism [must] be understood as a public good, a social value, and not the ideology of some special interest...By combining the dignity and security of occupational identity with the integrity and competence of social function, professionalism can be a major resource for rebuilding not just a dynamic economy, but a viable public order as well.
>
> *(Sullivan 2005: 124–125)*

With these definitions in mind, we can return to our first two questions. How does college prepare students for the sustainability challenges they will face in their chosen professions? Second, does this process of professionalization support or dissuade students from pursuing broader and deeper conceptions of professionalism? Answers to these questions depend upon whether students learn, at the foundation of their professional education, problem-setting as well as problem-solving (Schön 1983), and upon whether their professionalism encourages an opening outward toward contexts or a funneling inward towards greater specialization and professional autonomy (Sullivan 2005). In order to ensure that professional education *does* adequately prepare students, we must ensure that the relationship between theory, technique, and practice inform one another interdependently, rather than merely building sequentially (Schön 1983), and that the problems students study are not severed from their contexts.

Identity Formation

Our third question remains. How does education for sustainability fit within the processes of professionalization? We have already seen that by the time they are juniors, engineering majors seem to have relatively strong professional identities. To ensure that an understanding of sustainability suffuses their developing sense of themselves as engineers, we will have to integrate the *practice* of sustainability into the curriculum at a foundational level, probably even in the first weeks of the first year. But how?

The curriculum is an important site for teaching professionalism, particularly if individual courses are integrated, so that rather than assimilating discrete pieces of information, students are immersed in an experiential, interdisciplinary body of knowledge-in-practice. "On a day-to-day basis during the novice's most impressionable period, the faculty, the curriculum, and the teaching practices of the school represent the world of the profession" (Sullivan 2005: 196). Students learn the profession not only by accumulating skills and concepts, the so-called body of knowledge, but also by interacting with professionals who model professional behaviors, and by practicing those behaviors. Beyond becoming professionals by *what* they learn – design principles or hard science – engineering students become professionals by *how* and *where* and *with whom* they learn. Here, the preponderance of evidence from student affairs professionals and from engineering educators suggests that "attention to changing curriculum design, course content, or teaching methods may be insufficient for improving education without simultaneous attention to the formative experiences of faculty and subsequent intentions for students" (Hooper 2008: 238). The curriculum, in other words, must itself be seen contextually, nested within the dynamic operations of identity formation that shapes the process of professionalization. "Professional education is about *identity formation*, which involves helping students form the character, dispositions, beliefs, values, ways of knowing, and ways of seeing that are characteristic of their chosen profession" (Hooper 2008: 228).

For sustainability to be integrated into the professional curriculum, in other words, it must not just consist of a particular body of knowledge. The behaviors that faculty practice, the interactions students have with one another, vocabularies and methodologies – all of these contribute to deep professionalization, the "formation of a distinctive habitus aligned with the deepest values and priorities of the tradition" (Foster *et al.* 2006: 112). Our students, Morton, Douglas, and Emily have likely been influenced by "the 'implicit curriculum' more than… through the explicit curriculum" (Eisner 1985; Foster *et al.* 2006; Sullivan 2005).

The literature on professional education accords with what the scholarship in student affairs says about the pedagogical implications of the first year of college. Ernest Pascarella cites consistent examples in which

> students learning under one of the various constructivist approaches [those based on the premise that students learn best when they actively construct knowledge in socially interactive contexts that are problem-based rather than passively receiving it from an 'expert'] had a statistically significant advantage
>
> *(Pascarella 2005).*

Peer interactions having the strongest net influence on various measures of first-year cognitive growth (e.g. critical thinking, reflective thinking) are those that: (a) extend and reinforce the ethos of the academic program, and/or (b) expose one to people, ideas, and perspectives that challenge his or her assumed views of the world.

(Pascarella 2005: 126)

Thus, the answer to our third question would appear to be that a professionalism that incorporates sustainability must extend far beyond the classroom. The classroom and the residence hall must work together.

HERE: A Home for Environmentally Responsible Engineering

Rose-Hulman's Home for Environmentally Responsible Engineering (HERE), an interdisciplinary living-learning community defines the early college experiences of a freshmen cohort of 44 students. In so doing, it grounds their identity as engineering professionals in personal and communal life as well as technical education. The cohort approach has proven successful at a large number of schools in numerous contexts, and much evidence recommends the approach regardless of its key content areas or thematic focus. A 2008 Department of Education report records positive impacts in and outside the classroom for high schools that developed cohort programs (Bernstein *et al.* 2008); at least one university reported "meaningful positive effect on both GPA and retention" (Jamelske 2009; see also Schroeder *et al.* 1999). Studies have observed increased levels of student engagement and academic performance for students in living-learning environments (Newell 1992; Stassen 2003).

The interdisciplinary nature of sustainability issues is especially fitting for a learning communities approach – particularly at the outset of an undergraduate education, when new students are satisfying requirements throughout the curriculum. HERE thus focuses on the first year of college. Each year, a group of volunteer first-year students live together in a designated campus residence hall. In addition to living space, the residence hall provides space for office hours, project planning, and for informal discussion .The goal "is not simply to teach concrete facts about the environment but to create an active, transformative process of learning that allows values to be lived out and debated, and permits a unification of theory and practice" (Warburton 2003). Academic and social needs can be met without requiring – or allowing – students to sever their life from their work.

The freshmen in each year's cohort take a sequence of four core courses, in specially designated sections taught by faculty who have chosen to take part. College and Life Skills, a one-credit course for freshmen, is taught by Student Life staff. Introduction to Design is required of all engineering majors. Rhetoric and Composition, a required writing course, and Sustainability and its Global Contexts help students meet two of their required liberal arts courses. Because all four courses are interdisciplinary and sequential, they can be linked iteratively and conceptually to build for increasing confidence and competencies.

Of course, HERE is not the first program to tie sustainability education to a residential community. Engineering education is an important new context for such programs, however, and potentially a difficult one. As engineering educators concerned with sustainability, we habitually consider the impact that our students may produce. One might restore a wetland, helping to conserve biodiversity. Another might advance the state of the art of low-emissions vehicles, others might introduce more material-efficient manufacturing processes, or serve as organizational educators, introducing their colleagues to bodies of knowledge such as green chemistry. Our own work can be enhanced by mindfulness that the process works in the other direction as well: that encountering environmental problems may have a salutary effect on our students as professionals and as thinking, acting, reflecting agents of change. Ultimately, we contend that those two capacities need not be so different as is often supposed, and that emphasizing their connection may be the greatest service that we can perform for the engineering profession and for the natural environments that will be affected, for good or for ill, by the work of its practitioners.

Notes

1 See M'Gonigle and Starke (2006) for context on campus initiatives that are sometimes called "greening the campus." See also Calhoun (2006) and Gruenewald and Smith (2008).
2 On this kind of muddle as an example of cognitive dissonance, see Kagawa (2007).
3 Most notable have been the Boyer Commission (1998), the National Research Council (2003), the National Academy of Sciences (2004), and the National Academy of Engineering (2004).

References

ABET, 2009. *Criteria for Accrediting Engineering Programs, 2010–2011 Review Cycle*. www.abet.org/forms.shtml

Alabaster, T. and Blair, D., 1996. Greening the University. In J. Huckle and S. Sterling (eds), *Education for Sustainability*. London: Earthscan, pp. 86–104.

American Society of Civil Engineers, 2009. Code of Ethics. www.asce.org/ Content. aspx?id=7231

Anderson, A., Chenoweth, S., DeVasher, R., House, R., Livingston, J., Minster, M., Taylor, C., Watt, A. and Williams, J., 2008. Communicating Sustainability: Sustainability and Communication in the Engineering, Science, and Technical Communication Classrooms. *Proceedings of IEEE Professional Communication Conference*, 13-16 July 2008. Montreal: IEEE International.

Ashford, N.A., 2004. Major challenges to engineering education for sustainable development. *International Journal of Sustainability in Higher Education*, **5**(3): 239–250.

ASME, 2009. Code of Ethics of Engineers. http://files.asme.org/ASMEORG/Governance/3675.pdf

Association for Computing Machinery, 1992. Code of Ethics. www.acm.org/about/code-of-ethics

Barth, M., Godemann, J., Rieckmann, M. and Stoltenberg, U., 2007. Developing Key Competencies for sustainable development in higher education. *International Journal of Sustainability in Higher Education,* **8**(4): 416–430.

Bernstein, L., Millsap, M.A., Schimmenti, J., and Page, L., 2008. Implementation Study of Smaller Learning Communities: Final Report. Cambridge: Abt Associates.

Boyer Commission on Educating Undergraduates in the Research University, 1998. *Reinventing undergraduate education: A blueprint for America's Research Universities.*

Calhoun, T., 2006. *A (recycled, of course) six-pack of sustainability lessons from the past year in higher education.* Ann Arbor, MI: Society for College and University Planning. www.scup.org/csd/3/pdf/SCUP-CSD Report.pdf

Dall'Alba, G., and Sandberg, J., 2006. Professional development: a critical review of stage models. *Review of Educational Research,* **76**(3): 383–412.

Eisner, E.W., 1985. *The Educational Imagination: On the design and evaluation of school programs,* 2nd edn. New York: Macmillan.

Fenner, R.A., Ainger, C.M., Cruickshank, H.J., and Guthrie, P.M., 2005. Embedding sustainable development at Cambridge University Engineering Department. *International Journal of Sustainability in Higher Education,* **6**(3): 229–41.

Foster, C.R., Dahill, L.E., Golemon, L.A., and Tolentino, B.W., 2006. *Educating Clergy: Teaching practices and pastoral imagination.* San Francisco, CA: Jossey Bass.

Gruenewald, D.A. and Smith, G.A. (eds) 2008. *Place-based Education in the Global Age.* New York: Lawrence Erlbaum.

Hooper, B., 2008. Stories we teach by: intersections among faculty biography, student formation, and instructional processes. *The American Journal of Occupational Therapy,* **62**(2): 228–241.

Jamelske, E., 2009. Measuring the impact of a university first-year experience program on student GPA and retention. *Higher Education,* 57: 373–391.

Kagawa, F., 2007. Dissonance in students' perceptions of sustainable development and sustainability: implications for curriculum change. *International Journal of Sustainability in Higher Education,* **8**(3): 317–338.

Lourdel, N., Gondran, N., Laforest, V., and Brodhag, C., 2005. Introduction of sustainable development in engineers' curricula: problematic and evaluation methods. *International Journal of Sustainability in Higher Education,* **6**(3): 254–264.

M'Gonigle, M. and Starke, J., 2006. *Planet U: Sustaining the world, reinventing the university.* Gabriola Island: New Society.

National Academy of Engineering, 2004. *The Engineer of 2020: Visions of engineering in the new century.* Washington, DC: National Academies Press.

National Academy of Sciences, 2004. *Facilitating interdisciplinary research.* Washington, DC: National Academies Press.

National Research Council, 2003. *Evaluating and improving undergraduate teaching in science, technology, engineering, and mathematics.* Washington, DC: National Academies Press.

National Society of Professional Engineers, 2007. NSPE Code of Ethics for Engineers. www.nspe.org/Ethics/CodeofEthics/index.html

Newell, W.H., 1992. Academic disciplines and undergraduate interdisciplinary education: lessons from the School of Interdisciplinary Studies at Miami University, Ohio. *European Journal of Education,* **27**(3): 211–221.

Norgaard, R.B., 2004. Transdisciplinary shared learning. In P. Barlett and G. Chase (eds), *Sustainability on Campus: Stories and strategies for change*, Cambridge, MA: MIT.

Pascarella, E.T., 2005. Cognitive impacts of the first year of college. In R.S. Feldman (ed.), *Improving the First Year of College*. Mahwah, NJ: Lawrence Erlbaum, pp. 105–134.

Project Kaleidoscope, 2006. *Report on reports II: Recommendations for urgent action: Transforming America's scientific and technological infrastructure.* http://www.pkal.org/documents/ ReportOnReportsII.cfm

Rowden, K. and Striebig, B., 2004. Incorporating environmental ethics into the undergraduate engineering curriculum. *Science and Engineering Ethics*, **10**: 417–422.

Schein, E.H., 1970. *Professional Education: Some new directions*. New York: McGraw-Hill.

Schön, D.A., 1983. *The Reflective Practitioner: How professionals think in action*. New York: Basic Books.

Schroeder, C.C., Minor, F.D., and Tarkow, T.A., 1999. Freshman interest groups: partnerships for promoting student success. *New Directions for Student Services*, **87**, 37–49.

Shils, E. 1978. The order of learning in the United States from 1865 to 1920: the ascendancy of the universities. *Minerva*, **16**(2): 171.

Stassen, M.L.A., 2003. Student outcomes: the impact of varying living-learning community models. *Research in Higher Education*, **44**(5): 561–613.

Sullivan, W.M., 2005. *Work and Integrity: The crisis and promise of professionalism in America*, 2nd edn. San Francisco, CA: Jossey Bass.

Thomas, I., 2004. Sustainability in tertiary curricula: what is stopping it happening? *International Journal of Sustainability in Higher Education*, **5**(1): 33–47.

Vanasupa L. and Splitt, F.G., 2004. Curricula for a sustainable future: a proposal for integrating environmental concepts into our curricula. *Proceedings of Symposium BB, Materials Research Society*. www.mrs.org

Warburton, K., 2003. Deep learning and education for sustainability. *International Journal of Sustainability in Higher Education*, **4**(1): 44–56.

9

IMPLEMENTING ENVIRONMENTAL SUSTAINABILITY IN THE GLOBAL HOSPITALITY, TOURISM, AND LEISURE INDUSTRIES

Developing a Comprehensive Cross-Disciplinary Curriculum

Michelle Millar, Chris Brown, Cynthia Carruthers, Thomas Jones, Yen-Soon Kim, Carola Raab, Ken Teeters, and Li-Ting Yang

Introduction

The United Nations declared 2005–2014 the Decade of Education for Sustainable Development to encourage schools around the world to incorporate sustainability into their curricula (Bardaglio 2007; Lozano-Garcia *et al.* 2008). Schools of higher education in particular, have made some progress on this front by greening their campuses and conducting research about sustainable development. Progress for incorporating sustainability into the classroom, however, has been slow (Calhoun 2005). That is not to say, however, that universities have been completely complacent in changing curricula. There are examples of universities in the United States that are in the process of integrating, or have successfully integrated, the topic into all types of classroom subjects (e.g. Emory University, Northern Arizona University). It is unclear, however, the extent to which sustainability is infused into hospitality higher education curricula (Tesone 2004).

Graduates of hospitality higher education programs will be called upon to shape future managerial practices and consumer behavior in an increasingly complex, competitive, and global hospitality and tourism industry (Goodman and Sprague 1991; King *et al.* 2003; Telfer and Hashimoto 2001). They are our future decision makers, and as faculty, it is our responsibility to prepare them for a successful venture out into the "real world." To do so, it is imperative that faculty teach, and college courses, curricula, teaching methods and syllabi reflect, the learning outcomes or competencies that are relevant today (Chen and Jeong 2009).

Students must acquire the competencies that enable them to succeed (Horng 2004; Millar *et al.* 2010). Such competency-based education (CBE) is directed at enhancing attitudes, skills and knowledge of students in pursuit of specific outcomes (Burns 1972).

To undergo a change in curriculum related to sustainability, it is imperative to identify the competencies that promote intentions and behavioral change related to sustainability among students, both personally and professionally. Hospitality competencies, in general, have been identified and well-studied in the hospitality education arena (Mayo and Thomas-Haysbert 2005; Millar *et al.* 2010). Very few of the competencies, however, are related to sustainability or sustainable managerial practices. The implementation of sustainable managerial practices requires that graduates acquire the competencies necessary to balance the three pillars of sustainable development, namely, economic, environmental, and social sustainability (Bardaglio 2007; Lozano-Garcia *et al.* 2008).

The purpose of this chapter is to provide a case study of the process of incorporating sustainability, thus far, into the curriculum at a major US hospitality college. The college recently decided that all of its undergraduates should have the sustainability competencies necessary to function effectively in the industry. In order to develop the curriculum, it became a priority to determine exactly which sustainability competencies students should acquire, as well as the receptivity and readiness of the faculty to address these competencies through the curriculum (Bardaglio 2007). Assessment of faculty knowledge is important because, while faculty may be familiar with sustainability, they may not be familiar with incorporating it into curricular and extracurricular activities. It is important for faculty to develop pedagogically sophisticated learning activities that engage the students' attitudes, knowledge, and skills.

According to the Theory of Planned Behavior (TPB), individuals' willingness to take action in any arena, including sustainability, is predicted by their knowledge, which, in turn, shapes their attitudes. Individuals' attitudes toward an issue, such as sustainability, together with their perceptions of behavioral control and social norms shape their behavioral intentions to act (Ajzen 1991). Attitudes are the overall positive or negative evaluation of the importance of sustainability efforts and are shaped by individuals' beliefs about sustainability (e.g., human behaviors affect sustainability of the planet; sustainable hospitality practices can conserve resources) (Armitage and Christian 2003). Therefore, faculty members' beliefs may determine the importance that they place on addressing sustainability competencies in their classrooms. In addition to holding positive attitudes about sustainability, it is imperative that faculty believe that they have the knowledge and skills necessary to be efficacious in teaching about sustainable practices (i.e., behavioral control) (Ajzen 1991). Even if faculty believe that it is important to address sustainability competencies, if they do not believe that they have the knowledge, skills, or curricular influence to constructively address sustainability issues, they are unlikely to behaviorally address those issues through the curriculum.

Finally, social norms may impact faculty members' intentions to enact behaviors (Ajzen 1991). Social norms refer to the perceived pressure from significant others to perform the behavior (Armitage and Christian 2003). An academic climate that establishes a social norm for addressing sustainability through the curriculum is likely to promote changes in faculty members' intentions to address sustainability, and, ultimately, their behaviors.

A sustainability committee of seven individuals was formed to lay the groundwork for the curricular change. The committee consisted of at least one representative from each department at the college (hotel management, food and beverage management, tourism and convention, and recreation and sport management), as well as one student representative. Some of the committee members were already diligent about infusing sustainability into their courses, others were fairly new to the topic, and others were somewhere in between. The varying degrees of "expertise" provided well-rounded input for the competency-development process. The goals of the committee, over the course of 2 years, were as follows:

1. The identification of curricular competencies related to sustainable professional practices;
2. The assessment of the faculty members' knowledge, attitudes, intentions, behaviors, and constraints relative to the implementation of sustainability competencies in the hospitality curriculum;
3. The education of faculty and staff on sustainability issues in which they are deficient;
4. The development of a comprehensive sustainability curriculum that includes service learning and extracurricular activities;
5. The assessment of students' attitudes, knowledge, skills, and behavior relative to sustainability;
6. The evaluation of curricular outcomes.

The results for the first two goals are presented in this chapter. On the surface, the goals are straightforward and clear, but delineating and defining them, especially those related to the competencies, proved much more time-consuming than was originally thought. In the end, however, both the competencies and the survey of faculty attitudes, intentions, and behaviors are tools that can be used by other hospitality and tourism colleges to help guide them through a curricular change for sustainable development education.

Development of Competencies

The sustainability competencies represent the specific sustainability knowledge and skills that were deemed important for the students to acquire. To undergo a change in curriculum related to sustainability, it was necessary to develop general education sustainability competencies, as well as identify specific competencies that were applicable to all of the disciplines within the hospitality college, i.e., hotel management, food and beverage, tourism and convention, and recreation and sport.

We started by conducting a thorough literature review about sustainability competencies. Many approaches to defining competencies (also commonly referred to as learning outcomes) were found, and many of those approaches varied from discipline to discipline, and university to university. We narrowed the search down to three key studies/projects from which to draw our competencies. These three studies primarily informed the development of the general education competencies, rather than the hospitality-specific competencies. The United States' Partnership for Education for Sustainability (2009) provided three general-education-sustainable-development learning standards for children in kindergarten through 12. Although the learning standards were not geared toward college students, the basic content applied to our efforts. The learning standards were:

1. Students understand and are able to apply the basic concepts and principles of sustainability (i.e., meeting present needs without compromising the ability of future generations to meet their needs).
2. Students recognize the concept of sustainability as a dynamic condition characterized by the interdependency among ecological, economic, and social systems, and how these interconnected systems affect individual and societal well-being. They develop an understanding of the human connection to and interdependence with the natural world.
3. Students develop a multidisciplinary approach to learning the knowledge, skills, and attitudes necessary to continuously improve the health and well-being of present and future generations, via both personal and collective decisions and actions. They are able to envision a world that is sustainable, along with the primary changes that would need to be made by individuals, local communities, and countries in order to achieve this (p. 3).

Svanstrom *et al.* (2008) developed sustainable education competencies for an international institute for higher learning. The competencies are currently being implemented and tested. Below is a summary of their most basic competencies:

1. An understanding of the ethical responsibility toward present and future generations.
2. An understanding of the carrying capacity of ecosystems, in order to provide services to humankind.
3. An understanding of one's social responsibility as a future professional and as a citizen.

4. An understanding of the impact that human activities have on the planet, regarding sustainable and unsustainable resource appropriation.
5. Knowledge of global trends that impact the life quality of present and future generations (pp. 344–345).

These competencies recognize the importance of personal and professional lives, combined, and that people and the planet are inseparable. In addition, there is recognition that sustainability is global. This point is very pertinent to hospitality and tourism education since it is a global industry.

Hines *et al.* (1986) provided four goals of environmental education (their version of education for sustainable development). Namely, students should have:

1. A working knowledge of environmental issues;
2. Specific knowledge of approaches to those issues;
3. The ability to make appropriate decision; and,
4. Possession of certain affective qualities (attitudes) that make people care about and pay more attention to environmental conditions.

Although very general, these four goals were helpful to our committee when formulating the general education competencies.

Finally, we drew our competencies from a list of learning outcomes drafted by the Higher Education Associations Sustainability Consortium and the Disciplinary Associations Network for Sustainability. Their list was more specific than the aforementioned competencies and began to reflect the importance of creating a competency that was actionable. The learning outcomes, as combined by the American College Personnel Association (ACPA) College Student Educators International Sustainability Taskforce (2006) are:

1. Each student will be able to define sustainability;
2. Each student will be able to explain how sustainability relates to their lives and their values, and how their actions impact issues of sustainability;
3. Each student will be able to utilize their knowledge of sustainability to change their daily habits and consumer mentality;
4. Each student will be able to explain how systems are interrelated;
5. Each student will learn change agent skills;
6. Each student will learn how to apply concepts of sustainability to their campus and community by engaging in the challenges and solutions of sustainability on their campus;
7. Each student will learn how to apply concepts of sustainability globally by engaging in the challenges and the solutions of sustainability in a world context (pp. 1–4).

Although gathered from multiple sources, the competencies reflect many similar assumptions. Sustainability is a pertinent topic of which all students must be aware, and there is a connection between humans and nature. The change process leading to sustainable behaviors requires changing students' hearts, as well as minds. In addition to individual behavioral change, systems must be changed. Sustainability should be taught across all disciplines, thus students will determine the future sustainability of the planet.

Once we identified the competencies from various sources, we began the task of developing what we refer to as general education sustainability competencies that all of the students in the hospitality college were to acquire prior to graduation. We realized that the hospitality college's faculty might not be adequately trained to teach the general competencies. To address this obstacle, we found general education courses on campus, such as an environmental studies course, that students could take during their first academic year in school. The logic behind this was that if students entered their advanced coursework in the hospitality college with the ability to define and explain sustainable development at a general level, they would then be in a better position to learn competencies that were specific to their industry. The general education competencies we developed are as follows:

1. Describe the core concepts of ecology;
2. Identify global trends that impact the life quality of present and future generations;
3. Define sustainability and the principles of sustainable development;
4. Explain the impact of societal values, actions, and culture on sustainability;
5. Examine how personal lifestyles affect environmental, social, and economic sustainability;
6. Examine how the adoption of personal and community sustainability practices impacts their individual quality of life.

We then created a second set of competencies specific to the hospitality industry. The hospitality college has roughly 2700 undergraduate students, all of whom can choose different majors/minors within the college. However, the college was going through a broader revision of its curriculum in conjunction with our sustainability competency development. The college identified six core classes that all students within the college must take (e.g., Introduction to the Hospitality Industry), regardless of major. As the process of developing the sustainability competencies evolved, the sustainability committee also identified the specific college/major classes that would be most suitable to address each competency.

We created each competency using verbs (e.g., define, analyze) that could be assessed by the instructor in the form of a quiz, project, or other form of assessment; then more specific and measurable competencies were developed to further delineate each of the primary competencies. For example, competency number three states (See Table 9.1) that students will "demonstrate knowledge of professional ethical, legal, and regulatory responsibilities for environmental, economic, and social sustainable practices." We clarified the primary competency by elaborating how students will be able to demonstrate their knowledge. For this competency, as one example, we delineated "describing local and national legal and regulatory requirements related to sustainability" as one way students will demonstrate their knowledge of it. Table 9.1 provides the complete list of the hotel college sustainability competencies.

TABLE 9.1 Hotel college sustainability competencies

1. Calculate a personal carbon footprint, and identify:
   - The environmental impact of that footprint and the environmental benefits realized from reducing it
   - The societal impact of that footprint and the societal benefits realized from reducing it
   - The economic impact of that footprint and the economic benefits realized from reducing it
   - Strategies for reducing one's personal carbon footprint
2. Recognize the global impact of the hospitality, tourism, and leisure industries on environmental, economic, and social sustainability by:
   - Identifying current issues related to the global impact of the hospitality, tourism, and leisure industries on environmental, economic, and social sustainability
   - Identifying future trends that may influence the global impact of the hospitality, tourism, and leisure industries on environmental, economic, and social sustainability
   - Identifying resources that can be used to assess the global impact of the hospitality, tourism and leisure industries on sustainability, including sustainability indices, indicators, and annual reports
3. Demonstrate knowledge of professional ethical, legal, and regulatory responsibilities for environmental, economic, and social sustainable practices by:
   - Describing local and national legal and regulatory requirements related to sustainability
   - Articulating cultural and governmental differences in global regulatory practices
   - Applying ethical principles to decision-making and problem solving related to sustainability
   - Articulating the importance of responsible consumerism in hospitality, tourism, and leisure
4. Describe design concepts and principles for hospitality, tourism, and leisure facilities that promote the principles of economic, social, and environmental sustainability. These principles include:
   - Promotion and use of sustainable design standards developed by government and other public and private organizations
   - Use of low impact and non-toxic materials that consume minimal energy when produced for the building's construction materials, furniture, fixtures, equipment, and supplies

- Design of better functioning and more durable building materials, furniture, fixtures, and equipment
- Use of more energy and water efficient equipment
- Construction of "closed loop" service delivery systems enabling the constant reuse of materials, or the ability to compost materials when their usefulness has been exhausted
- Selecting a facility site that ensures a minimal negative impact on the environment and the surrounding community
- Employment of building architecture and landscape design principles that reduce energy and water usage

5. Analyze the consumptive practices of the hospitality, tourism, and leisure industries, specifically in one's area of responsibility, by:
   - Conducting a waste audit
   - Measuring water quantity and usage
   - Examining purchasing practices
   - Examining energy practices
   - Identifying mechanisms that offset contributions to the carbon footprint
   - Examining the impact of consumptive practices on the community

6. Develop resource management techniques that will address the consumptive practices of the hospitality, tourism, and leisure industries, and reduce excess use of resources, specifically in one's area of responsibility, by:
   - Developing a waste management program
   - Formulating purchasing policies that are sustainable
   - Designing water conservation programs
   - Designing energy conservation programs
   - Formulating sustainable marketing strategies
   - Applying an appropriate capital budget strategy that encompasses total life-cycle cost, and reflects a commitment to sustainability
   - Applying instructional techniques that educate employees and customers about sustainable issues and practices

Development of Faculty Survey

After the competencies were developed, the committee then had to determine faculty attitudes, intentions, and behaviors, and whether they had the knowledge to teach the competencies. It was important to assess the attitudes and knowledge related to sustainability as applied to hospitality education and professional practice, because if students are to acquire sustainability competencies, the faculty must be willing and able to teach those competencies. A survey was developed to assess faculty members' attitudes, knowledge, intentions, and behaviors relative to teaching sustainability. To determine what kind of survey to use, the members of the sustainability committee reviewed both existing attitudinal surveys and sustainability surveys in order to develop the survey instrument used in this study. It was difficult to identify one scale that measured exactly what we wanted to measure, so we developed a survey specifically for this project. The final faculty survey included six questions designed to measure faculty attitudes toward teaching sustainability in hospitality curricula, in general, as well as teaching sustainability in their assigned classes. The survey also assessed faculty members' intentions of addressing hospitality competencies in their classes, the degree to which they currently addressed sustainability in their classes, as well as their perceptions of their knowledge related to sustainability, current constraints to addressing sustainability competencies in their classes, and resources they would need to develop their knowledge and appropriate pedagogies for teaching sustainability in hospitality. The faculty survey took approximately 15–20 minutes to complete.

The survey was administered to all of the hospitality college's 56 faculty members through their campus mailboxes. Due to a relatively low initial response rate, a few weeks later, the survey was also administered at a college meeting with another follow-up request for participation placed in faculty mailboxes.

Results

Of the 56 faculty, 32 responded to the survey. In the first section of the survey the faculty rated their level of agreement to 12 statements, using a scale from 1–7 (1 = strongly disagree; 7 = strongly agree), regarding attitude toward, and behavior in, sustainability. With a mean of 6.21, the respondents most strongly agreed with the statement, "I think it is important that hospitality *industry professionals* implement sustainable business practices." The next highest score (6.00) was for "I think it is important that hospitality *courses/curricula* address sustainability issues." "I regularly address sustainability issues in my classes," received the lowest mean score (4.88) indicating that faculty members' actual teaching behaviors were not completely reflective of their espoused attitudes related to teaching about sustainability. For a complete list of means and standard deviations for each statement, see Table 9.2.

The purpose of the next section of the survey was to determine how likely respondents were to incorporate sustainability into their courses. The respondents were simply asked "If you are *likely* to incorporate sustainability into any of your courses, will that be within the next: 6 months; 12 months; 18 months; 24 months; or, Already doing it (please circle one)?" Twenty-one respondents indicated, "already doing it," while five said 6 months, and three said 12 months. Six people skipped this question. The next question then tried to determine what factors might constrain faculty from incorporating sustainability into their courses. They were presented with eight constraints; they could check all that applied. The most often cited constraints were "lack of confidence in teaching sustainability" and "it's not a priority for me" each with four responses, followed by "nothing constrains me." Other constraints included "lack of knowledge of teaching techniques," "lack of time to prepare," "lack of time in class," and "lack of

TABLE 9.2 Means and standard deviations for faculty attitude toward sustainability in the hospitality industry

Statement	Mean(n = 32)	SD
I think it is important that hospitality *industry professionals* implement sustainable business practices.	6.21	1.45
I think it is important that hospitality *courses/curricula* address sustainability issues.	6.00	1.50
I think it is urgent that hospitality *industry professionals* implement sustainable business practices.	5.69	1.47
I think hospitality *industry professionals* have an ethical responsibility to implement sustainable business practices.	5.69	1.67
I think sustainability is very relevant to the courses that *I* teach.	5.53	1.87
I think it is important that *I* address sustainability issues in *my* hospitality classes.	5.50	1.92
I think hospitality *educators* have an ethical responsibility to teach sustainable business practices.	5.50	1.74
I think it is urgent that hospitality *courses/curricula* address sustainability issues.	5.34	1.81
In the future, I plan to stay current about sustainability issues related to my classes.	5.31	2.03
I stay current about sustainability issues that relate to the courses I teach.	5.19	1.91
I think it is urgent that *I* address sustainability issues in *my* hospitality classes.	4.91	1.91
I regularly address sustainability issues in my classes.	4.88	2.01

knowledge in sustainability." The least cited constraint was "lack of instructional resources."

The last part of this section was introduced to assess the faculty members' actual knowledge of sustainability. On a scale from 1 to 7 (1 = very low; 7 = very high), respondents rated their level of sustainability knowledge. Respondents were most familiar with sustainability in their field of study (M = 5.20). They were least familiar with pedagogies for teaching sustainability (M = 4.06). "How would you rate your general knowledge of sustainability?" received a mean score of 4.69.

Finally, the last section of the survey was used to ascertain what tools faculty might need to either develop general knowledge of sustainability or develop knowledge of sustainability in their own field of study. To develop general knowledge, they believed that information on sustainable organizations and movements would be helpful, as would bibliographies of seminal works on corporate social responsibility, and energy, water, and waste management. Access to workshops and/or faculty retreats about sustainability issues was also an important tool. To develop knowledge related specifically to their field of study, faculty wanted similar information that related to their field. Information about sustainable organizations and movements in their field of study was cited most often, followed by workshops. They also wanted bibliographies specifically related, for example, to meetings and events, sports, recreation, and leisure studies, and pedagogical approaches to teaching sustainability, to name a few.

Discussion/Conclusion

From the beginning, the committee realized that not all faculty would be on board with incorporating sustainability into either their classes, or the college as a whole. To engage these faculty in sustainability efforts will require winning their hearts and minds, just as with the students. However, many of the faculty strongly endorsed the importance of sustainability for the industry and in hospitality curricula. They indicated a need for information and resources to support their sustainability efforts. We will provide the information and resources to faculty that were interested in sustainability.

We are still in the process of analyzing and digesting some of the faculty's responses to the survey. After an initial review, the responses do prove quite interesting. There seemed to be a trend toward putting more pressure on the industry to implement sustainable practices than on educators to teach the practices. Respondents also indicated that it was important to incorporate sustainability into hospitality curricula, yet were less committed to staying current in such issues. Others thought the incorporation of the competencies was important, overall, but not necessarily important to them and their classes personally. "I regularly address sustainability issues in my classes" received the lowest level-of-agreement mean score. On the surface, this may appear disappointing, but the reason for not addressing sustainability now may be that faculty may not have the knowledge or tools to incorporate it more often. Therefore, providing faculty with relevant hospitality sustainability resources may help to remedy this apparent gap between interest and current teaching behaviors.

With competencies identified and faculty's attitudes/knowledge assessed, our next step will focus on changing the curriculum to require a general education environmental science class, identifying the sustainability competencies that will be addressed through six core hospitality classes, and helping to prepare the faculty to teach them. This will include compiling the necessary resources for faculty to enhance their knowledge of sustainability. In the near future, we will help to develop sustainability competencies for each major in the hospitality college; each committee member will work to identify the articles, books, and other seminal readings and organizations that provide information on sustainability in their particular field of study. The compiled information will then be passed along to the faculty interested in the information. At that point in time, appropriate pedagogies, service-learning activities, or extracurricular activities can be created and incorporated into the classroom.

Providing the appropriate resources will address some of the constraints some faculty identified. There are some challenges to alleviating some of the constraints, however. The respondents who held that incorporating sustainable education is not a priority for them may require additional information about the importance and urgency of sustainability education, or an organizational climate that has clear expectations for faculty involvement, before a meaningful change occurs. In addition, in today's economic climate, many faculty members are required to teach more classes than normal, and thus they may not have enough time to prepare a class that incorporates new competencies. Despite these barriers, as late adopters see other faculty addressing sustainability in their classes, they may get on board. It is imperative that the initiative moves forward in order to address effectively the compelling sustainability challenges of the twenty-first century.

The hospitality leaders of the future will be challenged increasingly to implement sustainable professional practices, and hospitality educators must prepare them accordingly. Yet, there is little in the hospitality literature to guide these efforts. We hope that the initial process presented in this chapter may help lay the foundation for other hospitality programs curricular initiatives.

References

ACPA College Student Educators International Sustainability Taskforce, 2006. http://www.myacpa.org/task-force/sustainability/docs/Learning_Outcomes_Sustainability_Map.pdf (accessed 1 August 2009).

Ajzen, I., 1991. The Theory of Planned Behavior. *Organizational Behavior and Human Decision Processes*, **50**: 179–211.

Armitage, C. and Christian, J., 2003. From Attitudes to Behavior: Basic and Applied Research on the Theory of Planned Behavior. *Current Psychology*, **22**(3): 187–195.

Bardaglio, P., 2007. A moment of grace: integrating sustainability into the undergraduate curriculum. *Planning for Higher Education*, **36**(1): 16–22.

Burns, R., 1972. Behavioral Objectives for Competency-Based Education. In R.W. Burns and J. L. Klingstedt (eds), *Competency-Based Education: An Introduction*, Englewood Cliffs, NJ: Educational Technology Publications, pp. 42–52.

Calhoun, T., 2005. A (recycled, of course) Six-Pack of Sustainability Lessons From the Past Year in Higher Education. http://www.scup.org/asset/48672/scup-csd-report.pdf (accessed 27 May 2010).

Chen, C. and Jeong, M., 2009. Students' Perspectives of Environmental Education Needs in the Hospitality Curricula. *Journal of Hospitality and Tourism Education*, **21**(2): 41–47.

Goodman, R. and Sprague, L., 1991. The Future of Hospitality Education: Meeting the Industry's Needs. *Cornell Hotel and Restaurant Administration Quarterly*, **32**(2): 66–70.

Hines, J., Hungerford, H. and Tomera, A., 1986. Analysis and Synthesis of Research in Responsible Environmental Behavior. *Journal of Environmental Education*, **18**(2): 1–8.

Horng, J., 2004. Curriculum Analysis of Foods and Beverage Management of Technological and Vocational Education in Taiwan. *Asia Pacific Journal of Tourism Research*, **9**(2): 107–119.

King, B., McKercher, B., and Waryszak, R., 2003. A comparative Study of Hospitality and Tourism Graduates in Australia and Hong Kong. *International Journal of Tourism Research*, **5**(6): 409–420.

Lozano-Garcia, F., Gandara, G., Perrni, O., Manzano, M., Hernandez, D. and Huising, D., 2008. Capacity Building: A Course on Sustainable Development to Educate the Educators. *International Journal of Sustainability in Higher Education*, **9**(3): 257–281.

Mayo, C. and Thomas-Haysbert, C., 2005. Essential Competencies Needed by Hospitality and Tourism Management Graduates as Determined by Industry Professionals and Hospitality Educators. *The Consortium Journal*, **9**(2): 5–16.

Millar, M., Mao, Z. and Moreo, P., 2010. Hospitality and Tourism Educators vs. the Industry: A Competency Assessment. *Journal of Hospitality and Tourism Education*, **22**(2): 38–50.

Svanstrom, M., Lozano-Garcia, F. and Rowe, D., 2008. Learning Outcomes for Sustainable Development in Higher Education. *International Journal of Sustainability in Higher Education*, **9**(3): 339–351.

Telfer, D. and Hashimoto, A., 2001. Environmental Education in Tourism – a Comparison Between Canada and Japan. *Journal of Hospitality and Tourism Education*, **13**(1): 18–24.

Tesone, D., 2004. Development of a Sustainable Tourism Hospitality Human Resource Module: a template for teaching sustainability across the curriculum. *Hospitality Management*, **23**(3): 207–237.

United States' Partnership for Education for Sustainability, 2009. http://www.uspartnership.org/resources/0000/0081/USP_EFS_standards_V3_10_09.pdf (accessed 15 November 2009).

SECTION 4
Problem-Based Learning

10

EVERYBODY'S BUSINESS

Addressing the Challenge of Team-Teaching Partnerships in the Global Seminar

Tamara Savelyeva

Introduction

Sustainability has become a very important concept in the life of universities. To bring meaning to this term, institutions create new programs and related courses, provide research funds, and create new policies that directly and indirectly reflect principles of sustainability. Because of the overlap between environmental research, green planning, and the creation of new curricula, universities face the challenge of simultaneously launching sustainability efforts in all the dimensions of academic life.

One of the ways universities address this challenge is through fostering partnerships among faculty and students on sustainability-related projects. Teaming up faculty and students through research and campus greening projects, as well as mixing natural sciences and humanities in new sustainability programs, builds a common sustainability vision across disciplines and generational divides. This promising approach is based on the assumption that academic partnerships overcome disciplinary disconnects and make sustainability a common experience for everyone. However, advancing new sustainability curricula models through teaching collaborations remains a rare practice among faculty members.

We built this study upon the idea that campus sustainability efforts, particularly greening, education for sustainability (EfS), and sustainability research encourage new curricular models, which strive for genuine academic collaboration and aim to create a unique type of academic scholarship. The over-arching goal here is to provide a clear outline of a successful curricular model that promotes "a different kind of scholarship that systematically focuses on [collaborative] *interactions* in a comprehensive and purposeful way" (Aber *et al.* 2009: 4). Our sincere hope is that the model will serve sustainability educators, who will utilize it in their teaching.

We used the case of the Global Seminar (GS) course curricula, a collaborative and participatory initiative, which was facilitated by faculty and run by students from 40 universities from around the world. Designed by an international and interdisciplinary faculty, the GS curricula model embraced holistic and constructivist approaches to sustainability education. Its unique features allowed participants to construct their own understandings of the complex issues by learning about sustainability principles from each other and utilizing different disciplinary expertise and cultural views. For over 10 years, the GS participants have promoted a unique way of teaching sustainability through collaborative teaching and learning.

Our intent was to address the need for new educational models, which extended the idea of academic collaboration to university teaching practices. Following this purpose, we shaped our inquiry with an assumption that teaching partnerships formed around the context of sustainability do exist; however, these instances have rarely been documented because such inquiries depend on indicator-based research. The usual set of campus sustainability indicators counts research, greening, and curriculum initiatives in numbers rather than focusing on nuances of sustainability teaching processes. By means of experiential analysis we aim here to provide an insightful description of our curricular model, which allows participants to practice holistic thinking, to apply this thinking to real-world situations, and to create meanings for sustainability via intense international and interdisciplinary interactions. Before discussing the study, it is necessary to introduce a broader context that reflects on campus sustainability practices and underlines the conditions for team-teaching in academia.

Campus Greening, EfS, Sustainability Science, and the Challenge of Team-Teaching

Sustainability in higher education encompasses many overlapping spheres of concern and professional specialties. Interdisciplinary collaboration is of a major importance, because it merges the primary ways of advancing sustainability principles in academic institutions: going green, promoting EfS, and supporting sustainability-oriented science projects. These three movements address the complexity and uncertainty of socio-economic/environmental relationships and serve the goal of creating and applying knowledge in support of sustainable decision-making. In this regard, interdisciplinarity appears to be the key concept, which allows "such knowledge to be truly useful…through close collaboration between scholars and practitioners" (Clark and Dickson 2003: 8059).

Campus greening includes the process of introducing environmentally friendly practices in university operations and facilities. EfS refers to the set of ethical standards that encourage universities to become sustainable. Sustainability science refers to a vibrant arena of research that merges different disciplinary perspectives and scholarship related to sustainable development.

The widespread campus greening movement started with a group of university presidents who were the first signatories of the1990 Talloires Declaration. This document, which helps to develop, implement, and evaluate a personalized plan of greening action on their campuses, provided a common starting point for sustainability efforts at universities, though the specific action plan depended on the university's type, history, culture, and mission. Julian Keniry (1995) listed the following strategies as those most commonly used in the American universities to promote campus greening:

- updating campus infrastructure with new technologies that help increase energy efficiency and reduce water consumption;
- constructing new Leadership in Energy and Environmental Design (LEED) certified buildings and retro-fitting old campus facilities to meet higher environmental standards;
- redirecting university food services toward "environmentally preferable" meal options, including complete vegetarian meals;
- directing a part of the campus expenditures toward local and organically produced foods;
- organizing campus recycling programs;
- including environmental impact specification in procurement contracts for cleaning products, paper, laboratory equipment, and building materials;
- participating in a sustainability audit program.

The second campus sustainability movement, EfS, appears to be more holistic than campus greening, as it aims to embrace the sustainability values in educational practices from the broader national and international context. This objective is guided by multiple United Nations declarations, including those signed in Stockholm (1972), Tbilisi (1978), Rio de Janeiro (1992), and Johannesburg (2002). In its essence, EfS is oriented more toward environmental education and natural sciences disciplines, which hampered interdisciplinary applications of the EfS. Stephen Sterling (2004) proposed an operational system-based staged model, which takes EfS beyond these disciplinary boundaries and allows institutions to integrate EfS principles in a more holistic way. Sterling's model proposes a systemic interconnectedness within an educational system and therefore favors collaborative practices. The cases of its practical applications, however, are scattered and not well evaluated.

The discourse on sustainability science represents another way of advancing sustainability in academia. It mobilizes the research from various disciplinary fields, such as ecology, biology, complexity science, sociology, psychology, demography, science and technology studies, and history. Although often not considered an autonomous field,[1] this movement constitutes the most interdisciplinary and collaborative efforts in the context of higher education and sustainability. Sustainability science is part of a research dimension of academia. It is not concerned with the teaching or curricular planning aspects of academic life. In contrast, EfS relates mainly to curricular and instructional activities of the university.

Greening, EfS, and sustainability science movements aim to overcome the discrepancies within and between disciplines, and to bring faculty and students together to create a common vision of sustainability. However, these three discourses do not interconnect – in part, because they involve collaboration on different levels of an institutional structure. This raises the question of whether interdisciplinary collaborations really aid simultaneous integration of sustainability principles within a university setting. We believe that one can find an answer by placing the inquiry within a framework of advancing academic partnerships, specifically, team-teaching. In the context of our research, we adapted Buckley's understanding of team-teaching, which means that all faculty "attend several or all of the class sessions to observe, interact, question, and learn" (2000: 5). Dean and Witherspoon stressed that the structural features of team-teaching should serve "the essential spirit of cooperative planning, constant collaboration, close unity, unrestrained communication, and sincere sharing" (1964: 4). They pointed out another defining feature of team-teaching: its ability to provide faculty with an increased degree of flexibility that creates "an invigorating spirit of freedom and opportunity to revamp programs to meet...educational needs" (quoted in Bair and Woodward 1964: 22). Our understanding of team-teaching complements a broader notion of academic collaboration, which is generally viewed as a discourse, conversation, or communication between two of more professionals who share the same goal and "work together to provide the best academic experience for their students" (Bush 2003: 6).

Although our findings indicate that team-teaching might re-enforce the introduction of sustainability principles at all academic fronts, across disciplines, and cultures, it is also true that team-teaching is not without its challenges. Team-teaching requires crossing the boundaries of disciplinary thinking and forces faculty and students out of their comfort zones to an "unknown territory" called sustainability. It also involves faculty developing new teaching techniques based on collaboration that, most likely, overwrite "signature pedagogies" common in their original fields (e.g., lectures, colloquiums, labs, seminars). Team-teaching might challenge one's professional identity as faculty are expected to give up some of their authority in the classroom and open up new channels of communication and negotiation.

Despite its obvious challenges, team-teaching should be seen as an opportunity, not an obstacle. One of the great potentials of a well-formed team-teaching partnership is its ability to create curricula structures which encourage holistic thinking and enrich participants' understandings of complex phenomena. Gary Poole advocated the importance of a holistic curricular approach, which allows balancing different metacognitions within and across disciplines:

> Divergent views regarding the nature of thinking within a discipline should
> be encouraged because these views enrich the discipline. Similarly, as educators,

we need to strike a balance between curricula that socialize students into a way of thinking and curricula that welcome new forms of discourse and thought

(Poole 2009: 54).

We believe that the detailed description of the GS course curricula model, as it is presented in this study, serves the goal of broadening the opportunities for faculty to integrate campus sustainability efforts into their teaching in a new, innovative way. We argue that the GS structure promotes holistic thinking and enhances team-teaching partnerships, which "focus on the potential interactions between the innovation and the relevant characteristics of local cultures, their teaching and learning regimes" (Trowler 2009: 194).[2]

Research Scope

We used the case of the GS project as an example of sustainability curricula that involve team-teaching. The GS project was launched in 1999 by seven agricultural colleges from the US, Sweden, Denmark, Austria, Australia, and the Netherlands. Over the course of one semester, the participating faculty piloted a series of virtual lectures, which were simultaneously delivered to their classrooms. Within two years, the international faculty team worked together to develop course content and a synchronized curricular model, which has continue to evolve through a truly participatory format. Currently, the GS is a consortium of over 40 universities, agriculture and technical colleges, community colleges, high schools, and professional institutions.[3]

The two research objectives of our study were: (1) to determine the aspects of the team-taught course which were successful and sustainable within different educational systems; and (2) to provide a detailed description of its curriculum model. Based on these objectives, we established a guiding research question: How do faculty members integrate the principles of sustainability into their practices in the context of team-teaching?

Research Design

We conducted a descriptive study of the GS using a qualitative research design, which helped us to construct a detailed and comprehensive description of the course's curriculum model. This experiential approach for examining the GS facilitated an empathic and open-minded entrance into the participants' frame of reference. We situated our study within a Constructivist theory (Vygotsky 2004 [1976])[4] and Hanvey's (2004/1976)[5] global perspective. The integration of elements from these two frameworks provided a broad perspective by which we examined the characteristics of a sustainability curricula model across the following course elements: course structure and academic leadership/management, stakeholder involvement, institutional support, course conducive-content, and teaching and learning practices (Savelyeva 2009).

We used a purposeful-intense sampling method of particular persons, settings, and activities in order to identify those best suited to provide detailed information about the GS. The pool of participants included faculty from the US, Mexico, Costa Rica, Italy, Australia, Sweden, Honduras, South Africa, Germany, Austria, and Denmark. We used three forms of data collection: (1) twenty in-depth, open-ended interviews that consisted of direct quotations from GS faculty about their course perceptions and experiences; (2) eleven direct observations of the GS classroom, which included institutions from the US, Germany, Mexico, and Italy; and (3) written documents available on the course website, at meetings, and in class. We addressed the trustworthiness of this study through three data-quality indicators: research credibility, transferability, and dependability (Table 10.1).

Instrument and Data Collection

The interview instrument consisted of open-ended questions created based upon the data about curricula modeling available in the literature. For observations, we adapted and modified Creswell's (2003) template by including specific items to capture the instances of constructive and participatory practices. Our choice of observation items reflected the information found in the literature and derived from the interviews. For the document analysis, we used a summary form adapted from Miles and Huberman (1994). We conducted the interviews during the GS annual meeting in Arlington, Virginia, USA in July 2005. The observations and

TABLE 10.1 Trustworthiness of the study

Qualitative term for assessing trustworthiness	Strategy employed
Credibility	Prolonged engagement in the field
	Pilot study
	Method triangulation (interviews, observations, documents, and artifacts)
Transferability	Purposeful-intense sampling technique
	Thick, rich description of the context, participants, and the findings
Dependability	Method triangulation (interviews, observations, documents, and artifacts)
	Research transparency (explicit explanation of the data analysis, management, and findings)
	Audit trail (keeping accurate records, research codes, interview recordings and transcriptions, and all other forms of documentation)

document analysis of the classroom took place during the 2007 spring semester at Virginia Polytechnic Institute and State University, USA.

The multicultural composition of the study group required participants' involvement. To ensure the clarity of the interview topics and questions, we engaged participants in the design of the interview questions. Prior to the interviews, the interviewees helped to modify individual questions to make them clear for non-English speakers. This prevented any terminological, linguistic, and cultural misunderstanding of the research issues that were discussed in English during the personal interviews.

Data Analysis Procedures

First, we analyzed the interview data using an open-coding feature of the ATLAS.ti (v3)® qualitative data analysis software for reading the transcripts and coding passages in the margins. We applied a coding-recoding strategy to the analysis to ensure the dependability of the findings. Next, we analyzed the observation data and course documents for an appearance of common themes and topics related to the research question.

Results: The Description of the GS Curricula

The team of GS course participants worked on sustainability case studies in conjunction with other international universities connected via educational technology. The faculty and students used one synchronized curriculum. The faculty team taught the course and facilitated learning within the international group. The students needed to produce a joint final project based on constant negotiation of different perspectives and sources by the end of the course.

The GS Curriculum Elements

Goals and objectives. The goal of this course was to build an understanding of sustainability through the analysis of different perspectives on global issues and the interdisciplinary scholarship of faculty and students. It included the following sets of objectives:

(1) Learning objectives
- Promote the development of participants' metacognitive and learning skills needed to address problems of global proportion and to enhance their awareness of sustainability;
- Encourage participants to take actions that reflect their commitment to sustainability;
- Encourage participants to construct an in-depth understanding of a sustainability concept.

(2) Institutional objectives
  • Apply a new teaching, research, and outreach model that networked partners around the world;
  • Refine our model for other universities interested in creating effective international educational collaborations based on a fully interactive delivery system;
  • Build linkages with and foster participation by institutions and faculty from around the world.

Organization and stakeholders. The GS was an ad hoc network of interested parties with minimal formalization of the participants' actions. Within the project, participating universities were clustered into groups of three to six institutions. One of the faculty members coordinated the cluster's course logistics and guided his/her colleagues' instruction at their respective universities. The course involved the principal investigator, enrolled students, cluster coordinators, teaching faculty, college programs, administrative units, sponsors, and the communities surrounding each university.

Faculty support. GS utilized a newcomers' informal mentoring program to assist faculty's introduction to the project and its dynamics. An experienced GS faculty-volunteer helped new participants to optimally manage the personal and professional partnerships within a course cluster.

Course structure. The course structure included three-week learning cycles (Table 10.2), which were built around different sustainability case studies. This structure allowed in-depth exploration of several sustainability-related topics during one semester. The learning cycles included both in-class and virtual sessions.

Course methodology. The class worked with case studies, which were developed by the participating faculty and presented through videos, readings, and other documentation that were realistic and complemented by background materials. The case study topics included: food safety, genetically modified organisms, water quality and use, fisheries, global climate change, sustainable tourism, food safety, natural disaster management, population, biodiversity, and sustainable agriculture. The participants used a Blackboard® courseware hosted by Cornell University, USA. This website was password-secured, and it contained readings, links, images, and mini-biographies of faculty and students. The courseware also included a discussion board, a link to library documents, course activities, announcements, and case study resources.

Assignments, grading, and evaluation. Throughout each semester, students wrote reflective essays on each case study and a final course paper, which were graded by the faculty at their universities. The grade assigned by

TABLE 10.2 The GS learning cycle

Week	Actions
Week One (local classroom)	Introduce a case study
	Identify sources to inform the case
	Define a group role in the overall case discussion.
	Divide responsibilities in preparation for a virtual discussion
	Create/respond to discussion questions
Week Two (local and virtual classrooms)	Develop recourses and analyze a problem
	Gather information and clarify perspectives
	Prepare a group view statement
	Discuss viewpoints with peers from other universities via live chat and discussion board
	Distribute videoconference schedule
Week Three (virtual classroom)	Present solutions at a videoconference
	Evaluate different points of view during the videoconference
	Discuss issues and negotiate final solutions with peers
	Create group memoranda
	Reflect on the videoconference
	Re-formulate conclusions

the faculty was confidential and it corresponded to a grading system used in a local university. The course employed formative evaluation sessions, conducted via online surveys at the end of each learning cycle. At the end of the semester, students filled out a faculty evaluation form. The faculty presented and discussed students' suggestions for the course at the GS bi-annual meeting.

Aspects of the GS Curricula Model

As a result of their collaborative efforts, the participants created a GS curricular model, which included the following unique features: they were international, interdisciplinary, innovative, and interactive. The culture of mutual learning served as the guiding principle that linked these distinctive aspects together.

International. The international scope of this course ignited team teaching that involved faculty from different cultures and educational systems. It also initiated collective conversations about sustainability and developed a fully functioning teaching partnership among the faculty from the Americas, Europe, Australia, Africa, and Asia. The international scope of this course linked the participants' experiences together with two major sustainability aspects: diversity and complexity. Within their course cluster, the participating faculty were present in the classroom at the same time, and acted as a team of teachers. They learned about diversity by dealing with each other's idio-syncrasies, specifics of class procedures, and work habits. They observed, toler-ated, appreciated, and respected cultural differences by recognizing each other's biases and stereotypes. At the same time, the diversity of views aided the faculty's understanding of the complex nature of sustainability.

Interdisciplinary. In addition to linking participants with different cultural backgrounds, this course connected faculty and students from different disci-plines. Simultaneously offered in over 40 colleges around the world, the GS course has extended the idea of academic collaboration across cultural peda-gogies. The international faculty who were engaged in course partnerships had little prior teaching experience outside of their own discipline, college, or country. The course's disciplinary mix and the novel teaching partnership experience offered GS faculty a sense of greater challenge and professional satisfaction. It also enriched their learning by facilitating a constructive envi-ronment within the course. By addressing sustainability as an interdisciplinary team of international scientists of agriculture, economics, education, art, medicine, and soil sciences, the participants learned sustainability from each other.

Innovative. The innovativeness of this model was three-fold, evidenced in course methodology, structure, and the use of technology. In terms of new methodology, the GS faculty employed a case study method. The same case studies were offered simultaneously to all participants throughout the course. Most of the GS faculty were researchers exposed to "signature pedagogies" common in their disciplines. In this course, the faculty learned about the case study method first-hand from their team members. Team-teaching eased their adaptation to this teaching method in this and other courses they taught. Taking the case study method to the next level, the faculty learned the art of composing sustainability cases based on real events and people in their home countries. The innovative student-led nature of this course advanced faculty teaching partnerships, because all faculty needed to undergo the challenge of adapting to the non-traditional constructivist approach, where students organized discussions and led the videoconferences while faculty acted as facilitators. The innovative course structure consisted of a series of three-week learning cycles. The learning cycles enriched teaching collaboration by providing local faculty with examples of teaching autonomy offered in dif-ferent academic cultures, yet engaging them in interdependent scholarship and cross-cultural teaching. This structure allowed flexibility in shaping in-class sessions and facilitating global student-led videoconferences in the respective universities. At the same time, faculty operated within a definite course framework and followed the rules and schedules of the course. The third innovation – an advanced technology – was used as a teaching and learning tool. The technology tools added to the "realism" of teaching partnerships by making personal and professional connections possible in virtual environments.

Interactive. The highly interactive nature of this course developed and sustained teaching partnerships. Faculty built various lines of personal and group communication: international participants communicated virtually, both synchronously and asynchronously, via e-mails, the course Blackboard® site, live chat rooms, discussion boards, and videoconferences. Local teams of faculty members met and communicated on a regular basis in their universities. Intense interaction facilitated the development of scholarly and personal relationships that grew out of a sense of professional stewardship within the group. At the beginning of this project, some of the GS faculty were required to teach this course and were randomly partnered up with a GS cluster. As the project progressed, the participating faculty recruited new partners via their professional networks and the GS faculty voluntarily joined the course. The participants' interactions established ongoing dialogues and discussions about the organization of the course, course logistics, and contents. These conversations often continued beyond faculty's offices and classrooms. The faculty members met in person at biannual GS conferences to plan the course, reflect on its progress, and train newcomers.

International, interdisciplinary, innovative, and interactive features of the GS model were linked by the culture of mutual learning established in this course. The success of the team-teaching resulted from mutual learning, which implied a learning curve for both faculty and students. Mutual learning engaged the participants in a continuous process of better understanding the course itself and the theme of sustainability. The faculty and students developed this understanding for two reasons: (1) participants were encouraged to challenge each other's fundamental assumptions about the course and their understandings of sustainability; and (2) they constructed individual and group meanings based on their practices and experiences.

Discussion

The two important features of the curriculum model identified as a result of this study included: the holistic structure of its curricular elements, which are perceived together in a nonlinear fashion, and the transformative nature of its pedagogy. These features signified the conditions required for a team-teaching partnership of international faculty to grow and sustain this course over the years. A sense of scholarship and stewardship, which faculty developed during the course, arose from team-teaching practices. It allowed faculty to build an understanding of sustainability as a concept through the shared teaching application of the course and simultaneously situate this initiative in different campuses, within different disciplines, and cultures.

The first unique feature of the model – the holistic structure of its elements – implies simultaneous perception of all of its aspects and processes. When perceived together, the international, innovative, interdisciplinary, and interactive aspects of the GS model create a notion of a sustainability curriculum as a nonlinear entity. This notion is opposite to that of the common sequential teaching process, which is based on an input-process-output model. A holistic approach to conceptualizing the sustainability curricula model acknowledges the complexity of its processes and interactions, which inspire collaboration and ensure faculty's engagement in a sustainability discourse. The holistic perception of GS elements involves considerable negotiation regarding team-teaching idiosyncrasies, use of an innovative case study method, application of course pedagogy, and the place of this course in the university curricula. The flexibility and interconnectedness of the GS elements ease the introduction of this model into different disciplinary and cultural contexts, and make it highly applicable to different educational systems. One of the important GS elements, considerable negotiation, empowers the process of interpersonal engagement and ensures GS cross-cultural effectiveness.

Each area of the GS model is constructive and participatory in style, structure, management, and content. The application of constructive and participatory principles (Table 10.3) supported the transformative nature of the GS pedagogy by moving the participants toward mutual development of their sustainability views and innovation of pedagogical actions. We argue that the GS's transformative pedagogy created what Goodman called "a fusion of horizons," when the ongoing collaborative process inspired pivotal decision moments, in which "the present, past, and future possibilities [were] related in a dialectical and explicitly value-based way" (2003: 190). The transformative power of the GS pedagogy stemmed out of the process of team-teaching, meaning making, and knowledge-construction. Oriented toward a transversal communication of differences, the model exemplified the "convergence without coincidence" approach (Schrag 2004) to educational action. It allowed the diversity of the GS elements to mutually enrich the practice of teaching and learning by promoting the emergence of transcendent decision-making.

The holistic structure and transformative power of this model ignited a sense of scholarship and stewardship among GS faculty, who ensured its lasting application within different disciplinary and cultural contexts. The model is characterized by open, flexible, and fluid properties that generate a flow of transformative interactions based on differences of educational and cultural contexts, contradictions of participants' views, and possibilities for potential resolutions.

Although the model appeared sustainable, this course also had vulnerabilities. The first weakness was its dependency on faculty's altruistic commitment to the GS scholarship. The success of this unique model rested in the hands of dedicated GS faculty, whose efforts and activities remained unrewarded within their own university systems. This course required significant investment of time and effort, as faculty promoted the innovation of sustainability team-teaching under the

TABLE 10.3 Transformative characteristics of the GS

Constructive	Participatory
Based on intrinsic values of the GS's participants	Based on scholarly networks of GS's participants
Promotes educational goals and practices that encourage the growth of students' responsibility, initiative, and development of generic metacompetencies	Develops sense of camaraderie among participants
Promotes learning through intense interaction and communication within cultural contexts	Operates within a flexible and non-centralized structure
Facilitates self-regulation and promotes independent learning	Develops participants' academic potential and autonomy
Establishes a culture of mutual learning	Promotes constant application of new ideas based on an immediate internal feedback
Encourages use of local resources to solve real-life problems	Promotes practices that imply integrity, ethical consideration, respect, and equity
Process oriented	Ongoing process
Uses case study methodology	Cultivates collaboration among participants
Responsive and dynamic	Utilizes participants' creativity based on the GS's dynamics and interdisciplinary
Focused on conceptual understanding and capacity building	Relies on the participants' expertise
Provides opportunities for multicultural and interdisciplinary learning	

constraints of their own university systems. Another vulnerability was the model's reliance on the availability of advanced educational technology. The challenge of using technology for virtual communication across national boundaries overwrote the challenges of cross-cultural and cross-disciplinary interactions, team-teaching, negotiations of course content, and course adaptation to local contexts.

Conclusion

The GS curricula model offered faculty a unique pedagogical space for developing a hands-on sustainability initiative that advanced them both personally and professionally, individually and as a group, through the process of formed team-teaching. The defining features of this model – it is international, interdisciplinary, innovative, interactive, and fosters a culture of mutual learning – ensured the success and longevity of this collaborative initiative. The holistic structure of the GS curricula elements and the transformative nature of its pedagogy extended the idea of academic collaboration to university teaching practices. The participatory and constructive characteristics empowered its participants in a transformative way by inspiring their holistic thinking and real-life applications of their sustainability understandings. The team-teaching method used in this course assisted the establishment of the unique faculty scholarship, which featured a can-do spirit that created educational opportunity, collaborative planning, unity, and a sense of sincere stewardship. The flexibility and interconnectedness of the GS elements promoted the simultaneous infusion of sustainability values in all the dimensions of academic life across different cultures and disciplines. This made the model highly applicable to different educational systems. The vulnerability of this model was its high dependency on faculty's altruistic commitment to the GS scholarship, as well as the reliance on advanced educational technologies. Inspired by the unique faculty scholarship, this model suggested an open approach to sustainability teaching that has the potential to transform the field of sustainability education.

Notes

1   Kajikawa viewed sustainability science as a vibrant arena that brings together scholarship and practice, global and local perspectives, and various disciplines (2008: 216).
2   Trowler suggested the following dimensions of an academic environment that, perceived together, shape teaching and learning regimes within a discipline: tacit assumptions; implicit theories; recurrent practices; conventions of appropriateness; codes of signification; discursive repertoires; subjectivities in interaction; and power relations (2009: 186–187).
3   For more information about the GS, see www.globalseminar.org (accessed August 2010).
4   The Vygotskian view of constructivism emphasizes cognitive and social development as practices achieved both through the work of an individual consciousness and through collective cultural mediation. Simply put, constructivism views education through a set of mechanisms by which learners internalize knowledge and construct their own meanings of a reality.
5   Hanvey's dimensions of educational reorientation toward global perspective include: perspective consciousness, state-of-the-planet awareness, cross-cultural awareness, knowledge of global dynamics, and awareness of human choices.

References

Aber, J., Kelly, T. and Mallory, B. (eds), 2009. *The Sustainable Learning Community: One university's journey to the future*. Lebanon, NH: The University of New Hampshire.
Bair, M. and Woodward, R., 1964. *Team Teaching in Action*. Boston, MA: Houghton-Mifflin.
Buckley, F., 2000. *Team-teaching: What, Why, and How?* Thousand Oaks, CA: Sage.
Bush, G., 2003. *The School Buddy System: The Practice of Collaboration*. Chicago, IL: American Library Association.
Clark, W. and Dickson, N., 2003. Sustainability Science: the Emerging Research Program. *Proceedings of the National Academy of Science, USA*, **100**(14), 8059–8061.

Creswell, J., 2003. *Research Design. Qualitative, quantitative and mixed approaches.* Thousand Oaks, CA: Sage.

Dean, S., and Witherspoon, C., 1964. Team teaching in the elementary school. US Department of Health, Education, and Welfare, Office of Education. *Educational Briefs* No. 38 (January).Washington, DC: Government Printing Office.

Goodman, A., 2003. *Now What? Developing our future. Understanding our place in the unfolding universe.* New York: Peter Lang.

Hanvey, R., 2004/1976. *Attainable Global Perspective.* Repr. New York: American Forum for Global Education.

Kajikawa, Y., 2008. Research core and framework of sustainability science. *Sustainability Science*, **3**: 215–239. DOI 10.1007/s11625-008-0053-1.

Keniry, J., 1995. *Ecodemia. Campus Environmental Stewardship at the Turn of the 21st Century.* Washington, DC: National Wildlife Federation.

Miles, M. and Huberman, M., 1994. *Qualitative Data Analysis: An expanded sourcebook.* 2nd edn. Thousand Oaks, CA: Sage.

Poole, G., 2009. Academic disciplines: homes or barricades? In C. Kreber (ed.), *The University and its Disciplines.* New York: Routledge, pp. 50–57.

Savelyeva, T., 2009. *Global Learning Environment: Innovative concept and interactive model for changing academia and academics.* Saarbrücken: VDM.

Schrag, C., 2004. *Convergence Amidst Difference: Philosophical conversations across national boundaries.* Albany, NY: State University of New York.

Sterling, S., 2004. Higher education, sustainability, and the role of systematic learning. In P. Corcoran and A. Wals (eds), *Higher Education and the Challenge of Sustainability: Problematics, promise, and practice.* Dordrecht: Kluwer, pp. 47–70.

Trowler, P., 2009. Beyond epistemological essentialism: academic tribes in the twenty-first century. In C. Kreber (ed.), *The University and its Disciplines.* New York: Routledge, pp. 181–195.

Vygotsky, L., 1999 [1925]. Consciousness as a problem in the psychology of behavior. *Soviet Psychology*, **17**(4), 3–35, 1925; Repr. New York: Peter Lang, 1999.

11

THE MORAL ECOLOGY OF EVERYDAY LIFE

James J. Farrell

In a beautiful essay called "The Politics of Storytelling," William Kittredge (1999: 52–53) writes that "We live in stories. What we are is stories. We do things because of what is called character, and our character is formed by the stories we learn to live in. Late in the night we listen to our own breathing in the dark and rework our stories. We do it again the next morning, and all day long, before the looking glass of ourselves, reinventing reasons for our lives. Other than such storytelling there is no reason to things."

Right now, Americans – and American college students – live in a set of stories that are increasingly unworkable. We structure our lives around stories, explicit and implicit, that threaten the lives of more-than-human others who share the planet with us, and increasingly, the lives of people who are more susceptible to global weirding, climate change, rising ocean waters, freshwater shortages, soil depletion, deforestation, toxic pollution, and biodiversity loss. In Environmental Studies, we often teach classes about these topics, but we seldom root them in the cultural and personal patterns of college culture. St Olaf's Campus Ecology class does just that.

This story began in the Spring of 2001 when I taught a course called "The Culture of Nature." In an attempt to show students a few local examples of the culture of nature, I invited Gene Bakko, our curator of natural lands, and Pete Sandberg, our facilities director, to talk about their environmental work on campus. That week, on our course website, an enthusiastic first-year student named Elise Braaten wrote about how amazing those stories were, and how you could teach a whole course on that.

Two years later, Elise declared an independent major called "Wild and Precious Life: Educating for an Ethic of Sustainability." The title came from Mary Oliver's poem "The Summer Day," which asks us all, "Tell me, what is it you plan to do with your one wild and precious life?" (Oliver 1992: 94). In the fall of her senior year, as part of her senior project, Elise designed a course called Campus Ecology, and in the spring she team-taught the course with me as an American Studies seminar. The following year, I team-taught the course with another student, and the year after that, it moved into the college catalogue, where it resides in the Arts and Humanities track of the Environmental Studies major.

Because it began as a combination of American Studies and Environmental Studies, Campus Ecology is a strange amalgam of academic and personal approaches to ecology, education, and sustainability. At St. Olaf, our American Studies program focuses on what we call "the moral ecology of everyday life," the ideas and institutions that shape the common sense of our culture. In *Habits of the Heart*, Robert Bellah defines moral ecology as "the web of moral understandings and commitments that tie people together in community." (Bellah *et al.* 1985: 335) In its Campus Ecology variation, moral ecology also includes the web of social values that tie people and nature together. It's the stories we live in.

In American Studies, we teach a lot of our classes using "dense facts," specific facts or artifacts that contain critical cultural values and assumptions within them. Using a "connecting mind," for example, a student might understand a shower *simply* as a way of getting clean in the morning, and *complexly* as a kind of cultural work reinforcing ideas and ideals of cleanliness, beauty, attractiveness, and hetero-sexuality, as well as the institutions of a hydraulic, fossil-fueled civilization that can create an artificial waterfall anywhere we want. As this suggests, Campus Ecology focuses on everyday life. According to what we might call "the law of inverse importance," academics often write extensively about things that most people do not do. American Studies, at least at St. Olaf, is intensely interested in the significance of the seemingly insignificant, making the familiar unfamiliar and vice versa.[1]

In the introductory class, for example, we open an American Studies Museum in the student center to teach other people on campus the cultural messages of everyday artifacts like Cheetos and cell phones, credit cards and a cup of coffee, a remote control and a baseball cap, a condom and a banana, a football and a pink Victoria's Secret bra. Preparing for the museum, we spend a whole day reading a can of Classic Coke in order to decipher what this strange object can tell us about our culture and civilization. What is the liquid in this container? What is it made of? What is it for? How do we think about it? We look at the container itself. What is it made of? What does it tell us about mining, metallurgy, and manufacturing, or about embodied energy in aluminum? Why is it red? How could we explain the script? Why is this stuff "classic?" What stories are being told about this liquid? Why is it "the real thing?" Why is there a recycling symbol on it? What is a cor-poration, a copyright, a trademark? How else are politics and policies involved with this bubbly liquid? How did this particular can of Coke get here? Why isn't Pepsi sold on our campus? And what's the environmental impact of this refreshing drink?

Campus Ecology builds on this foundation, asking even more broadly about the moral ecology of everyday life. The main question of the class, as far as I can figure it out, is this: What are the cultural patterns on this college campus that reflect and affect the natural patterns of this place and the planet? We answer these questions by contemplating a day in the life of a college student, with classes on waking up and using the bathroom, assessing the stuff in a dorm room, getting dressed, eating in the cafeteria, driving a car, going to a wild party, hooking up sexually, and framing life in religious and political terms. Such topics allow us to consider larger issues like time poverty and convenience, comfort and materialism, work and alienation, automobility and televisions, Facebook and placebooks, play and *fun*damentalism, sex and love and biophilia, religion and spirituality, sitizenship and public policy.[2] They let us see the "ordinary consumption" and assumptions of American college students, and the extraordinary problems that flow from our everyday lives. Environmentally speaking, a college campus is an organic machine for converting natural energy to human thoughtfulness, and Campus Ecology helps us understand that.

When we designed the course, Elise and I had several things in mind. We wanted students to confront what Robert Bellah *et al.* call "the problem of invisible complexity" (1985: 207): the ways in which our visible lives depend so much on things we cannot see, on people and cultural patterns we do not understand, and on natural processes we usually take for granted. We wanted students to think the unthinkable – or at least the unthought – and to confront their complicity in their culture, including its consuming culture of nature. We wanted them to notice the tensions between the Romantic conceptions of nature that we routinely express, and the resourcist conceptions that animate much of our lives.

From the beginning, we planned the course to create "a space where imagination can happen," so we invited students to combine the personal and the academic. We required journals, where students could take ideas personally and look for cultural patterns in their own idiosyncratic experiences. We asked students to "go deep," thinking not just analytically but introspectively about their lives and their culture. We wanted students to ask "What are people for?" What is education for?" "What are my deepest values?" "What are my operative values?" "What's my real relationship with nature?" and "How can I change my life (and my institutions) so that they reflect my deepest values?"

In doing this, we hoped to break down the mental barriers between college and the so-called "real world." We wanted to teach students that a college campus is as real as any other place, so I wrote an essay called "The Real World of College" (Farrell 2005), which we use early in the semester. And we suggest that environmental experiments enacted on college campuses can be models for the wider world.

We also wanted to provide a space where students could act on their thinking, a place for what we came to call "practical idealism." We wanted to help students to apply their ideas and ideals to the "real world" of college, to learn how to research problems, organize ideas, propose solutions, work collaboratively, and accomplish some good work *before* they graduate.

We created some unconventional assignments in this class, because we believe that education is more about what students *do* than about what they read or hear in class.[3] For example, we assigned students to audit their dorm rooms, making an inventory of all the stuff they found there, and trying to assess what it all means. Here are a few excerpts that suggest the kind of deep learning that can happen in such an open-ended assignment:

> All of the stuff in my dorm room tells a story. The story is about a group of people who call themselves Americans. By carefully reading the story that my dorm room tells, it is possible to learn who Americans are, how they live their lives, and how they feel about the world around them. So although a dorm room may be a very small space, it can and does say very big things about Americans and their values.
>
> Whenever I pay for a piece of clothing, it sends a message to the entire commodity chain from the advertisers to the retailers to the transporters to the dyers to the factory owners to the farmers of the material (or chemists if it's synthetic). This message is "Keep doing exactly what you're doing. It works."
>
> Now, as I've listed off my possessions, I'm feeling a bit guilty, like I do indeed have lots of useless crap. In all honesty, I think more of my things collect dust than get used.
>
> The appreciation of nature is innate, but has been gradually pushed to the side by piles of clothes and shoes and other clutter in American culture. We yearn for a relationship with nature, but other "stuff" so often obscures our vision.

On another day, we assigned students to read a J. Crew catalog. We asked them to think about the catalog as an artifact advertising not just clothes but American values, including American environmental values. We asked them to consider the *nature* of consumer culture revealed in the catalog, from Romantic representations of nature in the background of photographs to the natural resources woven into the clothes and into the catalog itself – made at that time of 100% virgin paper, with no recycled content. Students generally think of themselves as savvy consumers, but I think every one of them got wiser in the course of this exercise.

For class, another day, students used Mapquest to calculate the mileage of one round trip for each member of the faculty and staff listed in the college directory. We were able to calculate mileage for 763 people. We knew that some people walk, and not all members of the faculty and staff come to campus every day. We knew that some people carpool. But we also knew that some people go home for lunch or a nap, and they run errands in town. We know that visitors come to campus every day, and that freight trucks add miles that aren't included in our calculations. In any case, while our calculations are hardly exact, our mileage figure offers a rough estimate of our automotive environmental impact. Each day, we discovered, the St. Olaf community is responsible for 19,788 miles of driving, almost enough to circumnavigate the earth. That's no small environmental impact.

Our class takes "field trips" on campus to learn how our small city works. We tour the college cafeteria with the food service director, and learn how carefully he thinks about the environmental impacts of our meals. We tour the power plant with the Director of Facilities, who is justifiably proud of the efficiencies of our current system, but who has also installed a wind turbine on campus that generates almost a third of our electricity. We tour our LEED Platinum science building to see how architects design ecologically. We tour prairie and forest restoration projects with our curator of natural lands, who helps us to understand how the college is trying to make its land more sustainable, with wetlands, prairies, and forests. Off campus, we tour a home remodeled by a local nonprofit organization to provide green living for low-income families. These trips make our readings real, and they introduce students to people who teach them about American values and American institutions, and about the possibilities of social change. "I love the field trips," said one student, "because we are using and appreciating our human resources to a greater extent."

The first year, another assignment also helped to expand student perspectives. One of Elise's favorite essays is "Naming What You Love" in Paul Gruchow's *Grass Roots* (1995). Gruchow contends that there are few deeply loving human relationships that remain anonymous, and that the same is probably true of the natural world. He wants us to be able to name and love the organic others who inhabit the planet with us. Drawing on Gruchow, Elise wanted our students to know the names of the plants and animals on Manitou Heights. So we designed an assignment called "Other Eyes." We asked students to write a first-person account of life at St. Olaf from the perspective of a plant or animal nearby. We asked them to consider this organism's place in an ecological community, and we asked them to think about the organism's relationship with the human beings on campus, if any.

The results were amazing. We got essays on squirrels and skunks and white-tailed deer. We got stories from foxes and frogs and flies. We heard both from turf grass and from big bluestem, one of the grasses of the native tallgrass prairie. You'd be amazed (and amused) to know how the landscape looks to skunks and squirrels, bacteria and bugs, grass and evergreens, deer and foxes. You learn a lot about ecological niches and energy flows by thinking about the lives of flies and frogs, mice and men, and you learn a lot about human culture by looking at it from the perspective of another organism. To bacteria, for example, people are just places to hang out and reproduce.

In the last few years, we have assigned plot projects instead, asking students to pay attention to a particular place over the course of the semester, and to express the place in words and images that make it come alive as a connected part of an ecological community. Students *describe* their plot, of course, but they also *analyze* it ecologically, looking at inhabitants and their habits, plotting resource flows, and exploring the aesthetics of functionality. Sometimes they invite other authors into the project, with poems, quotations, or songs. Sometimes they take photographs, but other times they produce sketches, paintings, color maps, or collages. Usually, the projects look like scrapbooks, but sometimes they're mobiles, sculptures, or webpages. Almost always, they're inventive and imaginative – and emotional, as students develop affection for the places they've come to know so well.

The main assignment for the class, though, usually involves research on resource flows at the college and explanations of the environmental impacts of our everyday lives. Students have produced reports for the college's Sustainability Task Force, while they learn about the environmental implications of cars, the curriculum, architecture, energy, food, purchasing (including paper), water, waste, and the landscape, both on the campus proper and on our prairie and forest restorations. They have investigated the ways that religion, past and present, is a resource shaping campus ecology – and America's culture of nature. In the process, they define the *operative values* of St. Olaf students, discovering, for example, that fun may be a more important value of college culture than serious study (although the two values do operate dialectically for many students), and noticing that – environmentally speaking – comfort or convenience may be the most important value of all. Feeling pressed for time, we often sacrifice environmental quality for quickness.[4]

During Earth Week, we share information with the college community. The class composes and presents a chapel service exploring the theme of caring for creation in its campus context. On Earth Day itself, we annotate the campus, posting hundreds of small signs on walls and in halls to reveal the invisible complexity of the campus environment. Here are a few samples of the annotations:

Going Up? While this elevator gets you from floor to floor, it is designed to move slowly and thus encourage people to use their own energy to walk up stairs.

The Peace Coffee brewed in the Cage and the cafeteria makes good things happen because it's fair-trade, shade-grown coffee, supporting workers and the environment in countries like Guatemala and Costa Rica.

Nice view? South-facing windows allow radiant heat to warm your napping body in the winter. Trees allow winter rays to pass but provide shade to block the summer sun. On top of that, large windows mean that artificial lighting demands are much reduced all the year round.

See that stain on the Stav Hall carpet? No? That's because St. Olaf chooses to use Interface carpet tiles for high traffic areas so when one piece is damaged, they can replace it without redoing the entire floor. That stain you remember has already been replaced and the stained tile is being recycled.

This is the prairie. Despite popular opinion, prairies are the most endangered ecosystem, not rainforests. A natural prairie has over 150 types of grasses and wildflowers. Our restored prairie has between 30 and 50 species of wildflowers and grasses. Many animals make it their home including birds, small rodents, and insects.

The annotations were so successful that we've been asked to prepare permanent plaques so that this kind of on-site and ongoing environmental education will be a regular part of our campus life.

We can't say with absolute certainty what the long-term outcomes of this class will be for students. But we already have a pretty good idea of some of its immediate intellectual and environmental impacts. We know, for example, that students are enthused if not exuberant about applying ideas to their own lives and circumstances. "In this class," said one of our students, "I am able to study and observe what goes on around me daily and question and wonder why everything happens the way it does and for once it isn't considered daydreaming in class. And the ideas from this class have affected me a lot."

We know that students enjoy the opportunity to integrate the personal and the academic. We assigned journals to give them space to reflect on readings and class conversations, and to teach us by showing us where they see other connections. One of our science students, for example, wrote a wonderful entry on her joy at finding her chemistry labs employing techniques of "green chemistry." We also have an online discussion board that students use to continue class discussions, and to bring in perspectives from other classes and majors. Economics majors, for example, are good at critiquing the class from an economic perspective, and about approaching mainstream economics from an environmental perspective.

We know that students like the idea of seeing how ideas work out in real life. One of the students said, "I am learning that a class where you DO a lot is the most effective kind, and is really the only kind of sustainable education. It seems ironic that we are sitting here, paying $100,000 to be passive, as if it will be a sustainable experience. I am learning to demand more from life and my education, which is almost unheard of in American education." Another student added, "DOING something about our conversations is a great way to run this class. In my water report, I feel like I am making changes. I love it that this is demanded of me."

We know that this is not just a classroom course. We know that students talk about it all the time, and we delight that the course isn't merely an academic exercise – which is to say, an exercise that only a dork could care about. "To be honest," said one student, "I think that my friends and family are getting tired of me mentioning everything that I am learning and thinking about from this class. Instead of saying "This one time, at band camp...," I say,

"Today, in Campus Ecology...." Another student says that "Campus Ecology is a class that I look forward to everyday and talk about all the time outside of class. I never dread doing homework and reading for it, because it is so interesting." Another student adds, "For me the most important part of the class is that it teaches about where we are and what we can do as a part of our environment, but it also incorporates a philosophy that requires mindfulness anywhere. You don't have to be living on a hill on the outskirts of a small town to understand [David] Orr, but rather it calls you whoever you are, wherever you are."

We have discovered how valuable a student professor can be. Students like the *idea* of a student-professor, and they loved Elise's embodiment of that role. They loved her enthusiasm and engagement, and her sense of identification with them. And she was a wonderful role model of practical idealism, especially for the younger students. "When she gets excited," said one student, "I do too because I respect her hopes and dreams for the class and the school." The only difficulty with Elise was that she set such a high standard. But six other students have, in successive years, also brought their own personal and academic skills to professing, showing that academic thoughtfulness isn't restricted to older people with degrees.

We know that some of the success of Campus Ecology comes not from us, or from the syllabus, but from the students who constitute this learning community. One of the things that students get from the course is the knowledge that there are other students who care – and who care deeply – about things that really matter. As one student said, "This course has the most genuinely passionate people in it out of any class I've taken at St. Olaf. The class (and my classmates) inspires me every day, and I rarely get that from my other classes." Elise and I often talked about creating space for "imagining out loud," and I think students' environmental imaginations really flourish in this class.

Students are also developing what I would call "carryover skills": skills that they can take with them into the so-called "real world," where they can be environmentally active in their own homes and businesses and communities. By the end of the semester, they know how to do effective research, and how to shape that research into proposals for institutional change. We talk a lot about rhetoric, and the art of persuasion, so we think they can advocate ideas without alienating an audience. They know how to look at an organization to determine who has the capacity to change things, and to find ways to work with those people to make it easier for them to move in environmental directions. Typically, too, they also have some examples of constructive failure.

By combining learning and doing like this, we think we're involved in a tradition of American education that dates back to one of its founders, Thomas Jefferson. As he thought about the necessity of public education in the United States, Jefferson said that he wanted people educated "so much as may enable them to read and understand what is going on in the world, and to keep their part of it going on right: for nothing can keep it right but their own vigilant and distrustful superintendence" (1795). We're also in the tradition of Emerson, who said in "The American Scholar" that action was the completion and fulfillment of scholarship (1837).

Last – but definitely not least – we are teaching students the practice of hope. By design, this course is an exploration of hope. These days, American college culture is not generally hopeful. These students have watched too much news and too much late-night TV to be naïve about their world. They've grown up with the Simpsons, South Park, and MTV and acquired the skepticism that Michael Moffat calls "Undergraduate Cynical" (1989: 7). They have watched enough reality TV to wonder about the intelligence of the average human being. And they've grown up with each other, teaching each other that bitching and cynicism are signs of maturity.

The truth is that things are in bad shape, and we need to be clear about the state of the world. But if that's the only truth we tell our students, things will get even worse. We also need to tell the truth about people who have changed the world, about traditions of care and collaboration, about institutions with resources to conserve our resources, about real people engaged in the work of creating a culture of permanence on this planet.

In Campus Ecology, our reading helps us with what we might call histories of hope. The central reading of the class is David Orr's *Earth in Mind* (1994), which offers hope of re-thinking higher education for the ecological revolution of the twenty-first century. We read Paul Gruchow's *Grass Roots* (1995) for its Midwestern landscapes, including the landscapes of mindfulness. We read Scott Russell Sanders' *Hunting for Hope* (1998), in which he finds hope in simple, everyday virtues like wildness, embodiment, family, fidelity, skill, simplicity, beauty, and the spirit. We connect our campus hopes to the outside world by reading a book called *Stuff: The Secret Lives of Everyday Things* (Ryan and Durning 1997), which offers hope that we can become responsible for our consuming lives if we understand the full cost of it. We read *Sustainable Planet* (Schor and Taylor 2002) for examples of thinking and action that are making sustainability a genuine possibility in the twenty-first century world. Finally, we read a lot of poetry about nature and everyday life. In all of this reading, we're examining how our words construct our worlds – including the world of the self.

We have also *written* a book in this class. Over the years, I've been writing essays on the moral ecology of college culture, and *The Nature of College: How a New Understanding of Campus Life Can Change the World* (Farrell 2010) is the result. Exploring college culture, consumer culture and the environment by analyzing the everyday lives of college students, the book probes why college students act the way they do, and why it matters ecologically. Even though they think they're charting their own way in the independence of college culture, students are still subject to American culture's powerful stories, including its consumerism and its consumer forgetfulness. The book examines the everyday activity of Joe College and his sister Jo, as they wake up in rooms full of stuff, use the bathroom, get dressed, eat in the cafeteria, drive a car, watch TV, check Facebook, go to a party, contemplate sex, and consider their lives from religious and political perspectives. All the chapters begin with the common sense of college culture, and then turn to the culture of nature on campus. After considering the environmental impacts of Joe and Jo College, each chapter concludes with suggestions for students interested in exploring more sustainable college cultures.[5]

The book itself has been a collaborative effort with my students, as they teach me about the environ-*mental* life of college culture. Students in the class have been commenting on the essays that comprise the book for years; they love marking "CBS" (clever but stupid) in the margins and pointing out where the prose is obscure. One student wrote the first draft of the Facebook section, and another helped significantly with the religion chapter. A 2003 St. Olaf graduate is my editor at Milkweed Editions (At one point, I told him that the manuscript was perfect, and he said he was hoping to make it "perfecter"); a 2010 graduate drew most of the illustrations; and a 2008 graduate has designed the website. Together, we've explored the common sense of college culture and some uncommon alternatives that might lead to a new "commons sense" – a set of beliefs and practices that might accustom us to our creative and conserving role in the global commons.

In American culture, most of us learn a number of coping mechanisms to deal with the stress and the strain of daily life. In Campus Ecology and on the St Olaf campus, we're trying to develop hoping mechanisms (including our class) that allow us to transform the system instead of simply conforming to it.

I think we have made a good start. Here's the final journal entry from a student in the first Campus Ecology class:

> Oftentimes, when I talk with other people about the world we live in and the problems it faces, they agree with me but feel that there is nothing they can do to change it. "One person can't change the world," they say.
>
> Now I finally have concrete proof that they are wrong. As I sat in class during our final session on Monday, I looked around and saw of roomful of thirty people, all of them students and teachers, who know that the world needs to change and who, if nothing else, will be an example to others of the little things that can be done that make a big difference.
>
> The conversations that we have shared for the past three months will not stop now that we have left the classroom. There is not one of us who has not and will not continue to involve others in these conversations and the world will change because of that.
>
> I didn't think of this when I wrote my list of ten things that I learned from this class, but I feel that this is by far the most important thing I have learned in a classroom: A conversation can change the world. Elise started this conversation and I would not hesitate to say that by doing so she has changed St. Olaf and the world. As I leave college and enter "the real world"

I have great hope for the future because I know that by participating in this conversation, I have actually begun to change the world.

Thank you Elise and thank you Jim. Thank you for helping me find and love my places on earth. Thank you for teaching me to never lose hope. Thank you for teaching me to make mistakes but never mistake them for failure. Thank you for teaching me that teachers can be students and students can be teachers. Thank you for showing me that it is okay to hope and dream and imagine and love and that there are other people who feel the same way. And thank you for proving, once and for all, that one person can change the world. These are lessons I will never forget.

Not all students are as effusive as this, but in recent years, we have used a survey to gauge what's happening in the course of the course. Before the semester begins, we ask students to look at a very long list of learning outcomes and to tell us if they're sure, or half-sure, or not sure all that they know or understand the concepts. At the end of the semester, they repeat the survey.

The list includes basic statements like:

I can explain the meaning of "practical idealism."

I can explain "the social construction of common sense."

I can compare and contrast expressed and operative values.

I can explain the "cultural work" performed by concepts like "the real world" and "the St. Olaf bubble."

I know why college students have so many clothes.

I know why my clothes come from so many different countries.

I understand how to use product chains to talk about the out-of-sight environmental impacts of clothes.

I can describe the expressed and operative values of the clothes that collegians wear.

I can describe the environmental costs and benefits of peer socialization.

I know how to estimate my ecological foodprint.

I know what Wendell Berry means by the extensive pleasures of eating.

I know how American politics influences what I eat.

I can explain television as a system, not just a technology.

I understand the environmental impacts of electronic waste.

I know how to access some of the benefits of electronic environmentalism.

I know what "clean coal" means.

I know how an internal combustion engine works within the earth's carbon cycle.

I understand how my driving causes global climate change.

I understand the appeal of parties to college students.

I can explain the environmental impacts and cultural work of beer.

I can explain the importance of *fun*damentalism in college culture.

I understand some of the ecosystem services provided by St. Olaf's natural lands.

I can name ten native plants on the St. Olaf campus.

I know how to make sense out of any plot of land I find.

I can explain the tenets of free market environmentalism.

I can describe the recent greening of American business.

I understand the difference between a boycott and a buycott.

I can explain Michael Maniates' critique of consumer environmentalism.

I can explain the difference between citizenship and sitizenship.

I understand the disparities of environmental opportunity – why some people get the opportunity to live by the garbage dump, and others don't.

I understand how politics is the practice of loving all the children all the time.

I could explain the precautionary principle to my friends.

I see how "going green" can be as much about saving capitalism as saving the earth.

There are more unconventional statements like:

I know how to know a place well.

I know what wonder is for.

I know the assumptions of romantic love, and I know the other kinds of love in the world – eros, philia, agape and biophilia.

I know what it really means to "Get real!"

I can map out the concept of "moral ecology."

I can explain the difference between knowledge, understanding, and wisdom.

I understand the virtues necessary to a liberal education and a sustainable society.

I know what's good about "the good life" and what's not-so-good.

I understand why David Orr says that all values are environmental values.

I know why people don't usually talk about their deepest values.

I can explain how mainstream American values impact the environment.

I can explain two different meanings of materialism.

I could chart the operative environmental values of college students.

I can compare and contrast materialist and post-materialist values.

I know how to think about consumption as vocation.

I understand why asceticism is un-American.

I can explain college sex as an environmental issue.

I can describe why John Ryan considers the condom one of the seven sustainable wonders of the world.

I understand the pleasures of sex, including the extensive pleasures.

I understand "the tyranny of small decisions," and the hope of small decisions.

I can imagine the contours of a sustainable society – political, economic, cultural, psychological, and spiritual.

I understand the importance of "possidiction."

I understand the different rhetorical strategies of environmentalists, the ways that people use words to shape our worlds – past, present, and future.

I appreciate "the slow and difficult trick of living," and finding it where I am.

And they include attitudinal/application statements like:

I know how to practice empathy as a way of knowing.

I know how to be a part of a genuine learning community.

I know what a "designing mind" is, and how to use it.

When I go shopping for clothes, I know how to evaluate the ethical implications of my choices.

I know how to bake bread.

I know enough to eat well.

I know how to reduce my carbon consumption two percent this year.

I can explain how religion animates (or not) my own environmental values.

I understand the difference between doing things right, and doing the right things.

I can explain the relationship between the extravagant gesture and regenerative design.

I know how to think about my life as a design, as a story that I get to shape.

I know how to increase my repertoire of political activity.

Even though it's taboo, I know how to talk about values and politics.

I know the difference between hope and optimism.

I know how to be a hoping mechanism for people in my life.

If I had time, I could name 50 things that make me environmentally hopeful.

I know how to put hope to work.

I know how to become native to a place.

I know how to use my designing mind to change the world.

I know, more or less, what I intend to do with my one wild and precious life.

So far, the results have been overwhelmingly positive, as students transmute knowledge into wisdom, individually and collectively. Because Campus Ecology students engage so fully in making sense of their lives, they also engage fully in making sense of the relationships in their lives, including relationships to nature. They learn a lot about the cultural stories they live in, and how the moral ecology of their own lives affects the ecology of the planet. It's a model that could be replicated in American Studies, Environmental Studies, sociology, anthropology, and a number of other disciplines. At St. Olaf, it fulfills a credit in the Arts and Humanities track of the Environmental Studies major, but it could be adapted to other general education requirements as well.

In Daniel Quinn's novel *Ishmael*, a character contends that "you can't just stop being in a story, you have to have another story to be in" (214). Having learned the dominant stories of American culture by finding them in their own lives, Campus Ecology students know that they need to imagine another story to be in. They know that we need to start imagining it now, and because of the structure of the class, they have some experience of living in that new story (Quinn 1995).

In "Going to Walden," poet Mary Oliver contemplates making a visit to Walden Pond. Her friends tell her that she'd enjoy it (Oliver 1972). But her friend Henry David Thoreau reminds her "how dull we grow from hurrying here and there!" So she concludes that "Going to Walden is not so easy a thing/ As a green visit. It is the slow and difficult/ trick of living, and finding it where you are" (239).

In Campus Ecology and on the St. Olaf campus, we have been engaged in "the slow and difficult trick of living, and finding it where you are." It's ecology; it's education; it's hope. It's not yet sustainable, but it's a way to imagine new stories in a culture that desperately needs them.

Notes

1 I heard Leslie Prosterman use the phrase "law of inverse importance" at an American Studies conference years ago, and it stuck with me because it seems so often true.
2 "Sitzenship" is the widespread practice of sitting in front of the TV complaining about politics, but never doing anything about it.
3 The assignments can be found on St Olaf's black, gold, and green website at http://stolaf.edu/green/campusecology/
4 *Expressed* values are ones that we say; *operative* values are ones that we do, and the difference can lead to some illuminating ethical discussions.
5 For more on *The Nature of College*, see www.natureofcollege.org.

References

Bellah, R.N. *et al.*, 1985. *Habits of the Heart: Individualism and Commitment in American Life.* Berkeley, CA: University of California Press.

Emerson, R.W., 1837. The American Scholar. http://natureofcollege.org/essays/the-ecologicians-teaching/.

Farrell, J.J., 2005. The Real World of College. http://natureofcollege.org/essays/essays/the-real-world/.

Farrell, J.J., 2010. *The Nature of College: How a New Understanding of Campus Life can Change the World*. Minneapolis, MN: Milkweed Editions.

Gruchow, P., 1995. *Grass Roots: The Universe of Home*. Minneapolis, MN: Milkweed Editions.

Jefferson, T., 1795. Letter to Mann Page. Quoted in Wendell Berry, The Unsettling of America: Culture and Agriculture. 1977 (Page 144).

Kittredge, W., 1999. *Taking Care: Thoughts on Storytelling and Belief*. Minneapolis, MN: Milkweed Editions.

Moffatt, M., 1989. *Coming of Age in New Jersey: College and American culture*. New Brunswick, NJ: Rutgers University Press.

Oliver, M., 1972. *The River Styx, Ohio and Other Poems*. New York: Harcourt Brace Jovanovich.

Oliver, M., 1992. *New and Selected Poems*. Boston, MA: Beacon Press.

Orr, D.W., 1994. *Earth in Mind: On Education, Environment, and the Human Prospect*. Washington, DC: Island Press.

Ryan, J.C. and Durning, A.T., 1997. *Stuff: The Secret Lives of Everyday Things*. Seattle, WA: Northwest Environment Watch.

Sanders, S.R., 1998. *Hunting for Hope: A Father's Journeys*. Boston. MA: Beacon Press.

Schor, J.B. and Taylor, B., 2002. *Sustainable Planet: Solutions for the Twenty-First Century*. Boston, MA: Beacon Press.

12

THE LIVING HOME

Building It into the Curriculum

Braum Barber and Leona Rousseau

The Living Home was a project partnership between the City of Lethbridge, Cedar Ridge Quality Homes, and Lethbridge College to build a green home. The project was initiated to provide an occasion for public discussion on green building, and an opportunity for students of Lethbridge College to engage in authentic and practical design and research experiences. There are many approaches to designing environmentally friendly residential buildings: some focus heavily on existing and emerging technologies, while others emphasize behavioral change and eco-minimalism; some focus on individualistic "off the grid" goals, while others advance community efficiencies. Through the process, each of these factors became a locus for critical thinking about the concept of sustainability.

To guide the project, a mission statement was developed by the partnership that would best achieve the expectations of each stakeholder and provide clear direction for the students, but would leave the design flexible enough to ensure authentic experiences for responsible design and research. Criteria were then developed based on international rating systems,[1] which were used to frame project design goals. The decision-making process was based on what can be termed the "triple bottom line," in which student decisions considered not only traditional economic valuation, but also less quantifiable environmental and social values. This exercise in holistic decision-making proved to be a great challenge, but it was rewarding for the students involved.

The Students

Lethbridge College is located in southern Alberta, Canada and offers a wide range of programs in arts, sciences, trades, and technologies. The three programs directly involved in The Living Home were the School of Engineering Technologies, Interior Design, and Multimedia Production. The program curricula are centered on skills development suitable for employment in industry, and fostering problem solving, creative thinking, and innovation. The Living Home project spanned three years from concept to completion, and was organized into three stages: in Year 1 students were engaged in a dynamic discussion on design philosophy, materials research, and home orientation and layout; Year 2 involved the design of energy, water, heating, and ventilation systems as home construction began; and in Year 3, the home was completed and opened for public demonstration and student research.

Students were involved in the project through a number of mechanisms at the College. Multimedia students were assigned the task of framing the project and developing a logo as a class competition. As an extended project within the Properties of Engineering Materials class, students conducted research on building materials and chose the final products used for the building envelope (siding, roofing, insulation, and basement walls). Another group compared building systems including power generation, water heating, home heating, and water management as a component of their Environmental Engineering class. Each year an engineering technology student was hired by Lethbridge College to design and conduct research projects. And finally, the Research and Innovation department provided a grant to two Interior Design students for independent research on materials, lighting, and space design.

Delimiting Sustainability

The primary intention in developing the project mission and goals was to allow students some philosophical flexibility in directing the project. A cohort of multimedia students was asked to frame the project conceptually, and to design a logo that represented the project. A lively class discussion ensued around concepts of sustainability, environmental responsibility, the application of technologies, and the ethics of self-sustainability (off-the-grid) goals compared to community-oriented goals. Initially, the students related examples of people who had built straw-bale homes and earth-ships, and those who had achieved some level of off-the-grid living. The faculty then posed the following question to the class: "Why would someone build a 'green' home?" The responses predominantly fell within the stick-it-to-the-man category: to be independent of utilities, mainly to eliminate monthly bills and to avoid paying the rising costs of electricity, natural gas, and water. After further reflection, responses that related to reducing resource extraction, reducing the impact on the environment, and social recognition emerged. The classroom discussion indicated a strong tendency amongst the students to believe that technologies were the primary means to achieving sustainability. This discussion, however, tended to drift into conspiracy theories of corporations suppressing revolutionary technologies (invented in someone's basement or discovered on a UFO) that would provide "free" energy and solve our collective environmental problems. It is an interesting experiment to allow these discussions to emerge (as they invariably seem to do).

Why do students believe in highly improbable conspiracies? Shermer (2009) cites:

> patternicity (the tendency to find meaningful patterns in random noise) and agenticity (the bent to believe the world is controlled by invisible intentional agents). Conspiracy theories connect the dots of random events into meaningful patterns and then infuse those patterns with intentional agency. Add to those propensities the confirmation bias (which seeks and finds confirmatory evidence for what we already believe) and the hindsight bias (which tailors after-the-fact explanations to what we already know happened), and we have the foundation for conspiratorial cognition.

In the case of sustainability, emerging challenges are characterized by the *dispersion* of cause and effects – a coal plant in the United States contributing to flooding in Bangladesh; *fragmentation of agency* – each of us contributes; and *institutional inadequacy* - global problems without effective global governance (Gardiner 2010). The apparent randomness of events and the lack of a clear agent encourage patternicity and agenticity and seem to create an opportunity for manufacturing denial and conspiracy.

The students involved in this discussion clutched on to their theories, as they seemed to be conjoined to more fundamental beliefs. Out of classroom chaos, however, there was an opportunity to establish the qualities of good research that involve developing hypotheses and collecting good data to reject or fail-to-reject the thesis. This was also an opportunity for harnessing the enthusiasm for conspiracy and directing it toward a more productive creativity.

This group of students was given a series of research assignments relating to the definition of sustainability, an introduction to renewable technologies suitable for the home, and environmental responsibility. Interestingly, after the groups had presented their findings, there was a general seriousness about emerging environmental and energy challenges, and practically no chatter concerning suppressed technologies and conspiracy. There was still some advocacy for renewable technologies, but the discussion centered more on reduction (framed by the ecological footprint[2]), and social responsibility. Of the logos submitted by the class, the one chosen by the selection committee used earthy colors and showed three leaves representing the community partnership, a book representing research, and roots representing the environment, organically connecting student learning within The Living Home project.

This amorphous approach to introducing sustainability in the classroom was more formally structured for the engineering technology classes using a short research paper and class presentations. Each week, an assigned group developed the theme established by previous presentations and discussions. The first week offered the definition(s) of sustainability – "What is sustainability?"; the second week presented the reasons for sustainability – "Why do we need to consider sustainability?"; the third week discussed practical approaches to sustainability – "How can we achieve sustainability?"; the fourth week discussed the inertia between actions and effects for possible interventions "When must we begin to act?"; and the final week discussed the for-whom-and-by-whom of sustainable development – "Who are we doing it for? Who should act?" The first three questions are commonly used in environmental education and are fundamental to understanding the converging challenges of climate change, energy supply, food security, water quality and quantity, pest and disease vectors, and so on. By the third week, the students began to reveal their individual proclivities along the spectrum from technological to social-behavioral approaches, and a collective consensus on the scope of the issues began to materialize.

The foci of the final two weeks are less commonly incorporated into the scope of environmental discussions. During the fourth week that addressed the 'when' of sustainability, discussions focused on the inertia of social and behavioral change, the role of government, the application of incentives or penalties, and the long-term impact of decisions made today as they relate to building longevity (80+ years). After this week of presentations, the students seemed to manifest some symptoms of despair – the classic Kübler-Ross (1969) indicators of ideological denial, anger, bargaining, followed by general ennui before acceptance (and action).[3] It is important that emotional paralysis does not set in, so this week also served an opportunity to address feelings and behaviors, both within the student group and as observed in society in general.[4] The final week of presentations returned to empowerment and action as the desired outcome. The "for-whom-and-by-whom" presentation provides an opportunity to discuss who creates the pollution, issues around population, distribution of wealth, how to assign responsibility (nationally or internationally), mitigation versus adaptation interventions, and light-green versus deep-green ethics of environmentalism.[5]

It should be remembered that this curriculum was developed for technology-oriented students who traditionally have little exposure to social sciences like human behavior and ethics. The importance of these discussions for supporting the college objectives of fostering social responsibility is clear. What was not completely clear at the time, however, was how these discussions would promote critical thinking by broadening the analysis beyond single attribute problems (i.e. reducing energy consumption) and advancing more holistic, non-technical solutions, thus enriching traditional engineering approaches.

From Andragogy to Psychagogy

Students in engineering technologies and interior design respond well to constructivist techniques, in which learners construct their own models of understanding based on observation, activity, and experimentation. College students are best motivated by setting the tasks just beyond the learner's current capability, as suggested by Lev Vygotsky's Zone of Proximal Development. Self-efficacy is encouraged and developed, and resiliency of learning is enhanced as students overcome obstacles related to sustainability, the application of technologies, and social challenges. Because the students were expected to make the final decisions for The Living Home, they had the necessary incentive to be responsible in their learning. In the final analysis, the students had to justify their decisions to professional designers and the public. The project scope provided the real-life context, collaboration, application, and ramifications typical of a reflected practicum method of pedagogy.

Schön (1987) defines the reflective practicum where "students mainly learn by doing, with the help of coaching," which involves "reflection-in-action," or what he describes as "thinking what they are doing while they are doing it." Students learn not only how to solve new design problems, but also how to frame each problem in its unique context. This method of teaching and learning rejects a "narrowly technical perspective" in favor of a more realistic, holistic, contextual approach that combines discipline-based knowledge with "competencies required of practitioners in the field." It provides the framework for a curriculum that can truly "prepare students for competence in the indeterminate zones of practice," integrating existing knowledge with contextual research, problem-solving, design, and application.

Given the challenges facing new graduates, it is important to elevate the ability of the adult learner to contextualize problems and solutions. Finger and Asun (2001: 34) suggest three different functions for education:

> first, there is *education as preparation*. Its role is to update people, to socialize them into the dominant habits in order to make them full members of the community and the process.... Second, there is *education as potential*; its role is to instill innovation, creativity and imagination – to increase the potential to act creatively on reality. Third, there is *education as action*: its role is to increase capacities to act or, more precisely, to solve problems.

These functions require a transition from andragogical techniques to more psychagogical approaches that affect the behavior of the learner and their choice of desirable life goals. In other words, the learner must not only construct an understanding of how to approach sustainable design and solve problems, but they must achieve a level of self-governance that will allow them to affect real change (their own selves within society). This is not significantly different to the ideals of citizenship inculcated through the educational system; however, it implies more of an inward self-realization and ethics that will result in sustainable behaviors at a time when the cost of collective inertia is getting higher. Jamieson (2010) calls this "noncontingency" which:

> requires agents to act in ways that minimize their contributions to global environmental change, and specifies that acting in this way should generally not be contingent on an agent's beliefs about the behavior of others.... Instead of looking to moral mathematics for practical solutions to large-scale collective-action problems, we should focus instead on noncalculative generators of behavior: character traits, dispositions, emotions, and what I shall call virtues.

The Living Home

A full account of the project as it was developed by students at Lethbridge College may be found at The Living Home website (www.thelivinghome.ca). The following three studies describe less about the outcomes and more of the process, particularly the conceptual models developed.

Study 1: Choosing Construction Materials (or Choose your Pollution)

In the process of choosing the materials for the building envelope, including roofing, siding, insulation, and the basement, the task was divided into two phases: the first was to conduct a life-cycle assessment of each material, and the second was to compare the environmental impacts between available materials for each envelope function.

A life-cycle assessment describes the amount of energy used and the pollution (air and water emissions, and solid waste) produced from "cradle-to-grave" or, better, "cradle-to-cradle" over the product life. This assessment evaluates the amount of energy used and the source of that energy at each stage, including material extraction, refining, processing, manufacturing, distribution, installation, operation, and finally disposal or diversion back into the materials cycle. The source of energy is very important, as a low-efficiency coal-fired electricity generation plant will result in considerably different types and amounts of pollution than a renewable energy source like wind used to produce electricity. Each stage of the life cycle may impact the environment due to emissions to the atmosphere or the watershed; it may result in land degradation or destruction; and it may create large volumes of solid waste requiring safe disposal. Some of the emissions may have more local impacts, such as wastes discharged into water systems or air emissions settling through wet or dry deposition on the surrounding environment. Other emissions, like greenhouse gases, may remain in the atmosphere for decades and have a long-term global impact.

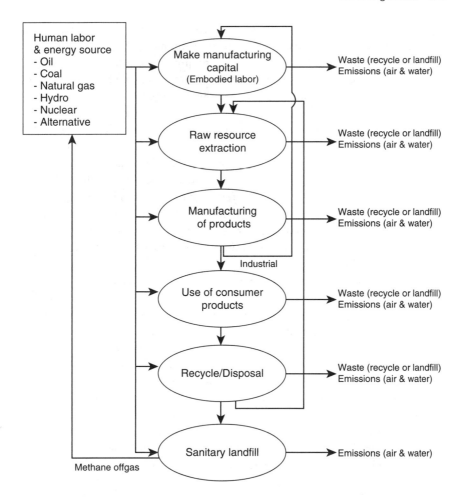

FIGURE 12.1 Life-Cycle Analysis

The amount of pollution created and the type of impact will depend on the source of energy and minerals (iron ore, bauxite for aluminum, hydrocarbons for plastics, etc.), the transportation distances, manufacturing processes, and disposal or diversion options. In other words, there is no single value for energy or any type of pollution that can be applied to a product as it depends on the specific process of making each product. The quality of information on life-cycle assessment, however, is improving with the application of international standards and methodologies. Software, like The Impact Assessor for Buildings from Athena Institute, may also be an effective learning tool as it distills complex results into comparable factors (e.g., acidification potential, eutrophication potential, ozone depletion, global warming potential, health effects, resource consumption).

The students were tasked to create a life-cycle flow chart for each product that identified the stages of the material process, from resource extraction to disposal. For each stage of the material process, the students investigated energy consumption and emissions based on a standard unit for the product, for example tons of concrete or square feet of roofing. Though improving, there are significant gaps in the information readily available, making student research a challenge. The flowcharts became a useful visual reference for the students as they assessed their options.

Once the flowcharts were completed, products used for each envelope function (roofing, siding, insulation, etc.) were compared. The students were asked to create a matrix of embodied energy (the total energy used in the life cycle) and embodied pollution (the total air and water emissions, and solid waste) generated per standard unit. An important consideration was the expected product life – for example, how long the roofing system or siding will last, based on the manufacturer's warrantee or empirical data from industry, compared to the 80-year design life of a residential home.

Each group made a final recommendation for the product with the lowest environmental impact over the design life of the home – easier said than done. If one product used more energy than another but could be at the end of the life cycle rather than disposed of in a landfill, or if one product created more greenhouse gases while another created more toxic waste discharged into the river, which would be worse for the environment? This dilemma suggested that it was a good time to review the discussion around sustainability. The development of the matrix that compared types of pollution also raised issues around social justice: Are emissions in China better than the same emissions in the United States? How does the manufacture of products in countries with lax environmental standards affect the decision? Where will the waste end up – in a local landfill, or shipped overseas? What are the impacts of using recycled materials in manufacturing?

The "correct" answer depends largely on the location of the project (the resilience of local ecosystems, type of climate, level of affluence), and it ultimately depends on values. In essence, the student must *choose their pollution*. Since a decision had to be made, our students chose durable cement-based roofing and siding, wood studs for the frame, and they used concrete for the basement with insulated concrete forms (ICFs). They also chose a hydrocarbon-based foam insulation product with an effective insulating value and good sealing properties. Other projects in environmentally friendly design have suggested different materials, based on different criteria. Comparing the student choices with other projects led to lively discussions and proved to be an opportunity for validating the decisions made.

Using the life-cycle assessment approach provided an effective framework for discussing the total impact of the materials that we use to build our homes – where the raw materials come from; how energy sources differ (electricity, natural gas, biofuels, etc.); the benefits of recycling; the distance products are transported;

why things are made where they are; where things go at the end of the useful life; and what impact these products have on our environment.

Study 2: Applying Technologies (or to Consume Is to Pollute)

There is a tendency in the engineering technologies to valorize technological solutions over other means of responding to challenges (i.e., behavioral change). This is generally true for addressing energy and environmental challenges that are escalating in significance. Students were assigned projects to evaluate systems for The Living Home, including electricity generation, heating and ventilation, heat recovery options, domestic hot water systems, greywater reuse, and rainwater management. The approach used was similar to the life-cycle analysis used for envelope materials; however, since these systems are typically marketed to save energy, the single attribute of energy became the focus of evaluation.

The concept used in the student research was Energy Return over Energy Invested (EROEI) – which means that one must create or recover more energy in the operation of the technology than the energy used to manufacture, maintain, and dispose of the technology. For example, a photovoltaic (PV) system (solar modules for generating electricity) requires energy to extract the materials, to manufacture the modules and balance-of-system, to transport, install, and maintain the system, and to dispose of the system at the end of its useful life. Over this life cycle, the PV system will generate energy in the form of electricity. The ratio of the electricity produced and the energy used to create and operate the system is called the EROEI. The performance of PV systems depends on the latitude of the installation, local weather, orientation of the arrays, the type of PV technology installed, and other variables, so the EROEI can vary widely between applications.

Contrary to common belief, alternative energy technologies are not pollution-free nor are they renewable. The confusion is that while the sources of energy (wind, sun, rivers) are renewable, the energy used to create the systems is not. The energy used to manufacture PV systems, for example, typically originates from non-renewable fossil fuel sources. As such, a lot of pollution is embedded within the system at the time of installation. A more useful schema for students to understand the efficacy of these technologies is a comparative evaluation of the emissions for each unit of energy produced by the technology over its useful life. For alternative energy technologies, most of the energy "invested" occurs in the extraction of raw materials and manufacturing the product, and the primary energy used for these processes (coal–fired electricity, natural gas, etc.) will vary between products, manufacturers, and locations. Once the alternative technology is installed, the operation of the system "pays back" the energy invested – in reality, however, the energy is never paid back and the pollution is never retracted (except, arguably, through natural ecosystem cleaning-services). Once the system is in operation, the best it can do is to dilute the initial embodied pollution per unit of energy produced by the system. The longer the system operates, the lower will be the emissions per unit of energy generated. If the system is removed prematurely or fails, it is possible that the emissions per unit of energy produced could be higher than the technology it was meant to replace. Social justice issues also emerge depending on where and how these technologies are manufactured and the minerals processed. A recent article described how a Chinese polysilicon (used in PV modules) manufacturer "is dumping toxic factory waste directly on the lands of neighboring villages, killing crops and poisoning residents" (Liu 2008), because they have not installed or are not properly operating pollution control devices. Is an alternative energy technology good if it reduces greenhouse gas emissions, but pollutes a local environment and harms the people living nearby?

The point is that it takes energy to produce energy, and each system contributes to greenhouse gas emissions and other forms of air and water pollution. Some systems are much better than others and some locations are much better for different types of technologies, but in the final analysis *to consume is to pollute*. As a critical thinking exercise in the curriculum the students evaluated their assigned system based on EROEI, as well as the implications of other pollutions and issues of social justice. The students rationalized the installation of 2 kW of PV modules to produce approximately 2500 kW of electricity each year; two solar thermal panels to heat domestic hot water; a heat recovery ventilator (HRV) that exchanges the heat from outgoing stale air to the incoming cooler fresh air during the heating season; and a rain harvesting system.

The students chose not to install a greywater system that collects water from showers and sinks and reuses the collected water for irrigation or for a second domestic use in toilets. The system requires a large plastic container, filtration and disinfection, and a small pump which results in an embodied energy that exceeds the energy that will ever be recovered (EROEI < 1). Furthermore, Lethbridge has a state-of-the-art wastewater treatment facility with a biogas recovery cogeneration system. It was decided that the community solution for treating wastewater was superior to independent systems installed in each home. In addition, the water returns quickly to the watershed to maintain minimum flows for aquatic health, whereas using the greywater for irrigating lawns would have delayed this return of water. In other regions, however, greywater systems may allow developers to reduce the size or eliminate sewer infrastructure and the concomitant environmental impacts of pipelines and treatment facilities. This decision also raised the question of the effectiveness of independent "life-ship" solutions compared to community solutions. Is it better to create a community electricity generation system (with greater efficiencies of scale) as opposed to each home having an independent system? What about heating domestic hot water or harvesting rain for irrigation? More importantly, since each of these technologies has an environmental impact, wouldn't an aggressive effort to decrease the consumption of electricity, domestic hot water, and irrigation water reduce the need for these technologies?

Another interesting outcome of the EROEI analysis for most "green" technologies is that the results become more attractive as the consumption increases. For example, a drain water heat recovery coil may be installed on the sewer stack before it exits the home. In principle, while a resident is showering energy from the hot water going down the drain is recovered by the cold water flowing to the water heating system. For the technology to be "green" it must recover more energy than the mass of copper used to produce the system. The student research found that the system worked quite efficiently, and the energy "payback" would occur after 3,000 eight-minute showers. The EROEI would, therefore, improve with the number and duration of showers; or from another perspective, the more one showers (wastefully), the more energy friendly the technology becomes. Such an assessment tends to value one attribute like energy efficiency over another attribute like water conservation. The more-you-waste-the-more-you-save becomes a common paradox in "green" technologies. If we were to shower only on special occasions (weddings, birthdays, etc.), this technology would never recover the energy used to make it – and there may be some social issues to consider.

In the classroom, critical thinking is challenged through concepts like life-cycle assessment, EROEI, social justice, independent versus community infrastructure, and the hazards of single attribute analysis (like energy) on decision-making. Furthermore, decisions are not generalizable, since the evaluation depends on the location, the context, and the behavior of the occupants. It is important, therefore, that the learner constructs a schema or process for sustainability-thinking, and that psychagogical outcomes supporting environmental ethics, self-efficacy and action be encouraged.

Study 3: Valuing Form and Function

The Interior Design students became involved with the Living Home project just prior to construction. They were responsible for conducting research on a range of sustainable interior materials, finishes, lighting, and furniture, fixtures and equipment (FF&E) based on given background information, specific selection criteria, and discussions with their faculty research mentor.

Sustainable product selection criteria included: life-cycle evaluation (energy, pollution, social impacts); durability and functionality; product materials (source and effect on indoor air quality); end-of-use considerations (up-cycled or down-cycled, biodegradability, etc.); corporate social responsibility of manufacturers; and cost compared to the benefits. The traditional cost benefit analysis is a blunt tool that tends to try to place value on the invaluable, so a process of product selection that incorporates other dimensions of value becomes an important learning experience.

The design students were also expected to contribute significantly to the aesthetic quality and marketability of the home. Throughout the research the students met with their faculty mentor to present and analyze potential materials, finishes, lighting, and FF&E for the home; wrote briefs on their findings and recommendations; collected materials samples; created selection boards; and met with the design team, builder and others involved in the project – approximating industry experience.

By Way of a Conclusion

The Living Home was a research project in itself and secondarily a means to integrate interdisciplinary sustainability research into the curricula of academic programs at the college level. For faculty, the project evolved into a case study on the integration of sustainability concepts and sustainability research into the engineering and design curricula. Students provided a design solution for a sustainable, practical, cost-effective, marketable home through the selection and application of unconventional, yet proven technologies that yielded significant energy and water savings as well as features, components, and renewable materials that optimized indoor air quality and comfort. The project demonstrated that sustainability was indeed compatible with mainstream living.

The students did not just learn how to solve a new design problem, however. They learned how to frame a design problem differently. Each context for green building is unique and cannot be solved with simple technical applications. Technologies change constantly, making their simple application an example of an education-in-obsolescence. Instead, they learned to adopt and adapt a broad range of knowledge acquired through many courses and experiences, and to apply it in the specific project context. Rather than lessons specific to the course or discipline, they learned lessons for life in a sustainable world – how to build that world and sustain it. This approach served as a catalyst for inspiring intangible learning outcomes like changing behaviors and attitudes by instilling values of sustainability, while fostering environmental and social stewardship, citizenship, and encouraging action amongst our future designers, leaders and decision-makers.

The preceding discussion was intended to illustrate how critical and creative thinking can be developed in a technology-oriented program. The understanding of environmentally friendly technologies and practices is foundational in engineering technology and interior design but, arguably, this understanding alone does not adequately prepare the graduate for the many emerging energy and environmental challenges. As illustrated, an introduction to life-cycle thinking and the importance of context in environmental decision-making will encourage the student to critically and holistically evaluate design problems, and to consider *as a first approach* reducing consumption, and advocacy for behavioral change through a reassessment of lifestyle values and expectations. It may be overly sanguine to expect each learner to "think like a mountain," as Aldo Leopold (1949) once famously suggested, but it is imaginable that together we begin to think like humans. In the words of Paulo Freire (1998: 26): "Insofar as I am a conscious presence in the world, I cannot hope to escape my ethical responsibility for my action in the world."

Notes

1   Rating systems that relate to these criteria include Leadership in Energy and Environmental Design (LEED) http://www.usgbc.org/DisplayPage.aspx?Category ID=19; National Association of Home Builders (NAHB) http://www.nahb.org/; BRE Environmental Assessment Method (BREEAM) (http://www.breeam.org/); and others.
2   The Ecological Footprint is a measure of human impact with the ability of the earth to regenerate as developed by William Rees in 1992. There are a number of easy footprint calculators available on the Internet. A more thorough summary and calculator may be found at the Global Footprint Network (http://www.footprintnetwork.org/en/index.php/GFN/page/footprint_basics_overview/).
3   The idea of grieving for the environment and our place within it is elaborated by Slavoj Žižek (2010).
4   Examples from the industry of denial, anger, and disinformation may be effective when addressing student concerns related to sourcing information and how to differentiate the objective from the biased. DeSmogBlog (www.desmogblog.com) or Greenpeace (2010) "Dealing in Doubt: the Climate Denial Industry and Climate Science" may be effective learning tools.
5   Suggested texts for facilitators includes Patrick Curry's *Ecological Ethics: An Introduction* (2006) and Neil Evernden's *The Natural Alien: Humankind and Environment* (1993).

References

Curry, P., 2006. *Ecological Ethics: An introduction*. Malden, MA: Polity Press.

Evernden, N., 1993. *The Natural Alien: Humankind and Environment*, 2nd edn. Toronto: University of Toronto Press.

Finger, M. and Asun, J.M., 2001. *Adult Education at the Crossroads: Learning Our Way Out*. London: Zed Books.

Freire, P., 1998. *Pedagogy of Freedom: Ethics, Democracy, and Civic Courage*. New York: Rowman & Littlefield.

Gardiner, S.M., 2010. A perfect moral storm: climate change, intergenerational ethics, and the problem of corruption. In S.M. Gardiner et al. (eds), *Climate Ethics: Essential Readings*. New York: Oxford University Press, pp. 87–98.

Greenpeace, 2010. Dealing in Doubt: The Climate Denial Industry and Climate Science. http://www.greenpeace.org/international/Global/international/planet-2/report/2010/3/dealing-in-doubt.pdf (accessed 5 August 2010).

Jamieson, D., 2010. When utilitarians should be virtue theorists. In S.M. Gardiner et al. (ed.), *Climate Ethics: Essential Readings*. New York: Oxford University Press, pp. 315–331.

Kübler-Ross, E., 1969. *On Death and Dying*. New York: Simon & Schuster.

Leopold, A., 1949. *A Sand County Almanac*. New York: Oxford University Press.

Liu, Y., 2008. The Dirty side of a "Green" Industry. http://www.worldwatch.org/node/5650 (accessed 14 June 2010).

Schön, D.A., 1987. *Educating the Reflective Practitioner*. San Franscisco, CA: Jossey-Bass.

Shermer, M., 2009. Why People Believe in Conspiracies: A Skeptic's Take on the Public's Fascination with Disinformation. *Scientific American*. http://www.scientificamerican.com/article.cfm?id=why-people-believe-in-conspiracies (accessed 31 October 2010)

Žižek, S., 2010. *Living in the end times*. New York: Verso.

SECTION 5

Transformational Approaches

13

SHAPING SUSTAINABILITY AT FURMAN AND MIDDLEBURY

Emergent and Adaptive Curricular Models[1]

Angela C. Halfacre, Jack Byrne,
Michelle Horhota, Katherine Kransteuber,
Steve Trombulak, Brittany DeKnight,
Brannon Andersen, and Nan Jenks-Jay

Introduction

One of the major challenges of the twenty-first century is balancing economic and human development and population growth with environmental quality, all in a context of increasingly limited or degraded natural resources. The challenge of sustainability is becoming ever more urgent as human transformations of the earth have overstepped at least three of nine critical thresholds (Rockstrom *et al.* 2009). Addressing this challenge requires examining complex problems from a variety of disciplinary perspectives and crafting holistic solutions (e.g. Dresner 2002; Edwards 2005; Orr 1992, 2002, 2004, 2009; Sayer and Campbell 2004). Institutions of higher learning provide an ideal venue for educating people about the importance of using interdisciplinary tools and perspectives to think systemically. Such holistic thinking, however, requires comprehensive, innovative approaches to integrating sustainability into the academic program (Aber *et al.* 2009; Bartlett and Chase 2004; Blewitt and Cullingford 2004; Creighton 1998; Cullingford 2004; Elder 2008; Kelly 2009). In its most fundamental sense, sustainability involves balancing the relationships among complex systems – environmental, political, economic, social, and ethical. These systems together generate ultimate questions of value: how does civilization sustain itself amid the challenges of environmental limits, social injustice, and political instability?

Sustainability is an amorphous concept in that it can mean diverse things to different people. It is at once a crusade, a movement, an ideal, a mode of thinking, and a simple description of whether or not a system can be sustained over time. At its core, it represents the urgent need for society to address the growing scarcity of natural resources by adapting human behavior to changing systems (e.g., environmental, economic, ethical/societal, political), in order to stay within the earth's biocapacity to sustain life.

As institutions of higher education have begun to integrate sustainability into curricular and co-curricular programs, three dominant views of sustainability have emerged. Some have seen sustainability as an urgent moral imperative, necessitating a compelling shift in methods of thinking and acting in a world whose population growth and economic development has collided with its natural environment (e.g. Bardaglio and Putman 2009; Cortese 2003; Kinsley and DeLeon 2009; Rappaport and Creighton 2007; Simpson 2008). Others have understood sustainability as a complement to existing disciplines and as a way to better understand the relationships among dynamic systems (e.g. Aber *et al.* 2009; Bardaglio 2007; Sherman 2008). Finally, sustainability – or sustainability science – has emerged as a discipline in its own right (e.g. Clark *et al.* 2005; Clark 2007; Cullingford 2004; Kates *et al.* 2001; Komiyama and Takeuchi 2006). As education professor Cedric Cullingford contended, sustainability is

> at once, an inescapable dilemma of our time, a matter of study and reflection, and a challenge to action. It raises questions about globalization and personal responsibility. It constitutes, in fact, all that a discipline calls for: a greater understanding and a basis for the moral authority of knowledge.
> *(Cullingford 2004: 250)*

The range of perspectives related to the nature of sustainability and its role in higher education presents a challenge for college campuses that have sought to practice sustainability in their day-to-day operations *and* educate students to address the complex, cross-disciplinary issues facing society (Bartlett and Chase 2004; Kelly 2009). In fact, this is a hallmark of sustainability science – developing more sophisticated, systemic ways to understand the problems generated by resource scarcity, while at the same time developing innovative solutions (e.g., Komiyama and Takeuchi 2006).

In many cases, the interdisciplinary nature of sustainability complicates efforts to integrate its concepts and methods into the curriculum (Baerwald 2010; Jones *et al.* 2010; Klein 2010). Most universities remain organized around disciplines, while interdisciplinary fields such as sustainability often struggle to gain acceptance into curricula. The effort requires cooperation, leadership, persistence, collaboration, and communication (Fullan 2005; Gordon and Berry 2006; Parkin 2010; Redekop 2010). The differing experiences of two very similar institutions – Furman University (Greenville, South Carolina) and Middlebury College (Middlebury, Vermont) – provide insight into the complexities and rewards that result from creative efforts to embed sustainability into the curriculum.

Furman University and Middlebury College are both small, private liberal arts colleges (approximately 2500 students at each institution) with explicit commitments to national leadership roles in promoting sustainability. The two institutions share many similarities. Both have long histories of environmental stewardship as well as efforts to conserve natural resources and promote energy efficiency, and have received numerous awards for their efforts. A strong moral imperative to instill the values of sustainability also exists at Furman and Middlebury, which permeates their campus cultures, from the administration to student life to facilities to alumni. These institutions also provide substantial curricular and co-curricular opportunities for students to engage in sustainability activities, on and off campus.[2] Both schools have strong undergraduate research programs that enable students to engage in community-based research.[3] In terms of size, structure, educational philosophy, and institutional commitment to sustainability, the two are truly sister schools.

Furman and Middlebury have, however, developed different approaches to incorporating sustainability into the curriculum. Middlebury's *adaptive* model grows out of its venerable Program in Environmental Studies, whereas Furman's more *emergent* model centers on interest among the faculty and senior administrators in providing new options to study sustainability. However different, the two models have both been effective in integrating the burgeoning field of sustainability into the colleges' academic programs.

Middlebury's Program in Environmental Studies, created in 1965, has facilitated the school's efforts to infuse sustainability concepts into existing courses and has provided an ongoing foundation for new initiatives. During the twenty-first century, the college has used environmental studies as the genesis for expanding the concept of sustainability into the broader curriculum without identifying sustainability as a separate field of inquiry. In this regard, Middlebury has largely followed an *adaptive* model – using an already strong program to meet growing curricular needs.

Furman's approach, on the other hand, is largely *emergent*. Although sustainability concepts have been examined in the Environmental Studies concentration, the Earth and Environmental Sciences department, and through curriculum infusion, in 2010 the university's faculty unanimously approved the creation of a new major in sustainability science. The new major was not based on existing programs; rather, it was designed to address a holistic definition of sustainability that centers on exploring the dynamic relationships among social, human, and environmental systems to better understand the resilience and vulnerability of modern societies and envision pathways to a sustainable future (Komiyama and Takeuchi 2006). The emergent model is most applicable to institutions that do not have an existing environmental or sustainability program, but which intend to create a curriculum dedicated to the new field of study.

Approaches to Sustainability Curricular Integration

In Figure 13.1, three categories for curricular integration of sustainability are depicted. Along the y-axis is a continuum between emergent and adaptive models.

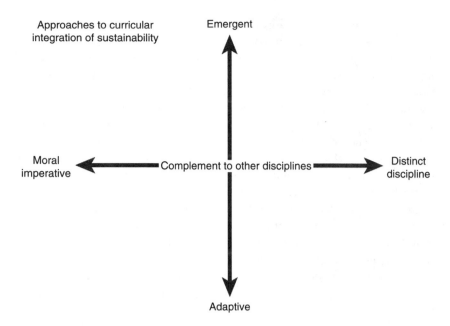

FIGURE 13.1 Approaches to curricular integration of sustainability.

Emergent programs are those that have been newly created as a result of holistic understandings of sustainability in the academic arena. Adaptive programs grow out of an existing major or program. Along the x-axis are three categories for sustainability integration: moral imperative, complement to other disciplines, and distinct program or discipline.

Curricular Approaches at Furman and Middlebury

Of course, the differing histories and contexts of Furman University and Middlebury College have shaped their different campus cultures and their institutional approaches to sustainability. Table 13.1 summarizes key data for each institution.

Campus Culture and Moral Imperative

Both Furman and Middlebury operate with a moral imperative for the core tenets of sustainability – ecological health, economic prosperity, and social equity – and relative to other colleges have long histories in this regard. Both schools were early signatories of the Presidents' Climate Commitment, have included sustainability as a strategic goal, have developed Climate Action Plans (CAPs), and in 2009 and 2010, the two colleges hosted national CAP workshops to train other institutions to create their own CAPs.[4] In addition, both institutions have support from the

TABLE 13.1 Relevant data for environmental studies and sustainability curricular development

	Furman	Middlebury
Campus		
Enrollment	2700 undergraduates	2450 undergraduates
Size of campus	750 acres (main campus is 450 acres; total includes surrounding areas and golf course)	6120 acres (main campus is 120 acres; total includes Breadloaf Campus and agricultural and forested areas)
Faculty size	265 roster faculty	320 roster faculty
Number of departments	24	49
Date of origin	1826	1800
Urban/rural	Suburban, five miles outside of Greenville, SC (Greater Metropolitan area, population 450,000)	Rural, Middlebury, VT (population 6300)
Moral imperative		
Environmental Awareness or Sustainability in University Strategic Plan	Yes (1996 Environmental Awareness; 2004 Sustainability)	Yes (1995)
Campus Climate Action Plan	Yes (2009)	Yes (2008)
Carbon neutrality goals	Neutrality by 2026	Neutrality by 2016
American Colleges and University President's Climate Commitment	2007, Charter Signatory	2007, Signatory
Campus Sustainability Master Plan	Yes (2009)	Yes (2008)
Campus-wide Sustainability Planning Council	Sustainability Planning Council (2006)	Environmental Council (1994)
Complement to other disciplines		
Sustainability Center or Office (academic)	Department of Earth and Environmental Sciences (renamed from Geology in 1996); David E. Shi Center for Sustainability (2008)[i]	Office of Environmental Affairs (est. 1997); Franklin Environmental Center at Hillcrest (2007)[ii]
General education requirement	Yes, "Humans and the Natural Environment" (2007)	No
Environmental studies concentration/minor	Yes, concentration (2001)	Yes, minor (1995)
Faculty development program	Yes (2009)	Yes (2009)
Faculty affiliate program	Yes (2010), Sustainability	Yes (1987), Environmental Studies

(Continued)

TABLE 13.1 Cont'd

	Furman	*Middlebury*
Program or discipline		
An environmental major	Earth and Environmental Sciences (since 1996)	Program in Environmental Studies (since 1965)
A specific major in Sustainability Science	Yes (2010)	No

ⁱ Furman established a focus on interdisciplinary teaching and research in the mid- 1990s, and in 1996, the Department of Geology (est. 1965) renamed itself the Department of Earth and Environmental Sciences to reflect its broader focus on earth systems science. A university sustainability coordinator was designated in 2005, and an Environmental Fellow as well as a faculty sustainability liaison were named in 2006. Two years later, the university created a Center for Sustainability to coordinate and promote the study of sustainability through teaching and research. The Director of the Center is a faculty member with joint appointments in Earth and Environmental Sciences and Political Science. The Center's administrative staff includes an associate director, program coordinator, and administrative coordinator. The Center also benefits from a large Student Fellows program.

ⁱⁱ Middlebury established a joint academic and administrative Office of Environmental Affairs and hired a director in 1997. An environmental coordinator position was created in 1999, which became sustainability coordinator in 2001. In 2007, Middlebury established the Sustainability Integration Office and created a new position of Director of that office when it also opened its new Franklin Environmental Center. At the same time, the Director of Environmental Affairs position became Dean of Environmental Affairs. The Franklin Environmental Center houses faculty and staff of the Department of Environmental Affairs, Program in Environmental Studies, the Sustainability Integration Office and Fellowships in Environmental Journalism.

students, faculty, staff, administrators, and trustees on issues of sustainability. Despite the similar moral imperative, sustainability initiatives on these two campuses have developed along very different pathways due to the different histories and campus cultures of each institution.

Furman's Campus Culture

Furman's dedication to environmental sustainability dates back over 15 years. Its former President, David E. Shi, and the Board of Trustees embraced the moral imperative of sustainability and designated it as a primary strategic goal in 2001. Such "top down" leadership, in turn, supported the faculty's development of strong interdisciplinary and environmental science curricular and co-curricular options for students, including student–faculty research projects, campus living/ learning laboratories, and sustainability engaged living programs.

Furman's approach to sustainability has been shaped in part by its distinct culture and history as a private liberal arts college located in the politically and socially conservative upstate region of South Carolina. For example, a 2009 Gallup survey rated South Carolina the sixth most ideologically conservative state in the nation (Gallup 2009). Although Furman faculty and students have participated in various forms of environmental activism since the 1970s, the wide array of initiatives related to sustainability and climate action planning did not begin at Furman until 1995. In 1999, the Board of Trustees began requiring that all new construction or major renovations meet Leadership in Energy and Environmental Design (LEED) Green Building Ratings System standards, and, in 2004, the Board of Trustees included the promotion of environmental sustainability as one of the university's five strategic goals. Since 2001, the campus has added numerous solar photovoltaic arrays, a campus vegetable garden (managed by students and staff), an ecological wastewater treatment facility, and other sustainability-related living and learning laboratories that facilitate place-based learning projects.

To formalize Furman's commitment to sustainability, in November 2009, Furman's Board of Trustees unanimously approved a comprehensive sustainability master plan, titled Sustainable Furman, which included an embedded CAP and set a goal of reaching carbon neutrality by the university's bicentennial – 2026. Sustainable Furman includes 8 goals and 90 strategies for addressing sustainability across the campus. The strategies focus on connecting sustainability goals with the student experience, from curriculum to research to co-curricular experiences. It is the result of 15 years of conversations by members of the campus community, and is reflective of the university's overarching strategic goals.[5] As part of the master plan, metrics and assessments have been developed to track progress over time.

To facilitate the achievement of increasingly refined curricular goals, Furman created the David E. Shi Center for Sustainability in 2008, named for its President from 1994 to 2010. The establishment of the Center was initially funded by the Andrew W. Mellon Foundation. The Center differs from many university clearing houses for sustainability in that it is housed in the Academic Affairs division. Its mission is to promote the study and practice of sustainability on campus and in the greater community. The Center supports significant local community partnerships and collaborations, including student–faculty research on community sustainability and service projects, and its focus is aligned with Furman's new major in sustainability science.

Middlebury's Campus Culture

Founded in 1965, the Environmental Studies program at Middlebury is the oldest of its kind in the United States. Middlebury's commitment to sustainability is also reflected in the daily operations of dining services and facilities services, student projects such as the organic garden, and as a cross cutting theme in both the College's Master Plan and Strategic Plan. In 1994, the president and trustees designated the environment as one of six areas of "peak" excellence based on existing strengths at the college. This emphasis has expanded to include the economic and social dimensions of sustainability.

Discussion about sustainability-related issues and challenges flows between the classroom, the administration and the boardroom, and to the broader community, forming a creative and innovative learning environment focused on practical solutions to these challenges. For instance, classroom discussions about adaptation to climate change spurred the formation of administrative decision-making teams, ultimately leading the Board of Trustees to adopt new policies and implement operational changes. This dynamic process is characteristic of how the college harnesses the hearts and minds of the entire learning community to help to solve sustainability challenges. Along the way, it informs and engages every level of the college community and maintains ongoing interest in sustainability.

Middlebury applied this process in 2003 to develop carbon reduction targets and strategies for meeting them, to assess progress toward sustainability goals, and to create new strategies as goals were met. This led to a 2004 commitment to reduce campus carbon emissions to 8% below 1990 levels by 2012, and a subsequent trustee resolution in 2007 that set Middlebury's carbon reduction goal to carbon neutrality by 2016. Middlebury's $12 million biomass gasification system, which reduced the College's carbon footprint by 40% and saved $800,000 in fuel costs per year, resulted from years of research and planning by teams of administrators, faculty, students, and staff working in conjunction with the board of trustees. This process also led to the creation of a new endowment fund for sustainability-related investing.

Middlebury's Janet Halstead Franklin '72 and Churchill G. Franklin '71 Environmental Center at Hillcrest promotes environmental sustainability both on campus and around the world, through lectures, campus events, and the support of programs like the Middlebury Fellowships in Environmental Journalism and a sustainable study abroad grants program. The Franklin Environmental Center is home to the Dean of Environmental Affairs, the Sustainability Integration Office, and the Program in Environmental Studies. The building also exemplifies Middlebury's commitment to sustainability with a LEED Platinum certification from the US Green Building Council. The Center serves as a community hub for sustainability-related ideas, initiatives, and collaboration, with its mission to engage and support all members of the College community in advancing leadership in sustainability and environmental citizenship.

Sustainability as a Complement to Existing Disciplines and a Distinct Discipline

Creative curricular development is an ongoing process on both campuses, although the strategies differ on each campus. What explains these different manifestations of sustainability-related curricula on two seemingly similar campuses? The culture of the geographic region, the interest of incoming and current students in sustainability, the curricular history, and institutional goals have all played roles in determining how sustainability could best be integrated in the curriculum.

As both Furman and Middlebury have advanced sustainability initiatives, student interest in sustainability has increased at both schools. In 2008, Furman conducted a baseline survey and focus group interview research project to assess student interest in sustainability; the same study was replicated in 2011 to monitor changes in perceptions and behaviors. According to the 2008 data, those students who expressed interest in sustainability believed that social and ethical aspects of sustainability were the most important, outranking environmental and economic aspects. In the 2011 survey, all aspects of sustainability were largely perceived as equally important. Middlebury has long attracted students interested in studying environmental issues. The longevity and popularity of the Program in Environmental Studies attests to this, as do the myriad of student activities and participation in student organizations which have been active both on and off campus in addressing sustainability-related issues like social justice, climate change, food systems, and poverty. In 2009, 54% of Middlebury students took a course with an environmental focus, and sustainability initiatives have proven to be a significant draw for prospective students.[6] Until recently, due to its location in an ideologically conservative region, Furman has had less student interest in sustainability than Middlebury; however, student interest in sustainability is growing rapidly. At Furman, a survey of the incoming 2010 first-year student class (714 students) indicated that approximately one-third of the class had an interest in sustainability curricular or co-curricular activities.[7]

To address growing student interest, both Furman and Middlebury have expanded their curricular offerings. Since 2001, Furman has offered a multidisciplinary concentration in Environmental Studies that includes a variety of courses exploring environmental issues from the perspectives of sciences, social sciences, and the humanities. The concentration is designed for both science and non-science majors and includes courses from nine different departments. Additionally, Furman transformed its academic program in 2008. The university-wide curriculum added a requirement that all students take at least one course that focuses on the relationship between "Humans and the Natural Environment (NE)." The NE credit, along with a World Cultures requirement, is part of a two-course requirement addressing Global Awareness. For Furman, the general education requirement approach was a timely way of meeting the institution's sustainability goals while also tailoring the requirements to students' personal interests. Within the span of two years, a dozen new courses focused on sustainability were added to the curriculum; in 2010–2011, 31 courses in 11 departments were offered to fulfill the NE credit, ranging from Biology to Religion, Sociology, and Philosophy. Furthermore, engaged learning, the hallmark of the university, is reflected in these sustainability curricular options as they promote interdisciplinary class experiences and community-based student–faculty research.

Since 2008, Furman has seen a growing student interest in studying sustainability in a more comprehensive and in-depth fashion. In response to both student interest and increasing recognition of sustainability science as an academic field of study,[8] Furman's Earth and Environmental Sciences department developed a major in sustainability science. The major is grounded by a core group of five courses that examine sustainability from the perspective of varying systems. The elective offerings for the major reflect 13 different departments, and students complete thesis research in their senior year. The sustainability science major, concentration in Environmental Studies, and the NE general education requirement provide a range of options for students to engage academically with sustainability.

The options at Middlebury grew out of the Environmental Studies program. Middlebury's distinguished Program in Environmental Studies attracts many students to the College and is consistently among the top five majors at the school. The program brings together a community of scholars and students engaged in the study of human relationships with the environment from 24 of the 49 departments on the campus. The 10 core faculty members and 53 affiliated faculty colleagues offer an interdisciplinary major and minor.[9] Both the major and the minor foster a shared base of knowledge across the humanities, natural sciences, and social sciences in students.

Because community involvement has been integral to Middlebury's sustainability efforts, internship experiences and honors theses take students' education beyond the classroom. The interdisciplinary senior seminar uses the campus and the surrounding region as an extended classroom, establishing partnerships with nonprofit conservation organizations, municipalities, and other departments on campus to collaborate on environmental problems.

There is strong support from both students and faculty for the Program in Environmental Studies. Students can choose a specific area of specialization within the major from among a wide set of options. Thus, students can choose an area of focus from 12 course options that span the environmental sciences, social sciences, and the humanities in addition to taking a common set of core courses. Because of the nature and history of the Program in Environmental Studies at Middlebury, the study of sustainability is available to interested students from within the existing program and not as a distinct major.[10]

Developing Faculty Sustainability Learning Communities: Strategy for All Campuses

Despite their contrasting approaches, Furman and Middlebury have addressed some similar challenges. How can an institution simultaneously meet the needs of both students and faculty with regard to demand for a sustainability curriculum? How can an institution create mechanisms for faculty to collaborate between and among disciplines to foster the teaching of sustainability?

Both Furman and Middlebury made a commitment to infusing sustainability into the existing curriculum. At Middlebury, professors across the curriculum were seeking opportunities to marry sustainability to their own disciplines. At Furman, the introduction of the general education requirement created the opportunity to infuse sustainability more broadly into the curriculum.

At both schools, meeting the needs of students interested in a more holistic concept of sustainability required effectively communicating this concept to faculty across the university. However, the lack of established mechanisms for linking faculty across the humanities, social sciences, and natural sciences presented obstacles to creating meaningful interdisciplinary academic opportunities in sustainability.

To address these obstacles, in 2009, Furman and Middlebury co-created faculty curriculum development workshops to support faculty members who were interested in infusing sustainability into existing or new courses. One of the primary goals of the workshops was to encourage faculty members to adopt a holistic understanding of sustainability involving the dynamic relationships among human, social, and environmental systems, and to examine the connections that exist between their disciplines and the concept of sustainability. Working with individual faculty members, the workshop leaders facilitated the development of creative approaches to incorporate the concepts and practices of sustainability across a wide range of courses. Additionally, students in each modified course completed pre- and post-course surveys in order to assess the impact of the sustainability infusion.

Fifty-nine faculty members at Furman and 30 faculty members at Middlebury have participated in three annual workshops. The workshops at Furman were funded by the Andrew W. Mellon Foundation, and at Middlebury, by the Department of Environmental Affairs. Participants represented 21 out of the 24 academic departments at Furman, and 19 of 49 departments at Middlebury.

In addition to discussing specific strategies that could be used within courses, faculty participants also developed sustainability learning outcomes. The main question asked of participants was, "What should our students have learned about sustainability by the time they graduate?" Six themes emerged in the Furman and Middlebury discussions across the years: (1) understanding the three interrelated primary aspects of sustainability (environmental, economic, and social);[11] (2) understanding the connection between sustainability and the student's primary discipline; (3) being a conscientious citizen and thinking about both local and global communities; (4) thinking and acting intentionally and recognizing that choices involve tradeoffs; (5) encouraging active leadership; and (6) fostering the ability to see issues and situations from multiple perspectives as an important element of developing solutions.

A critical goal of the workshops was to create a learning community where faculty members could share ideas and create a deeper dialog. To foster connections, participants spent much of the workshop in interdisciplinary groups that linked individuals who did not otherwise frequently interact with one another. Within institutions, an ongoing affiliate faculty program in sustainability (with faculty from over half the departments of each institution) was created to enrich faculty teaching and research in sustainability and to foster continuing interdisciplinary conversation after the workshop was completed.

Conclusions and Commentary

Emergent and adaptive models provide ways for colleges and universities to include sustainability in their curricula. Furman University and Middlebury College can be used as case studies for how sustainability can be incorporated into the undergraduate curriculum at small liberal arts institutions. However, the models at each of these schools and the lessons learned are relevant for schools of all types.

Furman's primarily *emergent* model has emphasized an array of curricular options from a general education requirement, Sustainability Science major, concentration in Environmental Studies, and the infusion of sustainability into a diverse set of offerings across a majority of the departments on campus. Institutions without a significantly strong history of student interest in interdisciplinary environmental studies may look to this emergent model as a way to introduce and to develop new programs and offerings.

Middlebury's primarily *adaptive* model has focused its efforts on its long-standing environmental studies program and offered sustainability as a complement to existing departments and disciplines. Institutions with strong, well-developed programs in interdisciplinary environmental studies may look to this adaptive approach to enhance and expand current offerings to meet new needs.

In Figure 13.2, the examples of programs that have been implemented to address these categories at Middlebury and Furman have been placed in the grid depending on how emergent or adaptive they are. For example, Furman's Sustainability Science as a major at Furman is emergent because it was created following a template discussed in the defining literature of sustainability science. The development of the major was the result of discussion among faculty members about how to best meet students' interdisciplinary interest in sustainability and reflects faculty understanding of the field of sustainability science. Middlebury's Environmental Studies program is closer to the adaptive side of the diagram due to its long history and culture. Though the Environmental Studies program at Middlebury has been the impetus for sustainability curricular efforts, the existence of the program itself has fostered an adaptive approach.

Regardless of whether the genesis of interest in sustainability is adaptive or emergent, the development of faculty sustainability learning communities, through workshops and ongoing conversations/collaborations, has been useful, relevant, and necessary for fostering meaningful interdisciplinary collaborations. The faculty curriculum development workshops and the resulting learning communities at and between Furman and Middlebury achieved the goals of providing faculty members with time to adjust their courses and facilitating lecture exchanges and collaborative thinking about assignments. Individual faculty members can infuse the ideas into their courses one by one; however, to create a broader shift in the way that colleges think about and teach sustainability concepts, the opportunity for faculty to engage in discussion and debate across disciplines is crucial.

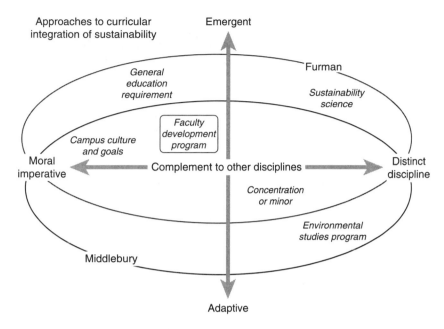

FIGURE 13.2 Furman and Middlebury approaches to curricular integration of sustainability.

In sum, one size does not fit all for sustainability curricular integration. Sister schools, regionally and inter-regionally, can learn from each other but are likely to take different pathways; collaboration with similar schools, however, creates connections and a more comprehensive learning community.[12] Sustainability curricular integration is likely to start with a campus commitment or moral imperative, but the pathway followed may be adaptive, emergent, or somewhere in-between. The resulting curricular pathways – from moral imperative to complement existing disciplines to distinct programs and disciplines – reflect the range of options for applying sustainability across the curriculum.

Notes

1 The authors thank Andrew W. Mellon Foundation for its generous support. We appreciate the collective contributions made by the faculty, staff, students, and administration across both colleges.
2 For more examples, please see www.furman.edu/sustain and www.middlebury.edu/sustainability
3 For an overview of the principles and practices of community-based research in higher education, please see Strand *et al.* (2003).
4 These workshops have been replicated, based on Byrne and Halfacre's model, by other institutions through the ACUPCC.

5 To read Sustainable Furman, please see http://furman.edu/press/sustain2.pdf
6 Data from 2009 shows that of 8000 applicants to Middlebury, 987 said the environmental program was their first or second interest. Of those 987 applicants, 188 were admitted and of those, 105 matriculated for a "yield" of 56%, which is significantly higher than the yield for any other academic interest area of the other students who matriculated (ranging from 27 to 46%).
7 Comparable data over time is not available.
8 For more information on sustainability science as a discipline, see for example Clark *et al.* (2005), Kates *et al.* (2001), and Komiyama and Takeuchi (2006). For more information on some of the key issues in sustainability science, see for example Layzer (2008), Reid *et al.* (2009), and Scheffer (2009).
9 For more information, see http://www.middlebury.edu/academics/es
10 Some have argued (Andersen *et al.* 2001) that environmental studies is an incredibly broad "field" of inquiry, but not a distinct discipline. Sustainability science, on the other hand, is a defined, though emerging, field with a clear set of research questions and approaches.
11 Some argue that economic and social should be combined. (e.g. Komiyama and Takeuchi 2006). The "three legs" of sustainability are often characterized as environment, social (political, economic, and non-government organizations), and human (individuals and families). For example, poverty and disease are often linked and the drivers are often a combination of political problems, economic structure and stratification, and environmental degradation. The key is that a systems approach allows the various drivers to be better understood.
12 Both schools have engaged in significant collaborations across institutions that are also grappling with how to best incorporate sustainability on campuses. Furman has worked closely with sister schools – Davidson College, Duke University, and Johnson C. Smith University – engaged in The Duke Endowment Task Force on Sustainability. Furman and Middlebury have been important contributors to national workshops and dialogs hosted by the Association for the Advancement in Higher Education, Second Nature, and The Duke Endowment. Both colleges are actively engaged in the regional networks in place to share sustainability innovation and curricular enrichment. The Associated Colleges of the South and the Northeast Campus Sustainability Consortium are two such networks.

References

Aber, J., Kelly, T. and Mallory, B., 2009. *The Sustainable Learning Community*. Lebanon, NH: University of New Hampshire Press.
Andersen, C.B., Worthen, W.B. and Polkinghorn, B., 2001. Humanism in the environmental sciences: a reevaluation. *Journal of College Science Teaching*, **31**: 202–206.
Baerwald, T.J., 2010. Prospects for geography as an interdisciplinary discipline. *Annuals of the Association of American Geographers*, **100**: 493–501.
Bardaglio, P.A., 2007. Moment of grace: integrating sustainability into the undergraduate curriculum. *Planning for Higher Education*, **36**: 16–22.
Bardaglio, P. and Putman, A., 2009. *Boldly Sustainable: Hope and opportunity for higher education in the age of climate change*. Washington, DC: National Association of College and University Business Officers.
Bartlett, P.F. and Chase, W.G., 2004. *Sustainability on Campus: Stories and strategies for change*. Cambridge, MA: The MIT Press.
Blewitt, J. and Cullingford, C., 2004. *The Sustainability Curriculum: The challenge for higher education*. London: Earthscan.

Clark, W.C., 2007. Sustainability science: a room of its own. *Proceedings of the National Academy of the Sciences*, **104**: 1737–1738.

Clark, W.C., Crutzen, P.J. and Schellnhuber, H.J., 2005. Science for global sustainability: toward a new paradigm. In H.J. Schellnhuber, P.J. Crutzen, W.C. Clark, M. Claussen and H. Held (eds), *Earth System Analysis for Sustainability*. Cambridge, MA: The MIT Press, 2005.

Cortese, A., 2003. The critical role of higher education in creating a sustainable future. *Planning for Higher Education*, **31**(3): 15–22.

Creighton, S.H., 1998. *Greening the Ivory Tower: Improving the environmental track record of universities, colleges, and other institutions*. Cambridge, MA: The MIT Press.

Cullingford, C., 2004. Sustainability and higher education. In J. Blewitt and C. Cullingford (eds), *The Sustainability Curriculum: The challenge for higher education*. Sterling, VA: Earthscan, pp. 13–23.

Dresner, S., 2002. *The Principles of Sustainability*. Sterling, VA: Earthscan.

Edwards, A.R., 2005. *The Sustainability Revolution: Portrait of a paradigm shift*. Gabriola Island: New Society Publishers.

Elder, J.L., 2008. Think systemically, act cooperatively: reaching the tipping point for the sustainability movement in higher education. *Sustainability: The Journal of Record*, **1**(5): 319–328.

Fullan, M., 2005. *Leadership and Sustainability: System thinkers in action*. Thousand Oaks, CA: Corwin Press.

Gallup, 2009. State of the States: Midyear 2009. http://www.gallup.com/poll/122333/political-ideology-conservative-label-prevails-south.aspx. Accessed 3 June 2010.

Gordon, J.C. and Berry, K.J., 2006. *Environmental Leadership Equals Essential Leadership: Redefining who leads and how*. New Haven, CT: Yale University Press.

Jones, P., Shelby, D. and Sterling, S., 2010. More than the sum of their parts? Interdisciplinarity and sustainability. In P. Jones, D. Selby and S. Sterling (eds), *Sustainability Education: Perspectives and practice across higher education*, Washington, DC: Earthscan, pp. 17–37.

Kates, R.W. *et al.*, 2001. Environment and development: sustainability science. *Science*, **292**(5517): 641.

Kelly, T., 2009. Sustainability as an organizing principle for higher education. In J. Aber, T. Kelly and B. Mallory (eds), *The Sustainable Learning Community: One university's journey to the future*, Durham, NH: University of New Hampshire Press, pp. 1–53.

Kinsley, M. and DeLeon, S., 2009. *Accelerating Campus Climate Initiatives: Breaking through barriers*. Rocky Mountain Institute.

Klein, J.T., 2010. *Creating Interdisciplinary Campus Cultures: A model for strength and sustainability*. San Fransisco, CA: Jossey-Bass.

Komiyama, H. and Takeuchi, K., 2006. Sustainability science: building a new discipline. *Sustainability Science*, **1**: 1–6.

Layzer, J.A., 2008. *Natural Experiments: Ecosystem-based management and the environment*. Cambridge, MA: The MIT Press.

Orr, D.W., 1992. *Ecological Literacy: Education and the transition to a postmodern world*. Albany, NY: State University of New York Press.

Orr, D.W., 2002. *Nature of Design: Ecology, culture, and human intention*. New York: Oxford University Press.

Orr, D.W., 2004. *Earth in Mind: On Education, Environment, and the Human Prospect*. Washington, DC: First Island Press.

Orr, D.W., 2009. *Down to the Wire: Confronting climate collapse*. Oxford: Oxford University Press.

Parkin, S., 2010. *The Positive Deviant: Sustainability leadership in a perverse world*. Washington, DC: Earthscan.

Rappaport, A. and Creighton, H.S., 2007. *Degrees That Matter: Climate change and the university*. Cambridge, MA: The MIT Press.

Redekop, W.B. (ed.), 2010. *Leadership for Environmental Sustainability*. New York: Routledge.

Reid, W.V., Bréchignac, C. and Lee, Y-T., 2009. Earth system research priorities. *Science*, **325**(5938): 245.

Rockstrom, J. *et al.*, 2009. A safe operating space for humanity. *Nature*, **461**: 472.

Sayer, J. and Campbell, B., 2004. *The Science of Sustainable Development: Local livelihoods and the global environment*. Cambridge: Cambridge University Press.

Scheffer, M., 2009. *Critical Transitions in Nature and Society*. Princeton, NJ: Princeton University Press.

Sherman, D.J., 2008. Sustainability: what's the big idea? *Sustainability: The Journal of Record*, **1**(3): 188–195.

Simpson, W. (ed.), 2008. *The Green Campus: Meeting the Challenge of Environmental Sustainability*. Alexandria, VA: APPA.

Strand, K., Marullo, S., Cutforth, N., Stoecker, R. and Donohue, P., 2003. *Community-Based Research and Higher Education: Principles and practices*. San Francisco, CA: Jossey-Bass.

14

STEPPING UP TO THE CHALLENGE – THE DALHOUSIE EXPERIENCE

Tarah Wright

Introduction

At the end of the last millennium, the United Nations Educational, Scientific and Cultural Organization released a document stating that, "education, in short, is humanity's best hope and most effective means in the quest to achieve sustainable development" (UNESCO 1997). The document also called upon higher education to take a leadership role in creating a sustainable future. Yet over a decade later, ecological footprint models demonstrate that it is the well-educated people of industrialized countries who continue to use the majority of the earth's natural resources and contribute the most to the world's sustainability problems.

How can an educated citizenry wreak so much havoc on the planet? Do we wake up in the morning with the intent to destroy another part of our planet or compromise another humans' ability to meet their own basic needs so that we can meet and often exceed our own? I suggest that this probably is not the case. What is more likely is that most well-educated individuals rarely think about their individual impact on the planet or how their actions affect the welfare of the global citizenry in anything but abstract or very general terms. While this, to an environmentalist, is deplorable, it is also a reality that has been created not by the individuals who are doing the most damage, but by the system of education that produced them. From an early age, typical Western education fragments knowledge and information into disciplines. If you look at the average grade school curriculum, you will likely see a schedule similar to this: mathematics from 9 to 10 am, music from 10 to 11 am, and physics from 11 am to 12 pm. The fragmentation and sectoralization of knowledge into separate subject matter from the beginning of formal schooling sends a message to Western-educated humans that subjects contain discrete bodies of knowledge that have little to do with the others. In this Descartian system, the integration of knowledge and experience is highly discouraged. Higher education perpetuates the myth, often producing disciplinary leaders incapable of addressing critical sustainability problems, because they are blindly contributing to them. How then can the United Nations list education to be humanity's best hope? As David Orr has pointed out, it is not education that will save us, but education of a certain kind (Orr 1992).

Einstein once observed "We can't solve problems by using the same kind of thinking we used when we created them." From a university perspective, educating for a sustainable future must involve new ways of thinking, teaching, researching, and being within the university. To this end, more than 1000 academic institutions worldwide have signed international declarations focused on implementing sustainability through environmental literacy initiatives; curriculum development; research; partnering with government, non-governmental organizations, and industry to develop sustainability initiatives; and "greening" physical operations (Bartlett and Chase 2004; Wright 2003).

This chapter tells the story of one institution amongst many who have joined the higher education for sustainability movement. It will describe why and how Dalhousie University created the first College of Sustainability in Canada, and the Environment, Sustainability and Society (ESS) program which is the most significant and far-reaching change to the way Dalhousie educates its students in recent memory, and one giant step on behalf of the university toward a sustainable future.

Haven't We Done Enough?

Dalhousie University is the largest university in Atlantic Canada with 11 faculties, 180 degree programs and a student body of approximately 16,000 students. It is a comprehensive university offering undergraduate and graduate education as well as professional programs such as law and medicine. Dalhousie University has a history of involvement and engagement in sustainability initiatives dating back to the early 1990s when it hosted a conference of university administrators that resulted in the Halifax Declaration (http://www.iisd.org/educate/declarat/halifax.htm) – a document that encouraged universities to become leaders and models of sustainability. The university has signed three international declarations related to environment and sustainability: the Halifax Declaration, the Talloires Declaration, and the United Nations Environment Programme (UNEP) International Declaration on Cleaner Production.

Environmental initiatives on campus include pesticide-free landscaping, a unique chemicals exchange program, a university-wide Sustainability policy, and a six-stream recycling and composting program. The campus is engaged in retrofitting projects and has reduced its chemical load through a recent change to green cleaners. The university bookstore stocks green products, encourages reusable bags, and the sale of reused books. Residence and food services have recently focused efforts on increasing local food content, fair-trade products, and sustainability education. In 2008, a University Office of Sustainability was created to lead in the continued reduction of Dalhousie's impact on the environment and to enhance sustainability efforts across the campus.

Student involvement in environment and sustainability issues has been strong for decades at Dalhousie University. Over the years, numerous student organizations have contributed to sustainability efforts through research, policy, and education campaigns such as Green Week, and action-orientated projects like "Dump and Run" campaigns. In fact, students at Dalhousie University are constantly walking the talk. For example, in 2007, students voted to establish a student Sustainability Office which continues to be funded through student fees.

Dalhousie University has also been a Canadian leader in academic offerings related to the environment and sustainability. With over 150 faculty members teaching and conducting research in related disciplines, Dalhousie has been the natural choice for Canadian students seeking educational opportunities in multiple environment and sustainability-related fields.

Given our success with environment and sustainability initiatives in the past, most observers might think that the university was adhering to its commitment to be a leader in modeling and creating a sustainable future. During the first decade of this century, however, a group of faculty members began to think that we might not yet be doing enough. The first problem lay in that the university was still not immune to the criticisms of traditional education, which fragments and sectoralizes information so that one discipline has no understanding of its impact on the other. For example, a student graduating with a business degree from the university might understand the financial benefits of oil extraction, but not the full environmental, political, and social ramifications and costs (and vice versa for a student in political science or biology). Further, if teaching and research about environment and sustainability remained within the disciplines, or at best within faculties, true interdisciplinarity would be hard to achieve.

With a belief that synergisms could occur by bringing sustainability experts from within the university together, the College of Sustainability was created. The ESS program is the first offering from the College and aims to allow students and professors from a multitude of disciplines to engage meaningfully with sustainability issues outside of their departments and faculties.

Putting our Best Foot Forward – The Environment, Sustainability and Society Program

Launched in 2009 the ESS program is a unique offering to the Canadian academic scene. While there are many sustainability-related graduate programs in

Canadian universities, there are very few at the undergraduate level, and none that we are aware of that are designed like the ESS program. ESS was intentionally launched as an undergraduate program, guided by the belief that in this century an understanding of sustainability will be critical for every person in a leadership role in every sector of society, and that students must be exposed to issues of sustainability from the beginning of their post-secondary careers.

The ESS program is unique, bringing together students from a wide variety of disciplinary backgrounds who share a common passion for the planet. Instead of creating a stand-alone program (which could be interpreted as another silo within the ivory tower), the ESS program is unique in that it is a mandatory double major program. Students are required to combine their ESS studies with another discipline. Currently, students can choose their second focus from the faculties of Architecture and Planning, Arts and Social Sciences, Science, or the King's School of Journalism, Management, and Computer Science. This means students from theater, business, biology, and computer science are all learning and working together on sustainability issues. It also allows students to pursue their passions in different areas (theater, computer science, planning, business, etc.) as well as sustainability, and enables them to make a difference in any profession they chose.

The curriculum in ESS also goes beyond what would typically be taught in an environmental class. While the ESS program recognizes the primacy of the environment in providing the raw materials for human society and the economy, it also embraces the tenets of sustainability and weaves together issues such as human rights, poverty reduction, sustainable livelihoods, peace, environmental protection, democracy, health, biological and landscape diversity, climate change, gender equality, and protection of indigenous cultures.

The ESS student body and curriculum is multidisciplinary in nature, and is echoed in the staffing for the core classes within the program. Professors who teach in the program are currently drawn from six faculties and dozens of academic disciplines. The core classes in the ESS program are exceptional in that each is team-taught with a minimum of two professors in the classroom at any given time. Students are therefore exposed to multiple ways of approaching sustainability from many different lenses. Course professors are required to co-develop lectures (rather than divide the classes between them), which to date has been a challenging, but very rewarding, experience.

Professors who teach in the ESS program have found that educating in the ESS program requires a different approach to teaching so that students translate knowledge into positive action. While traditional delivery methods have served to inform students, they can been criticized for failing to promote a full understanding or appreciation of sustainability issues as a whole. As a UNESCO publication put it,

> No amount of preaching to the citizenry about the perils of a polluted environment, the dangers of irresponsible disposal of wastes or deforestation

and the benefit to mankind [*sic*] of greening the environment will make people act to seek to forestall environmental degradation unless they are imbued with a deep concern for the common good, a sense of responsibility for maintaining a balanced and healthy ecosystem and a strong drive to achieve harmony with nature.

(UNESCO 1990, as cited in Clover *et al.* 1998)

In the ESS program, we are not only changing some of the content that we teach, but challenging traditional notions of how to teach. Classes in ESS emphasize teamwork, problem-based, and experiential learning.

The introduction of experiential learning into the ESS classroom has had implications for instructors and students. First, introducing experiential learning into the classroom fundamentally changes the traditional role of the professor from knowledge expert to facilitator of experiences. ESS professors shed their didactic cloaks and become participants in the learning process. Their role is to ask questions that encourage students along individual learning paths, offer advice and information, and provide relevant experiences for learning. This does not mean that our ESS instructors lose total control of the classroom or what is being taught, but it does change the dynamic of the classroom.

Bringing experiential learning into the classroom also means that both students and teachers become active learners. Research into the use of experiential learning in the university classroom has shown that student motivation and satisfaction is increased through active participation in learning (Acosta 1991; Baslow and Byrne 1993; Cranton 1989). Another benefit of using experience in the classroom is the increased ability of students to transfer salient learning to other settings and situations. One of the most significant critiques of traditional pedagogy is that students are required to memorize isolated pieces of information without understanding its practical application (Cantor 1995). Students who are involved in their learning through experiential techniques are better able to make connections between their education and their daily lives (Cantor 1995; Cranton 1989; Knowles 1977).

Further, research shows that university students who learn through active and experiential learning are more likely to translate their learning into action. It is very easy for students to keep a scholarly distance from changes in global temperature, the disappearance of species, or the effects of poverty on the lives of fellow human beings. The ESS program attempts to have students develop a sense of empathy for society, the natural environment, and an understanding of how to solve sustainability problems through hands-on learning. After four years, students can expect to graduate as critical thinkers, communicators, researchers, and effective team members. They will be leaders who will approach all they do with an understanding of sustainability and will contribute to a new generation of leaders.

The Journey Is as Important as the Destination

Colleagues often ask, "How did you do it?" There is no simple answer, but I can confirm that it takes a village to create a College of Sustainability. It is also important to note that despite appearances, it is very rare that anything in a university ever happens overnight. For more than two decades, sustainability-minded faculty members at the university had been informally discussing the potential synergistic effects that could be accomplished through broader collaboration. The universe must have been conspiring to favour sustainability initiatives on campus in 2006 when a grassroots ad hoc committee emerged and began to meet regularly to discuss how to forward the agenda of creating interdisciplinary sustainability educational opportunities on campus, and how to overcome the constraints and administrative barriers to collaboration. At the same time, the university released an institutional strategic focus document that listed sustainability as a major area of emphasis for the university. The ad hoc group seized the opportunity and approached the Provost to discuss various opportunities on campus. The Provost was very receptive to the idea of creating synergies, and directed the deans of each Faculty to nominate staff, faculty, and student members to a university steering committee. In September 2007, the newly formed committee was mandated with developing a proposal for academic programming related to sustainability with a focus on undergraduates where the impact to the university would be the greatest. The committee undertook global reviews of current sustainability programs, and held focus groups and interviews with key stakeholders on campus. The work of the committee was supported by a full-time research associate, paid for by the Provost.

The committee hosted a two-day university-wide workshop in February 2008. The event had over 100 attendees including members of the Board of Governors, community members, faculty, staff, students, and administrators. One of the major conclusions of the workshop was that everyone who takes on a leadership role in the future, no matter what the field, needs to understand issues of sustainability. Further, the participants concluded that the university must overcome traditional barriers to enable students of any disciplinary or professional interest to access sustainability education. In retrospect, this event was essential for constituency-building and allowing people to feel that they were a part of the process of creating the College.

In just over two years, the push toward sustainability grew from a grassroots effort to a centerpiece of Dalhousie's strategic initiatives, supported by upper administration, faculty, students, and staff. Working at warp speed for a university, a proposal for the College of Sustainability with full details on administrative structure and budget, as well as details of the new undergraduate ESS program was developed, submitted, and approved by the university senate in late 2008. In September 2009, Dalhousie opened Canada's first College of Sustainability and launched the unique interdisciplinary major in Environment, Sustainability and Society with an incoming class of over 300 students.

The Challenges

This is an honest account of the College's genesis, but the process described above is only half of the story. I have not yet shared some of the bumps along the road to curricular innovation. Anyone familiar with university settings knows that scholars love to debate, and there were many points of discussion in the development of the College and the ESS program that occasionally made for lively dialog and challenging disagreements. Some of these are detailed below.

Is Sustainability Just for Tree-Huggers?

One of the first challenges to the College came from a group of faculty members who believed that sustainability, as a field of study and research, is only for a small fringe group of tree-hugging environmentalists. This perception of sustainability is indeed one challenge that the sustainability movement as a whole faces constantly. How do advocates convey that sustainability is truly everyone's issue? We found that proponents within the College had to engage in thorough and often laborious sessions where they educated colleagues (nay-sayers and advocates alike) about the concept of sustainability and the benefits of a new approach to sustainability education. The challenge involved explaining that sustainability goes beyond environmental issues, and encompasses a new way of looking at the world where society, environment, and the economy are considered together. Further, many of the proponents of the College found themselves challenged to explain why higher education institutions should take a stance and become models and leaders of sustainability. "Why is sustainability more important than what I do?" was a sentiment often heard from colleagues. Proponents' responses varied depending on the audience, but the message was clear: the main purpose of the university has always been to prepare students for an active life and to solve the major issues of our time. When we weigh the balance of scholarly evidence, it is apparent that sustainability is most certainly the issue of our time. Ecological footprint models demonstrate that it is physically impossible for the earth to produce all of the goods North Americans consume for every person on the earth. According to footprint calculations, humanity would need at least three planets the size of our earth for all of humanity to attain the lifestyle of North Americans and live in a way that does not compromise the earth's ecosystems (Ewing *et al.* 2010). Further, sustainability does not focus solely on the natural environment (although it is commonly seen as such, and is often portrayed as being about the natural environment in rhetoric), but encompases human and economic development as well. The Human Development Report (UNDP 2010) suggests that while some developing countries have made progress in health, education, and the improvement of basic living standards in recent decades, as a species our most important tasks are still to address issues of poverty, inequality and inequity, and social unrest. While there continue to be nay-sayers within the university, the exercise of explaining what sustainability was (and was not) was not only helpful in creating more awareness within the university about the field, but also helped to clarify the *raison d'être* of the College.

Is Sustainability Too Soft?

Another challenge to the development of the College and the ESS program in particular was the idea that sustainability is too "soft," used pejoratively to imply that studies of sustainability are not rigorous enough to stand up to academic scrutiny. Scholars who have been "disciplined" by their own discipline may be blind to the limits of their own fields of study and may be unaware that traditional notions of reliability and validity are no longer the only useful concepts in paving the way to a sustainable future. It is my firm belief that scholars must stand up to academic scrutiny, but alternative ways of assessing work are necessary. New evaluation criteria that judge how individuals within the academy are contributing to a sustainable future must be adopted. One measure which could enhance or even replace archaic notions of validity, reliability, and rigor is catalytic validity: the degree to which a body of knowledge allows individuals to understand the world's systems and the way they are shaped, in order that they might be transformed. We have not yet formally tackled the issue of how to evaluate sustainability scholarship at Dalhousie University, and there are those who continue to critique the program for being too soft, but we collectively cope, knowing that what we are doing makes sense to our colleagues and has an impact on our students, and ultimately the planet.

What's the Best Way to Teach About Sustainability?

Other challenges came from within the group of faculty pushing for a new program. While these scholars all agreed to the "why" of the College and ESS program, there were many who disagreed on the how, who, what, and where aspects. For example, one of the first questions that emerged at our university-wide workshop was whether sustainability should be a single course that everyone takes before graduating from the university, a stand-alone program, or a concept that should be infused into every academic discipline.

While there may be some positive outcomes from having all students take a course that helps them learn about sustainability, simply adding a course to a disciplinary requirement has two possible negative outcomes. First, a mandatory sustainability class might generate resistance from the student population. Having taught a mandatory environmental studies class to management students at the beginning of my teaching career, I can attest to how difficult it was to change the hearts and minds of students in a class they attended only because they were told to. Second, a mandatory class isolates issues of sustainability, reinforcing the notion that the environment and sustainability are special interests rather than something relevant across disciplines. Such a course might teach students about the environment and society, but does not contextualize it within their chosen discipline (i.e. What do the environment and sustainability have to do with business, education, or engineering?).

Second, for many in the group of faculty, a stand-alone program in sustainability was seen as an attractive option. Sustainability is an emerging, multidisciplinary field of study, and degree programs in sustainability have begun to appear in universities globally (although most are housed in a traditional faculty). While interdisciplinary programs related specifically to sustainability would be welcome by most at Dalhousie University, such a stand-alone program could allow other disciplines to continue their fragmentary pursuit of knowledge, in many cases with little regard for their impact on the sustainability of humanity and the planet. Further, some in the group argued that sustainability could not, and should not, be a discreet subject or field of study.

Third, it was argued that an ideal university would infuse sustainability concepts and critical thinking skills into each of the disciplinary programs offered. Instead of adding an additional sustainability requirement or degree program, the ultimate goal is for the university to shift the dominant disciplinary paradigm and infuse environmental literacy, social responsibility, and civic engagement into all disciplines. As Tony Cortese says, "rather than being isolated in its own academic discipline…[sustainability] must become an integral part of the normal teaching in all disciplines" (1995).

In the end, however, I believe that it may not be necessary to choose one option over the other, but rather have all options available to students. The creation of the ESS program in the College of Sustainability should be considered only one initiative in the university which should be accompanied by many others if we are to become leaders in creating a sustainable future. The ESS program was not intended to replace other initiatives on campus, but rather complement them and add value to the many existing sustainability-related programs on campus. Students at Dalhousie may choose to take an individual course on sustainability, study in a sustainability-related program on campus (i.e., environmental studies, international development studies, environmental science or engineering), enrol in the ESS degree program, or all of the above. Students can choose their own adventure, depending on what path is right for them.

Bringing the Message Home?

In many ways the ESS program serves as a catalyst to impact disciplines not traditionally associated with studies in sustainability. Because students are required to double major in ESS and another discipline, they are able to specialize in a traditional field, but are made aware of the impact of their discipline on the planet. Anecdotally we are told that these students are bringing their sustainability knowledge back to their disciplinary programs and pushing their professors and fellow students to think about their discipline differently. The same can be said of our professors teaching in the program. Rather than hire sustainability specialists permanently into the program, the College of Sustainability offers limited term appointments (most of them 3 years) for instructors who wish to teach in one of the ESS core classes. Each of these instructors' home units are compensated for 33% of their time, and instructors in turn are expected to develop and co-teach a course and actively participate in the life and governance of the College and with the student body. The model of revolving instructors was an intentional approach to attempt to infuse sustainability into each instructor's home unit. It is anticipated that individual faculty members who teach for a couple of years in the ESS program will begin to think about their own discipline and how the curriculum in their program can be re-oriented toward creating sustainable solutions for the future. The continual flow of individual students and teachers through the College means an ongoing exchange of ideas, expertise, and passions.

It was important that our staffing model was attractive to both faculty members and their home units. A College that takes scholars away and harms their home unit's ability to deliver their own programming is not a sustainable model. The College's compensation of 33% of each instructor's actual salary during the time of secondment is beneficial to the College and the home units. Many departments are willing to give up their more senior professors for a three-year period of time if they know they will be compensated well (i.e., senior professor salaries are larger than junior, and thus provide more compensation to the home unit). The three-year term has allowed departments to date to hire post-docs or junior faculty on a short-term contract and infuse new thinking into the home unit. In turn, the College benefits from the experience and wisdom of senior faculty members seconded to teach in the ESS program.

Further, the College recognizes that co-teaching is often just as much work, if not more, than teaching a class alone. For this reason, each instructor co-teaching in an ESS core class receives full credit for their teaching. This model is more expensive for the university, but it was determined that co-teaching is so attractive to students that the class numbers would justify the expense.

Where Is Home?

Rather than house the College of Sustainability within a faculty, it was decided that the College should exist outside of the traditional silos within the ivory tower. The term "college" was purposefully selected to distinguish the College of Sustainability from existing, more disciplinary schools and faculties and to emphasize the collegial nature of the unit. The roots of the term "college" refer to a body of scholars and students within a university, and while such a body could exist only conceptually, the College also has a physical presence on campus. The directors, faculty and staff who work within the College, as well as the students enrolled in College programs have a common space to work and meet in. Faculty members with offices in other units are encouraged to work 33% of their time in offices at the College. To date this has been successful in the sharing of ideas and building community amongst all College stakeholders.

Who's the Boss?

While there were some original plans for the College of Sustainability to have a decentralized governance structure, the hierarchical model and chain of responsibility that has been adopted in the College will be familiar to most academics. The College is overseen by a full-time Director whose duties include the administrative and academic leadership of the College as well as a full credit of teaching within the ESS program. The Director is appointed on a 5-year term at 100% from within the faculty complement at the university. The College Director reports to a Council of Deans made up of partner faculties in which programs are offered.

The College also has three Associate Directors, each appointed to the College at 50% full-time equivalent for 2–4 year terms (staggered to prevent turnover of executive staff all in one year). The Associate Director (undergraduate) has duties to the College which include the administration of the ESS program; overseeing the curriculum development committee; managing cross-appointments, fellowships and adjunct faculty appointments; managing the appointments of teaching faculty and fellows in the undergraduate ESS program; and teaching a half-credit class. The Associate Director (graduate) oversees the development of graduate, certificate, and diploma programs of the College; the graduate curriculum development committee; assists the Associate Director (undergraduate) in managing the graduate dimensions of cross-appointments, fellowships, and adjunct faculty appointments; managing the appointments of teaching faculty and fellows in the graduate ESS offerings; and teaching within the College. Finally, the Associate Director (research and outreach) duties include liaison with government agencies, research agencies and community groups; identification of research project opportunities and development of research project teams and proposals; identification of community project opportunities and development of project teams and proposals; development of strategic and specific linkages of research and community projects to senior undergraduate and graduate classes in ESS; and teaching within the College.

It is important to note that other than staff, there are no permanent appointments to the College. The Director, Associate Directors, and faculty remain members of their original home units while serving in the College, and return back to their unit full-time at the end of their term. The thinking behind this was to use the resources and energy already available amongst the faculty complement at Dalhousie University and allow new ideas to flow into the College and out to associate faculty members home faculties regularly.

Stepping Up and Reaping the Rewards

While the creation and development of the College of Sustainability and the ESS program has not been without its challenges, we have also reaped many rewards. First, our university has benefited significantly from an influx of students into the university. In a survey of the first-year class, 64% of them said that the ESS major was influential in their decision to come to Dalhousie University, 43% said it was a major or primary factor, and 19.5% said they would not have come to Dalhousie if the ESS major was not available.

The development of the College of Sustainability has also been an amazing exercise in building community. The multiple consultations and democratic nature of the development of the College created an atmosphere of pride and ownership. At the launch of the College, over 300 university members gathered to celebrate. Using the mantra of "no academic left behind," the College intentionally remains open to ideas from all stakeholders.

The university is also pleased that the College of Sustainability has been recognized for its efforts to create a sustainable future. In 2009, UNESCO highlighted the College as one of 25 World Good Practices in Education for Sustainable Development. The College was also shortlisted for the Innovative Educational Practice Award at the first World Innovation Summit on Education, and is featured in the new book *Eco-Education for Human Survival in the 21st Century*, by Lin and Oxford.

Finally, the College has generated hope. As my colleague David Orr says, "hope is a verb with its sleeves rolled up." Faculty, staff, and students at Dalhousie University have already rolled up their sleeves and are digging in. Sometimes we might get disillusioned by the university and its propensity to work at glacial speed. At times we may be disheartened by the didactic style of lecturing adopted by so many, yet proved by education scholars to be so ineffective in creating change. Occasionally we may even contemplate leaving the university with the thought that what we do inside the ivory tower makes little difference to the rest of the blue planet. The College, while still a work in progress, demonstrates that a small group of people working together can make significant change. It shows that campuses can mobilize, that universities can become leaders in creating innovative solutions and future change agents that can help to ensure a sustainable future, and these developments fill us with hope.

References

Acosta, V., 1991. Integrating experiential learning and critical inquiry in health education. Paper presented at the Annual Meeting of the American Educational Research Association, Chicago, IL.

Bartlett, P.F. and Chase, G.W., 2004. *Sustainability on Campus*. Cambridge, MA: MIT Press.

Baslow, R. and Byrne, M., 1993. Internship expectations and learning goals. *Journalism Educator*, **47**(4), 48–54.

Cantor, J., 1995. *Experiential Learning in Higher Education: Linking Classroom and Community.* (Report no. 7). Washington, DC: The George Washington University, Graduate School of Education and Human Development.

Cortese, A., 1995. *The Essex Report: Workshop on the Principles of Sustainability in Higher Education.* Boston, MA: Second Nature.

Cranton, P., 1989. *Planning Instruction For Adult Learners.* Toronto: Wall & Thompson.

Dewey, J., 1960. *On Experience, Nature, and Freedom.* New York: The Liberal Arts Press.

Ewing, B., Moore, D., Goldfinger, S., Oursler, A., Reed, A. and Wackernagel, M., 2010. *The Ecological Footprint Atlas 2010.* Oakland, CA: Global Footprint Network.

Knowles, M., 1977. *The Modern Practice of Adult Education: Andragogy versus Pedagogy.* New York: Association Press.

Orr, D., 1992. *Ecological Literacy: Education and Transition to a Postmodern World.* Albany, NY: State University of New York Press.

UNDP, 2010. *Human Development Report.* Gland: Switzerland.

UNESCO, 1990. *The Talloires Declaration.* Gland: UNESCO.

UNESCO, 1997. *Thessaloniki Declaration.* Gland: UNESCO.

Wright, T., 2003. Ten Years and Counting: Examining the Implementation of the Halifax Declaration in Canadian Universities. *Canadian Journal of Environmental Education,* **8**(1), 217–234.

15

SUSTAINABILITY AS A TRANSFORMATION IN EDUCATION

Charles L. Redman and Arnim Wiek

We are in the early stages of a fundamental and globally pervasive transformation in the interactions of humans, their institutions, the technologies they have created, and the environment that provides both the home and the resources that make it all possible. In this new world, change is to be expected and desired as much or more than stability and this change will often be nonlinear, complex, and hard to predict with the tools we have at hand. Just as we may be frustrated in our attempts to predict the future we, as a global society, have been largely disappointed by the results of our concerted and enduring efforts to solve some of the major challenges already facing us. Continuing war, poverty, pollution, hunger, disease, social injustice, loss of biodiversity, and anthropogenic climate change have not been resolved despite decades of massive effort by the best minds, with enormous resources, and by well-intended nations. New ideas, new tools, new institutions, and new technologies must be part of any emerging solution. For it to succeed we also need a cultural transformation in the way we think, the way we interact, and the way we value the world. It will require that people have a respect for the environment and the services it provides; a respect for others – those we don't know as well as those we know; a willingness to take responsibility for our actions and inaction; and a determination to make difficult decisions in order to underwrite a better future. Taken together this is what many of us mean when we suggest that "sustainability" should be the goal of our efforts in education and in the broader society.

This article is a brief description of how faculty, administrators, and students at Arizona State University (ASU) have attempted to put sustainability into action in order to transform aspects of the educational system and to work toward a transformation in the broader society. Like ASU, many other colleges and universities are in the midst of their own transition to sustainability, each with their lessons to be learned. The ASU story is particularly interesting in that it has benefitted from the enthusiastic support of all sectors of the university (administrators, faculty, staff, and students); it declared very aggressive objectives, such as creating a complete academic program of the equivalent of Life Sciences or Engineering and assuming leadership in President's Climate Commitment; and it also benefited from early philanthropic support. This case study will only briefly outline the steps in the creation of the School of Sustainability at ASU, and will focus on the major issues that had to be confronted and the fundamental concepts that we believe should underlie any school of sustainability.

ASU has a long history of interdisciplinary environmental research; in many ways that was foundational for launching its sustainability efforts. The evolution of those projects over the past dozen years in particular made them a "training ground" for sustainability by encouraging social scientists to work with natural scientists. Especially in our urban Long Term Ecological Research (LTER) grant, bringing graduate education even closer to research through a series of National Science Foundation (NSF) Integrative Graduate Education and Training (IGERT) grants, and focusing on solving real-world problems in partnership with the community while conducting basic research (characterized by our Decision Making Under Uncertainty Center grant). The crystallization of these efforts came in the spring of 2004 when the President of ASU, Michael Crow, assembled a distinguished group of international "sustainability" scholars to discuss how to bring sustainability into the university system. This set in motion the creation of ASU's School of Sustainability (SOS), but the first step was to transform the existing Center for Environmental Studies into the Global Institute of Sustainability (GIOS). The mission of GIOS was to build on the former center and to expand the work to include more disciplines, more applied work, more geographic diversity, and most importantly, to incubate a fully fledged school of sustainability.

An interesting aspect of Michael Crow's nascent sustainability initiative was that it paralleled his larger initiative to change the university (and universities in general) into what he referred to as "The New American University" (Arizona Board of Regents 2005). He believes that the traditional education system is in urgent need of transformation and proposed eight "design aspirations" as a guide to change. In simple terms these are:

1. Leverage our place
2. Transform society
3. Value entrepreneurship
4. Conduct use-inspired research
5. Enable student success
6. Fuse intellectual disciplines
7. Be socially embedded
8. Engage globally

The soon-to-be-launched SOS was not just built around some of the same principles, but rather is an exemplar of how these aspirations could be achieved. The lesson for other schools is that a coherent sustainability initiative can serve as a pilot project for the type of larger change that many university administrations seek (Rowe 2007). From the beginning, it was clear that for SOS to be successful we must be in the vanguard of demonstrating how to accomplish the New American University.

Although the push for sustainability came from the President of the university, he stepped back when it came to designing the program and faculty took up the leadership role (Wiek *et al.* 2011). The process focused on a series of meetings of faculty who had expressed interest or had been recommended by their unit chairs. These meetings represented almost the entire spectrum of disciplines and colleges at the university. Although over 100 faculty participated in these meetings, about 40 were active contributors and because of this, level of involvement became the initial "faculty" of the SOS when it enrolled its first students in 2007. None of the faculty had formal training in "sustainability," but all of them believed that the challenges of the times required a more interdisciplinary and aggressive approach than currently existed. I do not know if it was the interdisciplinary success of the antecedent organization (Center for Environmental Studies), my own belief in the great potential of interdisciplinarity, or the structure of the faculty planning groups, but the end result was a consensus that created a school which reflected the belief that strong interdisciplinarity was the primary pathway to sustainability. Looking back today, one could see that this was a natural progression from where each of us were (in our training, current research, and objectives) to somewhere we wanted to go, but had not yet conceived of the roadmap to get there (even if we could agree on where we wanted to get to, which was a debate that we deferred for later). This initial framework for ASU's School of Sustainability could also be considered as representing an "eclectic" approach to sustainability. That is, if one brought together the appropriate disciplines and partners, one could effectively address sustainability challenges.

The curriculum that emerged in that first year was a series of "perspective" courses, each encompassing the views of a suite of traditional disciplines. The courses included social sciences, ecology, economics, policy, technology, and built environment; and students were expected to master at least three of these perspectives. Moreover, the introductory graduate course that all students would take as an entering cohort was initially comprised of six sections reflecting these perspectives on sustainability. The other feature of the curriculum, and in some ways the most effective, was a series of "solution workshops," where students and faculty from various disciplines/perspectives would work together on addressing a real-world problem. From the moment we established this curriculum on paper and began to offer it, the courses have evolved in response to student input and the experience of faculty working together. Students have been particularly important in questioning and redirecting our efforts as they are not just experiencing the curriculum, but have also risked their futures by committing themselves to a field and academic degree where there is no track record of careers and professional success. Whether or not this initial curriculum is the "best" approach to sustainability education is something we continue to debate, but clearly it was successful if one measures it in terms of student interest and in meeting the expectations of faculty. We limited the entering graduate class (Masters and PhD combined) to 25 students (a reasonable cohort for the introductory class), with 87 applicants the first year, 150 the second year, and 250 in the third and fourth years. In 2008, we introduced an undergraduate major in sustainability (based on roughly the same principles as the graduate degree) and by the second year there were 600 majors! Rather than allow the number of majors to continue to grow, it was decided to establish a three-prong approach to undergraduate sustainability: a major for those most committed, a minor (established in 2010) for those who want substantial exposure, and disciplinary-based sustainability courses for those who want to know about it in the context of their primary studies. Each of these "levels of intensity" has substantial audiences and satisfies an important need in our educational framework.

The success of any curriculum is most directly reflected in the impact on students and their future achievements. Clearly, we need sustainability graduates to be leaders, to be change agents, and not simply someone who wants to fit into already well-established career tracks. Given that in many ways students are ahead of faculty in their early commitment to sustainability, students should often assume the role of teachers, and professors should be students. Toward that end, students at the SOS are key to organizing solutions workshops, running their own reading groups on topics of their choice, and holding a monthly town hall where they raise questions and suggest solutions to faculty, staff, and administrators of the SOS. As an additional outlet for their creativity and to solicit input from those outside the SOS they have formed their own journal, *The Sustainability Review*, that is open source and available globally (http://www.thesustainabilityreview. org/). Our hope is that each graduate in their thesis work and in their career will demonstrate an understanding of and the ability to apply five basic elements of sustainability. Students should first possess an *awareness* of the challenges facing society and the interconnectedness of the world; second the *creativity* to deliver innovative solutions; third, they will be *stewards* of natural, cultural, and human resources; fourth, promote *institutions* that continuously learn, anticipate, and adapt; and finally, they should hold *values* that enhance inclusiveness, equity, and justice in all that they do.

Although the initial curriculum and structure of the SOS, albeit with continuing modest refinements, may be judged to be most effective to offer, the faculty and students of the SOS have immersed themselves in an all-encompassing inquiry as to whether to continue in the established direction or to once again fundamentally reorganize ourselves and what we are doing (see Miller *et al.* 2011 for a discussion of the reorganization of academic units as an example of the adaptive cycle from resilience theory [Gunderson and Holling 2002]). Although the SOS has been established as an independent administrative unit with a mandate to create a novel approach, the reality is that the inertia of traditional approaches is difficult to overcome. A major stimulus for change has come from the addition of new, junior faculty. These are the first faculty who were hired directly into the SOS and hence are more inclined to consider it as fundamentally new and distinct from existing disciplines rather than a transitional unit whose value derives from effectively joining together approaches developed in the antecedent disciplines. Whether the SOS ultimately develops into a more closely integrated set of previously established perspectives or a wholly novel and distinctive perspective of its own is yet to be determined, but in the act of self-evaluation a set of six "cornerstones" has emerged as defining the SOS and its aspirations.

First, we focus on identifying and addressing a series of sustainability challenges/opportunities that we refer to as "wicked problems" (Kates and Parris 2003). By that we mean they are important, urgent, and complex and do not yield to simple solutions or optimal tradeoffs. Eliminating poverty, protecting biodiversity, and mitigating human-caused climate change are all examples of sustainability challenges recognized for decades by many, but still without adequate solutions. Unfortunately, the tools of traditional science have proven to be ineffective in solving these challenges (Grunwald 2007; Ramo 2009) given their high level of uncertainty, the need to incorporate conflicting value systems, and the complexity of solving these types of global problems at one locality at a time. Sustainability science requires a new paradigm, and the educational system must be transformed to accommodate it.

Second, there are multiple ways of knowing, and in fact there may be more than one "truth" for each situation. A study that incorporates the methods of one discipline is almost certain to result in an incomplete picture of the phenomenon, despite most practitioners' belief that their disciplinary methodology produces complete knowledge. If multiple different perspectives are employed in an inquiry a fuller picture emerges, though sometimes aspects of the results may be in conflict. The goal is for sustainability scientists to employ epistemological pluralism to develop methodologies that encourage the maximum input while creating the means to integrate these findings (Miller *et al.* 2008). This approach to interdisciplinarity requires mutual respect among practitioners as well as a working knowledge of the collaborating perspectives. The goal is not necessarily to find the middle ground among the perspectives or to treat them as if each one would add its own unique data, but rather to provide a space for each one to enrich and alter the approach of the others so that a new approach is employed, distinct from the traditional approaches that preceded it.

The third cornerstone is that research and problem solving should not be seen as separate activities and that scientists, practitioners, and stakeholders should work together in the co-production of knowledge (Cash *et al.* 2003; Kates *et al.* 2001). We use the term transacademic to indicate the kind of work that goes well beyond the bounds of academia to enlist the help of people who have worked on a problem and who often have a direct interest in its solution. To be most effective, this type of partnership should start early in the process, when the problems are being defined and the investigative methods developed. In some cases the solution to pressing challenges may also result in new theoretical insights, as suggested by what Stokes has termed "Pasteur's Quadrant," a class of research methods that both solve scientific problems and generate societal benefits (1997). The distinction between "basic" and "applied" research that has emerged in traditional disciplines becomes much fuzzier (or non-existent) when viewed from a sustainability perspective. This has enormous implications for a reorganization of the faculty reward structure (especially promotion and tenure expectations), and how graduate students are encouraged to design their careers. It also means that conducting research and problem solving becomes more contextual since the times, places, and people involved in each situation are unique. In addition, it must be acknowledged that research and problem solving are reflexive activities in which the investigators may have both explicit and implicit impacts on the course of investigations and the ultimate results (Grunwald 2004). Despite the unrealistic expectation of complete objectivity and detachment often attributed to the "scientific method," sustainability scientists must accept the additional challenge of explicitly and intelligently dealing with the importance of context and the implications of reflexivity.

If the solution of real-world problems is at the core of sustainability science, then it is apparent that real-world learning experiences (RWLEs) should be an essential element of the educational process at every level (Brundiers et al. 2010). This is the fourth cornerstone. Effectively, working with problems and people in the real world necessitates a series of skills and experiences that are not often emphasized or even available in the normal academic career. RWLE promote working with students from different disciplinary backgrounds, working effectively in teams, communicating and working with those outside academia, and the ability to lead and find ways to bring together the differing values and opinions of those you work with or serve. At an advanced graduate level this may take the form of the "solution workshops" described in the SOS curricula, where real-world problems are identified, often specific clients are secured, and teams of faculty and students with diverse backgrounds collaborate to find sustainability solutions. RWLEs should be available in other forms such as internships, and we also believe that most classes should have some aspect of this in their syllabus, even if it is as simple as a visiting lecturer from the community, or a class visit to a local agency or company. At an even earlier stage in the curriculum one might have class projects that involved RWLEs on or off campus, role-playing activities, and team-building exercises.

The fifth cornerstone is an explicit concern with possible future states, with the objective of moving the system toward sustainability. Part of this is an emphasis on change as a normal condition and a willingness to consider even more dramatic transformations as essential to moving the system toward a more sustainable state. Another element of this approach is being able to work with possible, expected, as well as desired futures generated from a variety of methodological approaches such as simulation modeling, scenario analysis, and uncertainty analysis (Swart et al. 2004). Implicit in an emphasis on futures is recognizing the necessity of working with input from stakeholders, and an ability to incorporate diverse values attributed to alternate outcomes by different participants. The planning and managing for particular conditions in the future implies the ability to deal with numerous tradeoffs in which there will be winners and losers. Beyond that there is a high degree of uncertainty in what will happen even with the best planning, so the nature of the tradeoffs will continue to shift over time.

The final cornerstone of a sustainability education is that graduates have a series of additional competencies beyond the basic ones expected in most academic fields (de Haan 2006; Wiek et al. 2011). There are basic skills and abilities, such as critical inquiry, quantitative and qualitative analyses, and written communication that are widely promoted, and sustainability professionals will benefit from them as well. There are others that are essential to sustainability research and problem solving that may be valuable in other fields as well but are often not explicitly recognized or taught. In fact, for many disciplines specific competencies are not explicitly identified, but rather "good pieces of research" are cited as defining the field and what students should aspire to. Beyond specific methods of data collection and analysis, the student is not directed at the real personal competencies that may have made that research effective. This traditional approach to directing graduate education has the unintended consequence of promoting business as usual and equating quality research with an appeal to authority. Sustainability science education cannot rely on implicit objectives, assume that a student learns by "experience," nor should the field aim to replicate what has been achieved in the past. If transformatory research and problem solving is the objective, then we must be ready to break with past practices. From a review of the growing literature on key competencies in sustainability education and our own experience at the SOS we have proposed five competencies that are essential to successful sustainability research and problem solving (Wiek et al. 2011) (see Figure 15.1). *Systems thinking* is key to understanding the challenges, how they are situated in the larger world, and the cascading sets of implications of various actions. *Anticipatory competence* allows one to envision and construct possible, likely and desirable futures for the system under study. In thinking about alternative futures, and decision-making in general, it is necessary to weigh the values of various outcomes as they are held by the different stakeholders. This *normative competence* is rarely emphasized in scientific pursuits, but if we are to be effective in guiding the future we must be able to incorporate values, perceptions, and attitudes. In order to achieve the desired futures and values, one must have the *strategic competence* of being able to formulate the strategies to implement sustainability ideas in actual real-world settings. The final item on our list is *interpersonal competence*,

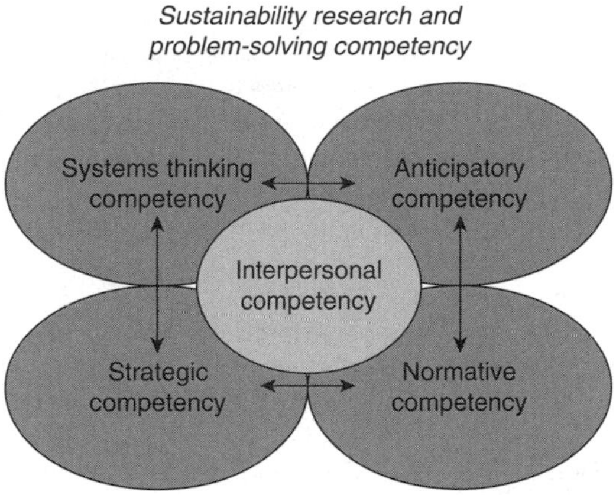

Sustainability research and
problem-solving competency

FIGURE 15.1 Sustainability research and problem-solving competencies (adapted from Wiek et al., 2011)

which involves teamwork skills, communication abilities, and leadership qualities. These skills are widely acknowledged as essential, but are rarely an explicit part of graduate science education.

The question that all of this has brought to the fore is whether sustainability education should be a gradual transition from current interdisciplinary programs adhering to and intensifying many of the approaches already current at research universities, or does it require a true transformation in our conduct of research and problem solving? Can we radically improve interdisciplinarity through epistemological pluralism, becoming disciplinary translators, infusing real-world learning experiences at all educational levels, valuing applied alongside basic research, and restructure our educational pedagogy around the five new core competencies of sustainability education?

These are difficult questions to answer without years of experience at attempting each alternative and tracking the success of graduates of both. It is likely that both positions have in training sustainability practitioners and should be pursued. One would expect that the first alternative of intensifying the interdisciplinary collaboration of current disciplines will be followed by the majority of programs and hence it is our belief that it is the obligation of SOS and other willing institutions to follow the radical program of experimenting with the developing of a tranformatory approach to meeting the grand challenges of sustainability.

References

Arizona Board of Regents, 2005. *A New American University*. Tempe, AZ: Arizona State University.

Brundiers, K., Wiek, A. and Redman, C.L., 2010. Real-world learning opportunities in sustainability: from classroom into the real-world. *International Journal of Sustainability in Higher Education*, **11**(4), 308–324.

Cash, D.W., Clark, W.C., Alcock, F., Dickson, N.M., Eckley, N., Guston, D.H., Jäger, J. and Mitchell, R.B., 2003. Knowledge systems for sustainable development. *Proceedings of the National Academy of Sciences of the United States of America*, **100**, 8086–8091.

de Haan, G. 2006. The BLK '21' programme in Germany: a 'Gestaltungskompetenz'-based model for education for sustainable development. *Environmental Education Research*, **1**, 19–32.

Grunwald, A., 2004. Strategic knowledge for sustainable development: the need for reflexivity and learning at the interface between science and society. *International Journal of Foresight and Innovation Policy*, **1**(1–2), 150–167.

Grunwald, A., 2007. Working towards sustainable development in the face of uncertainty and incomplete knowledge. *Journal of Environmental Policy and Planning*, **9**(3), 245–262.

Gunderson, L. H. and Holling, C.S. (eds), 2002. *Panarchy: Understanding transformations in human and natural systems*, Washington, DC: Island Press: 25–62.

Kates, R.W. and Parris, T.M., 2003. Science and technology for sustainable development special feature: long-term trends and a sustainability transition. *Proceedings of the National Academy of Sciences of the United States of America*, **100**(14), 8062.

Kates, R.W., Clark, W.C., Corell, R., Hall, J.M., Jaeger, C.C., Lowe, I., McCarthy, J.J., Schellnhuber, H.J., Bolin, B., Dickson, N.M., Faucheux, S., Gallopin, G.C., Grübler, A., Huntley, B., Jäger, J., Jodha, N.S., Kasperson, R.E., Mabogunje, A., Matson, P., Mooney, H., Moore, B. III, O'Riordan, T. and Svedin, U., 2001. Sustainability science. *Science*, **292**(5517), 641–642.

Miller, T.R., Baird, T.D., Littlefield, C.M., Kofinas, G., Chapin, F. III and Redman, C.L., 2008. Epistemological pluralism: reorganizing interdisciplinary research. *Ecology and Society*, **13**(2), 46.

Miller, T., Munoz-Erickson, T. and Redman, C.L., 2011. Transforming knowledge for sustainability: towards adaptive academic institutions. *International Journal for Sustainability in Higher Education*, **12**(2), 177–192.

Ramo, J., 2009. *The Age of the Unthinkable*. Chapter 1, The Nature of the Age: 3–19.

Rowe, D., 2007. Education for a sustainable future. *Science*, **317**(5836), 323–324.

Stokes, D.E., 1997. *Pasteur's Quadrant: Basic science and technological innovation*. Washington, D.C.: Brookings Institution Press.

Swart, R., Raskin, P. and Robinson, J., 2004. The problem of the future: sustainability science and scenario analysis. *Global Environmental Change,* **14**(2), 137–146.

Wiek, A., Withycombe, L. and Redman, C.L., 2011. Key competencies in sustainability – a reference framework for academic program development. *Sustainability Science*, **6**(2), 203–218.

16

TOWARD A RESILIENT ACADEMY

Richard M. Carp

Introduction

Peter Hay wrote that there are two schools of ecologists. One views ecology as a subdiscipline of biology; the other understands it to require a fundamental transformation of our lived, felt, and understood existence (2002: 132). I am among the latter; those who believe that, for example, better science or more technology will see us through will find little of interest here. Those who believe otherwise may find a greater understanding of our current situation as scholars and teachers, as well as some resources for working our way into more sustainable knowledge and action.

The human capacity to provide for ourselves and our progeny a congenial life of material sufficiency and experiential joyfulness is in peril, in large measure because of the effects of our own actions.[1] Our understanding of the world and our place in it is largely responsible for this peril, because people do what we do because it makes sense for us to do so.[2] For our doing to change, so must our understanding (though the reverse is surely true as well). The academy is largely, though not entirely, responsible for the official regimes of truth and meaning that permeate society. Historically, as well as in the current moment, academic knowledge practices are complicit in creating, justifying, maintaining, and applying the behavior that places us at risk. Those practices must transform, fundamentally and comprehensively. There are a variety of re/sources ready to hand to assist us with that task; they challenge the very bases on which our academic institutions, our academic disciplines, and our academic careers are based. They must do so, because those institutions, disciplines, and careers participate in patterns of relationships that fray, rather than support, the resilience of the social–ecological systems that provide the ecosystem services upon which our life depends.

This chapter, like its author, lives a dual life. On the one hand, this is a piece of academic writing, aimed at an audience of scholars/teachers and conforming to the protocols of the academy. On the other hand, it seeks to confound and disrupt those protocols, arguing that they participate fully in unsustainability. Such are the ironies of our time.

Academic Unsustainability

I argue here that the network of institutions that make up "the academy," which includes not only colleges and universities, but also (at least) professional and disciplinary organizations, its sources of funding, and its methods for distributing economic and status rewards, predominantly defray rather than support resilience. There are many ways in which this seems to be so. In a relatively brief chapter such as this we can only explore two of the most important. The first has to do with how we conceive and enact relationships between knowers and what is known, which are at odds with the lessons of ecology. The second has to do with the economics of the academy, which marry it to one of the primary engines of unsustainability.

Knower/Known Relationships

Oecos[3]-Logos

In the *oecos*, everything is related to everything else; everything is active, transforming in response to changes elsewhere, in turn effecting transformation through change, in an endless process. Change in one place changes everything, to some extent. Chaos theory warns us how hard it is to predict that extent, which may be more profound in a seemingly remote location than at a seemingly proximate one, in either time or space. Knowing participates in the *oecos*, and therefore changes it. There is nowhere "outside" from which to know. There are not two zones, one of ecology (nature) and one of culture (human), so that the question is of the impact of the culture on the ecology. Rather, cultural landscapes and their components participate fully in the developmental system of which they are a part. That is, culture participates in the process by which current activities "shape the context of development of their successors," a process joined into by all beings which engage in or affect "current activities," and one which, in its largest organic dimensions, we call evolution (Ingold 2000: 391).

Knowledge practices, therefore, are actions, and like all human actions they have practical and ethical, as well as conceptual, dimensions. Our knowledge practices are subject to judgments not simply of accuracy or adequacy, but of their effect on the health and well-being of social-ecological communities. Simply as a matter of survival, we are responsible to and for the *oecos* for our knowledge practices.

Acts of knowing are not acts of objectification (and correlative subjectification), but acts of participation which themselves enter into the ongoing cycle of transformation described above. For this reason, a sustainable (or a sustainability) curriculum would begin with the mutual interdependence and interpenetration of beings. As Thomas Berry put it, "The difficulty cannot be resolved simply by establishing a course or a program in Ecology, for Ecology is not exactly a course or a program; it is rather the foundation of all courses, all programs and all professions" (1996: 9). Moreover, as Ingold remarked, "ecology as presented in textbooks could be regarded as profoundly *anti*-ecological, insofar as it sets up an organism and environment as mutually exclusive entities (or collections of entities) which are only subsequently brought together and caused to interact" (19). Scholars "tend to study the system from a perspective of being outside whereas in fact they, too, are part of the system" (Walker and Salt 2006: 32).[4]

The logic of *oecos* (eco-logos) is a logic of dynamic relations, of transforming patterns composed of patterns in transformation.[5] The interconnection of what we study implies the interconnection of our knowledge about what we study and the practices by which we study; an ecology of being(s) requires an ecology of knowledge(s). This entails, at the very least, a sustained and consequential conversation among the various forms of study, what are now known as "disciplines," whereas today, "in the universities one discipline is rarely called upon to answer questions that might be asked of it by another discipline" (W. Berry 2001: 129; see also Walker and Salt 2006: 32).

The ecological crisis is not an "accident" of cultural development; it is a necessary correlate of our knowledge practices (cf. Carp 2001: 89; Lefebvre 1991: 412).

What Sort of Thing Is Truth?[6]

If ecological crisis results from our knowledge practices, we will have to alter them if we are to support resilience. "Truth" is a crucial component of knowledge, for "truth," or its analog, is used to distinguish understanding from error. In most academic work, we think of truth as a more or less accurate representation, in some dimension or set of dimensions, of an underlying reality. Truth is something like a map, and the most common touchstones of accuracy are replicability, prediction, and control.[7] If we take the science of ecology seriously, neither prediction nor control is possible (Walker and Salt 2006: 29).

I propose that a more adequate test of thought is not its "accuracy," but "its ability to contribute to practices of living well" (Carp 2001: 73). This raises many questions about the characteristics of "living well," but in the context of sustainability, it must include contributing to, rather than diminishing, resilience – supporting "the health and well being of human and natural communities [social-ecological systems]" (W. Berry 2001: 134). Subjecting our knowledge practices to this test and the critiques it implies would doubtless alter many of them.

Moreover, resilience thinking, rooted in evolutionary ecology, situates us in a world of dynamic and unpredictable change (Walker and Salt 2006: x–xi and *passim*). Our conduct emerges from the understandings and rationalizations that form part of our knowledge practices, while those practices (self justifying for the most part) are conduct themselves. This conduct effects unpredictable change, both because of the dynamic and uncertain character of the world, and because of the inevitably fallible and incomplete quality of our understanding, so that "part of what we need to know is how to change [adapt]. We must 'make room for surprises and ironies at the heart of all knowledge production; we are not in charge of the world.' (Haraway 1996: 125)" (Carp 2001: 73). Rather than "truth" (a collection of propositions or a set of maps) we should seek "truing" (the capacity for adaptive transformation) (cf. Carp 1991: 34–35).

This implies a new respect for the local and particular. Currently, that something can be done everywhere is a test of its truth (it is universal). In a truing context, something is valid only if it enhances the health of the social–ecological community in which it takes place. The sheer capacity to do is a test only of power, not of validity. The "larger" scale does not necessarily take precedence over the "smaller," since cross-scale effects take place in both directions (Walker and Salt 2006: 90–91). Kudzu certainly can grow in the American South (it *is* true); whether it contributes to the health and wellbeing of the region is another question altogether (it *doesn't* true). Expert knowledge often acts like kudzu. For truing, the social–ecological community is the final judge.[8]

The Socio-Cultural Oeco-Logos of Unsustainability

Unsustainable economic and political practices and systems have developed in dynamic relationship with the academy and its knowledge practices. From the standpoint of *oeco*-logic this is no surprise. Nothing is the result of a single cause; rather there is "the creative unfolding of an entire field of relations within which beings emerge and take on the particular forms they do, each in relation to the others" (Ingold 2000: 19). This pertains at each scale, and therefore characterizes social, political, and economic development as much as natural ecologies. We can best understand unsustainability as a resilient, but destructive, social–cultural system with an ecological form. The academy has from the beginning participated in the patterns of relationships that degrade the resilience of the social–ecological networks on which human life depends.

The history of unsustainability is also the history of particular understandings of and actions in the world. To the extent that this is a history of "the post-Enlightenment West" and its global effects, it is the history of the academy and its knowledge practices. Academic knowledge provided the technical means as well as the ethical rationales for the conquest of nature, women, and the non-European world (Carp 2001: 92). Meanwhile, the growth and development of academic knowledge has depended on a network of technical, economic, political, and military forces. The history of science parallels the history of technology; scientific advances rely as much on new technical laboratory capacities as technological developments in the wider society rely on scientific breakthroughs. Both require the complex economic, political, and military networks that have made them possible (Haraway 1996: 118).

The question before us today is whether we can transform our knowledge practices so that they move our socio-cultural ecology into a basin of attraction amenable to the long-term well-being of human individuals and our species. The economics of the academy (how we pay for knowledge workers and research and how we justify our work to students, parents, and other stakeholders) creates a substantial obstacle to doing so.

The Economics of the Academy

Paying for Knowledge Workers and Research

The academy is driven by what can be funded, who will fund it, and why. What economic interests does the academy serve? Predominantly those of the mainstream economic (and political and military) forces of our time; those very forces that fray resilience. Faculty members are evaluated, rewarded, retained, or fired, based in part on their ability to bring in external funding. This also affects who goes to graduate school, what paths they follow through it, and what they study. Because faculty members and graduate students teach undergraduates, the effects trickle down there as well.

As Wilson put it there is, "a cardinal principle in the conduct of scientific research: Find a paradigm for which you can raise money and attack with every method of analysis at your disposal" (1998: 157). This principle applies with equal force in the social sciences: work that can be done is work that can be funded. One might think the humanities would be exempt, but this is hardly the case: pressure for external funding in the humanities is high, though funding itself is scarce, and the humanities are subsidized by administrative funds raised by others.

Unsurprisingly, money available for research serves funders' interests. Money is predominantly available based on two criteria: economic worth (profit enhancement) or military application (state security). Yet it is vanishingly unlikely that either capitalism or the nation state will prove to enhance resilience, the former (at least) because limitless expansion in a limited system is impossible, the latter (at least) because national boundaries bear little resemblance to bio-regions or other ecological forms.[9]

"Professors," wrote Paul Feyerabend, "serve masters who pay them and tell them what to do: they are not free minds in search of harmony and happiness for all…" (1987: 315). As Wendell Berry put it, "The faculties and administrations of universities are inexcusably bewildered between the superstition that knowledge is invariably good and the fact that it can be monetarily valuable and also dangerous" (2001: 144, see also 122, 68, 63).

Selling Education to Students, Parents, Taxpayers, and Donors

Economic justifications are also the primary reasons education is held to be important. Students are told to go to college because it will increase their earning potential. Parents are asked to pay for education to enhance their children's financial capacities. Donors and taxpayers are enticed with promises of students' economic well-being and of larger-scale economic development. While we sell education to students on the promise that they will succeed in the world economy, that economy degrades the resilience of the *oecos* on whose ecosystems services we depend (Walker and Salt 2006). We promise students that they will contribute to unsustainability!

Articles in newspapers and online ask whether a college education is a "good investment," comparing the cost of college with graduates' lifetime earning power. A Google search of "is college worth it" (19 August 2010), displayed articles from *The New Yorker*, *The Washington Post*, *Business Week*, PBS, and *The Huffington Post*, on the first page, the oldest of which was 19 March 2010. The UNC System's *UNC Tomorrow Final Report* (Phillips, 2007) repeatedly stresses the importance of the UNC system in North Carolina's economy, focusing primarily on "global competitiveness." On page 4, the commission summarizes its findings in three points, each of which emphasizes this factor. Although the report repeatedly uses the phrase "personal and professional" (*passim*) to describe the purpose of education, nowhere in the first 15 pages was there any mention of educating students for non-economic components of quality of life, although page 8 seems to assume, without in any way demonstrating, that the education imagined in the document will lead to "improving the quality of life," including providing "an intellectual and artistic environment that makes for a full, meaningful life." How it will do so is left to the imagination. Page 13 of the report makes it clear that humanities and arts should be taught because they enhance the learning of "soft skills" necessary for career success, not because they have intrinsic or non-economic significance.[10]

In contrast, Csikszentmihalyi (1993) stated that the arts and humanities, properly understood and taught for their own significance rather than their contribution to economic success, may provide an antidote to our addiction to endless consumption. Material culture, he writes, "compete[s] with humans for scarce resources" (20); our survival depends on establishing a relationship with material culture that builds, rather than frays, resilience. The antidote to an "addiction to objects" is "a genuinely rich symbolic culture...poetry, songs, crafts, prayers, and rituals..." (28). If he is right, the doorway to resilience opens in a revised practice of the academic backwaters of art, music, theatre, religion, and philosophy.

Livelihood is of course necessary, as is governance. We and our students are faced with the conundrum of how to live in a process of continuous transformation that moves our economics and our governance toward forms that support resilience. An academy devoted to sustainability would commit its intellectual and financial resources toward resolving that conundrum.

Re/Sources for a Sustainable Academy

It is not at all clear that the modern disciplinary academy can transform into a sustainable institution. Perhaps we need a new locus of education, analogous to the rise of new knowledge practices associated with the humanities, enabled by the appearance of an economic and political counterforce to the Church and the divinities – the princely courts of mercantile capitalists (Carp 1997b). Perhaps new knowledge practices await an alternative contemporary political and economic locus; perhaps knowledge, politics, and economics must transform in tandem, mimicking the evolution of ecologies.

On the other hand, some may argue that even if the critique articulated above is correct, we will for a long time need transitional knowledge practices associated with the network of industry, science, technology, social science, and humanities currently practiced in the academy. This may be true, but it is, at best, a rearguard action which may provide additional time for more fundamental change. Like the argument that we need to continue to harvest and burn oil and coal and build nuclear reactors, an argument on behalf of the academy as it is may be correct in the short term, but is unsustainable in the longer term. Change is coming; we will either help to shape it and learn to ride it, or we will be inundated by it.

Below I briefly discuss four re/sources I find useful in imagining and beginning to instantiate new knowledge practices more likely to support resilience: contemporary indigenous education; scholars' bodies; reflexive commensality; and assets-based community relations. We can understand each as an academic knowledge, since I present them here as they have come to me in scholarly works. Yet these works point toward and attempt to embody extra-academic knowledge practices; any academy that took them seriously and made them central would be very different than the one we now inhabit.

Knowledge is not just (not even primarily) ideas in minds or media. It corresponds to practices "for organizing schemes of perception, appreciation, and action, and for inculcating them as tools of cognition and communication" (Lenoir 1993: 82). I invite you, as you read these brief introductions, to imagine putting these re/sources into effect. How would your knowledge practices change or stay the same? How might they affect the material conditions of your daily life: what you do with your body; where you do it and in relationship with what material culture; how would they affect your social relationships, both their form and also with whom you relate; how might your "perception, appreciation, and action" change or stay the same?

Contemporary Indigenous Education

The word "survivance" describes the fact that, despite substantial obstacles, many indigenous peoples are both surviving and thriving, without being crushed by or capitulating to modernity.[11] Many of these peoples engage in practices that seem better adaptive to supporting resilience than our own. Walker and Salt (2006) note that "many traditional societies and small scale farmers" engage in resilience thinking and practices (xi).

One primary contributor to indigenous resilience is the survivance (continuity and transformation) of indigenous knowledge practices, transmitted through indigenous education. Perhaps we have something to learn from contemporary indigenous education as we imagine how to transform our own?

Dr Gregory Cajete (Tewa), Director of the Native American Studies Program at the University of New Mexico, has articulated "an ecology of indigenous education" (1994). It is an example of the paradigm of locale: although he expresses what he believes to be universal phenomena, he knows that he does so in particular (not universal) terms; although he believes his principles apply in every indigenous context, he recognizes that each realization of them will be unique to those contexts (18–19). Beyond that, they are applicable to education in the "developed" world, "if our collective future is to be harmonious or whole, *or* if we are even to have a viable future to pass on to our children's children" (23; see also 25–26; 78).[12]

Cajete presents a genuine ecology of ideas and images. It would be as presumptuous to summarize it as it would be to summarize, e.g., the ecology of the giant redwood forests. Here I will make only a few remarks:

- The whole social-ecological pattern is sacred (individual and social human life depends on its well-being);
- Individual persons are always already social persons. Isolating individuals conceptually or practically violates their factual being;
- Education does not primarily take place in institutions, but in lifeways, which are always also cultureways and *oecos*ways. Institutions can support education;
- Education is a lifelong process and cultural forms must recognize and support education at all moments of life. People cannot appropriately be "graduated" from educational institutions and then left to themselves to be or not be "lifelong learners." Culture and society are organized to provide educational forms, and teachers, throughout life, though not necessarily constantly;
- Education is correlated with personal development (which is always also social and ecological development). Although education may facilitate development, people can only learn what is appropriate to (makes sense from) their developmental stage;
- Wisdom is more important than, though no substitute for, knowledge;

- Learning is, and depends on, ethical as well as cognitive factors (heart and mind together). Humility, respect, honesty (including about one's self), are necessary components of education;
- "True learning and gaining significant knowledge does not come without sacrifice and at times a deep wound" (228);
- Knowledge and action are inseparable;
- All the senses are necessary for genuine education.

For indigenous education, knowledge is always bodily; there is not a mind somewhere and a body somewhere else. Rather there is bodymind always already in relationship with social-ecological context. This directs us to consider our own bodies as they participate in knowledge practices.

Scholars' Bodies[13]

"As both Michel Foucault and Pierre Bourdieu have urged, attention to discipline is not merely a concern about institutions and professionalization; it is above all concern about bodies – human bodies" (Lenoir 1993: 82). In the academy, we dream of eternal, universal knowledge, of meaning without context. To maintain the dream as reality, the actual contexts of academic work must disappear, most especially scholars' bodies, since the academy can pretend to present universal knowledge only by claiming academic bodies require no special discipline, a claim we know from our own experience to be false.

A sustainable academy requires, in Paul Stoller's words, that we "reawaken profoundly the scholar's body" by fusing "the intelligible and the sensible" (1997: xv). Doing so requires that we "eject the conceit of control in which mind and body, self and other are considered separate. It is indeed a humbling experience…" (xvii), which necessitates becoming conscious of and responsible for, among other things, the "assembly of unarticulated, non-verbal skills" required to do various kinds of academic work, and their involvement in the appearance of their objects of study (Lenoir 1993: 71).

We live as bodied creatures, participating fully in material socio–ecological communities. We want to sustain our successors' bodily survivance, to enhance the resilience of material patterns of the *oecos* that support human well-being. To do so, we will have to acknowledge fully the bodily character of our knowledge practices, and adjust them accordingly, effecting "a mixing of head and heart…an opening of one's being to the world – a welcoming" (Stoller 1997: xviii).

Reflexive Commensality

Reawakening our scholar's bodies, we discover that they are social–ecological, always already formed by and forming other people and the material world, which is largely fashioned through human activity, taking the shapes of material culture.

Bodies participate in material culture; like all artifacts they are formed from raw materials (genetics, flesh) by its processes, structures, and forms (Carp 1997a: 288–299). Bodily activities, including perception and, therefore, the world perceived, are skilled practices "engendered from early infancy through culturally induced processes" that participate integrally in material culture (Carp 2001: 103; see also Carp 1997a). Because resilience is frayed by our material practices, achieving sustainability requires transforming those practices. Because our bodies are formed by those same material practices, achieving sustainability requires transforming our bodies. Because our perception, which gives us a world to know, is profoundly affected by our bodies' participation in material culture, achieving sustainability requires transforming our perceptual skills.

C. Nadia Seremetakis explores how memory, history, and sensation are embedded in and embodied by material culture. Skilled sensuous attention to material culture allows us to experience "*commensality…the exchange of sensory memories and emotions, and of substances and objects incarnating remembrance and feeling.* Historical consciousness and other forms of social knowledge are created and then replicated…through commensal ethics and exchange" (1994: 37).[14] Just as scholars' bodies have been anaesthetized, so commensality has been effaced in modernity, so that we experience our shared sensual exchanges as "banal, functional or literal and…private." Yet beneath the apparent universality of material modernity, other commensalities have "an underground existence as a repressed infrastructure of social knowledge" (Seremetakis 1994: 37–38). Underneath the dust of modernity, there are articulate sensory experiences that embody not only remnants of premodern worlds but also specific critiques of modernity. They produce and reproduce "social knowledge through the circulation of material forms" (38), embodying knowledge practices far removed from the academy, sites where "sensory memory is encapsulated, stored, and recuperated in…artifacts, spaces and temporalities of consumption, sharing and exchange" (128).

Learning to experience these commensalities provides both respite and insight. On the one hand, they can "constitute provisional refuge areas in the prevailing sensory cacophony" (125), a haven from the banal, private, mundanity of everyday life in modernity, which is largely devoid of metaphor or poesis, and is often experienced, ironically, as either anesthesia or as pain.[15] On the other hand, in their multiplicity, reflexive commensalities confound the academic dream of abstract universality, introducing us to "the reflexive interplay of multiple sensory realities" (125). These realities provide us with avenues to explore in our search for knowledge practices that support resilience.

They also introduce us to the politics of the senses (125–132), which is a pragmatic as well as an ethical concern. Diversity is a measure of ecological well-being, while the existence of multiple organisms that perform the same function strengthens resilience (Walker and Salt 2006: 69). Multiple commensalities work in a similar way in the social component of social–ecological systems, embodying a variety of lived understandings of the world and ensuring a range of potentially adaptive responses to disturbance, rather than a single "survive or die" response throughout the system. In knowledge practices, as in other components, the social–ecological world, "being efficient...leads to drastic losses in resilience" (7).

It is difficult to describe in a text how to tune into reflexive commensality, which must begin with sensory practices in social contexts. Patiently opening oneself to unfamiliar sensory experiences and practices, and returning to them until they begin to make sense is a start. Perhaps the simplest, though by no means the most enjoyable, starting point is to awaken to the commensalities of the academy, to the peculiar "nowhere" in which our work takes place. Abandoning the dream of a meaning independent of context, we can experience the sensory reality of the contexts of our meaning forms – exhibition spaces (museums and galleries), expression spaces (print pages and their electronic analogs), and learning spaces (classrooms, laboratories, and meeting rooms) – and of the meanings embedded in them. We need a close grained analysis, and an equally rigorous experience, of academic material culture and the bodies, spaces, and times associated with it.

Assets-Based Community Relations

If all you have is a hammer, all the world looks like a nail. If you are educated only to solve problems, all the world is filled with them; "solving" one only brings other problems to the fore. To achieve sustainability, we need a keen understanding not only of problems, but of the assets on which we can draw to resolve them.

In 1993, John Kretzmann (sociology and urban affairs) and John L. McKnight (human development and social policy) wrote "a guide about rebuilding troubled communities." In it they contrast two approaches, one focusing on "the community's needs, deficiencies and problems...the second...on a community's capacities and assets" (1). Although they focus on devastated neighborhoods, their approach is applicable to the whole *oecos*. They turn expertise on its head, focusing on the assets already present in a community, rather than on the knowledge experts bring into it. They recommend an "intense and self-conscious internal focus," which concentrates on strengthening relationships (9). Such work is inevitably particular and local, for each community's strengths and relationships (like those of each ecological community) are specific to it; another way of saying this is that diversity is recognized and valued. In this, as in many arenas, assets-based community development resembles the resilience thinking recommended by Walker and Salt (2006), who insisted that enhanced social–ecological resilience "needs to emerge through people working with their local systems" (151). As Kretzmann and McKnight insisted, the trick is to "*support* local invention... to *respond* to community rather than manage, replicate, and proliferate" (374). Diversity is a key value; each place and its components must be approached in terms of their local specificity, not as examples of larger categories to which they can be reduced (e.g. Walker and Salt 2006: 145–148; Kretzmann and McKnight 1993: 373).

Standardization (often embodied as expertise) is a problem, not a solution; local innovation is a key necessity, "one size doesn't fit all" (Kretzmann and McKnight 1993: 373; Walker and Salt 2006: 101). Knowledge practitioners can be helpful when they are servants of the community, understood integrally as social–ecological. Resilience is built when we "locate all of the available local assets [and] begin connecting them with one another in ways that multiply their power and effectiveness" (Kretzmann and McKnight 1993: 5).[16]

Looking Ahead

The contemporary academy is unsustainable. It participates in a socio-cultural pattern that has its own internal resilience (and therefore is difficult to change) but that degrades the sources of the ecosystem services on which it depends. If we are to transform the academy into something more sustainable, or to develop new institutions of higher education and research, we will need to find the assets for knowledge production available in every community in which we take place and to connect them in diverse and local ways to multiply their power and effectiveness. In this way, we may build genuinely sustainable academies.

Notes

1   Contemporary global economics and politics exhibit unsustainable characteristics, manifesting in increasing fragility in fundamental ecological support systems. "Sustainability" is a metaphor in which we try to imagine and enact modes of behavior that enhance, rather than degrade, the resilience of our social–ecological systems – their capacity to absorb disturbance and continue to function (Walker and Salt 2006). The problem is not only that ecosystem services on which we rely are diminished. Complex adaptive systems tend to settle into "basins of attraction," resilient conditions to which they return when disturbed. Under sufficient disruption, they will "flip" into a new, resilient basin of attraction, with different characteristics to the former basin (Walker and Salt 2006). We risk flipping the global ecology into a resilient basin of attraction far less amenable to human life.
2   I use "we" rather than the common "they" to empathize that you and I are part of the collective noun "people." If something is true of "people" it is true of you and me (us). Commonplace forms of language and experience routinely separate us from contexts to which we actually belong (ecologies, for example, as well as humanity). Talking and writing in ways that instead articulate our connections is one aspect of moving toward sustainability.
3   "Oecos," is a transliteration of the ancient Greek οἶκος (plural: οἶκοι), meaning "house" or "household." It forms the root of our "eco," as in ecology, economy, and ecumenical. I use "oecos" rather than "ecosystem" because of a critique of systems thinking which I cannot elaborate here, and because the metaphors we use to articulate

experience matter. "The *oecos*" as I use it refers to Earth's ecology in its largest context, "an *oecos*" refers to a more local ecology.

4 A critique of Walker and Salt (2006) would begin here; they often write as if people can manage or understanding as if outside.

5 In important ways, ecology and evolution imply one another. Perhaps we should talk about evocology or ecolution.

6 I have addressed this question at length elsewhere (Carp 2001: 72–74).

7 In the humanities, these may be replaced with adequate interpretation, measured by how convincing the argument is to other scholars, and the extent to which the argument is used and developed by them.

8 As my use of science indicates, I am not suggesting we simply abandon existing knowledge practices. We need what some have called a "successor science" (Haraway 1996: 111).

9 For the former, see, e.g. O'Connor (1994), Kovel (1988), and Harvey (2005). For the latter, see Princen (2005), Sagarin and Taylor (2008), and Anielski (2007). Giving up capitalist economics and nationalism may not be as painful as it seems at first. Anielski notes that, for citizens of the United States and Canada, the experience of well-being (including security and happiness) have not increased since WWII, despite the vast increase in monetary wealth (and armaments and other security apparatus) in those nations during that time.

10 We would find a similar pattern at almost any US college or university. See, e.g. Schmidt (2002).

11 *Survivance* combines survival and vitality, referring to culture's capacity to retain identity while adapting to continuously changing circumstance. It is formally similar to "complex adaptive system" (Bélanger 2000; Vizenour 1994; Rickard 2005).

12 There is no point romanticizing "noble indigenes"; indigenous peoples have harmed the *oecos*. Neither is there a point in dismissing their long-standing capacity to remain within stable and resilient basins of attraction. The difference in scale, scope, and impact on resilience between indigenous and modern and post-modern societies is massive.

13 This section draws heavily on Carp 2001: 99–104.

14 The ensemble of inarticulate skills required for academic work is a form of commensality.

15 The slow cities and slow food movements may be attempts to re-establish reflexive commensality in everyday experience (J. Carp 2012).

16 See Walker and Salt (2006) and Kretzmann and McKnight (1993) for examples.

References

Anielski, M., 2007. *The Economics of Happiness: Building genuine wealth.* Gabriola Island, BC: New Society Publishers.

Bélanger, C., 2000. Gérard Bouchard, the ideology of "*survivance*" and its corollaries. http://faculty.marianopolis.edu/c.belanger/quebechistory/readings/bouchard.htm (accessed 23 August 2010).

Berry, T., 1996. The university: Its response to the ecological crisis. Paper delivered before the Divinity School and the University Committee on Environment at Harvard University, 11 April 1996. http://www.spiritsdelight.com/berry2.html (accessed 14 August 2010).

Berry, W., 2001. *Life's a Miracle: An essay against modern superstition.* Washington, DC: Counterpoint.

Cajete, G., 1994. *Look to the Mountain: An ecology of indigenous education.* Rio Rancho, NM: Kivaki Press.

Carp, Jana. 2012. "The Study of Slow" in Bruce Goldstein, ed., *Collaborative Resilience: Moving Through Crisis to Opportunity*, pp. 99–125. Cambridge, Mass., MIT Press.

Carp, R.M., 1991. Rereading Coomaraswamy. *Art & Academe: A journal for the humanities and sciences in the education of artists*, 3(2): 24–37.

Carp, R.M., 1997a. Material culture and meaning: a historical and cross-cultural perspective. *Historical reflections/Réflexions historiques*, 23(3): 269–300.

Carp, R.M., 1997b. Metadisciplinarity: A provocation in the Humanities. *ERIC Clearinghouse* on Higher Education, ED#401 852. Abstracted in *Resources in Education*, April.

Carp, R.M., 2001. Integrative praxes: learning from multiple knowledge formations. *Issues in Integrative Studies*, 19: 71–121.

Csikszentmihalyi, M., 1993. Why we need things. In Steven Lubar and W. David Kingery (eds), *History from Things: Essays on material culture*. Washington, DC: Smithsonian Institution Press, pp. 20–29.

Feyerabend, P., 1987. *A Farewell to Reason*. New York: Verso.

Haraway, D., 1996. Situated knowledges: the science question in feminism and the privilege of partial perspective. In J. Agnew, D.N. Livingstone and A. Rogers (eds), *Human Geography: An essential anthology*. Oxford: Blackwell, pp. 108–128.

Harvey, D., 2005. *A Brief History of Neoliberalism*. Oxford and New York: Oxford University Press.

Hay, P., 2002. *Main Currents in Western Environmental Thought*. Bloomington, IN: Indiana University Press.

Ingold, T., 2000. *The Perception of the Environment: Essays in livelihood, dwelling and skill*. New York: Routledge.

Kovel, J., 1988. *The Radical Spirit: Essays on psychoanalysis and society*. London: Free Association Books.

Kretzmann, J.P. and McKnight, J.L., 1993. *Building Communities from the Inside Out: A path toward finding and mobilizing a community's assets*. Chicago, IL: ACTA Publications.

Lefebvre, H., 1991. *The Production of Space*. Trans. Donald Nicholson-Smith. Oxford and Cambridge, MA: Blackwell.

Lenoir, T., 1993. The discipline of nature and the nature of disciplines. In E. Messer-Davidow, D.R. Shumway and D.J. Sylvan (eds), *Knowledges:Historical and Critical Studies in Disciplinarity*. Charlottesville, VA: University Press of Virginia.

O'Connor, M. (ed.), 1994. *Is Capitalism Sustainable?: Political economy and the politics of ecology*. New York and London: The Guilford Press.

Phillips, J. *et al.*, 2007. University of North Carolina tomorrow commission final report http://www.northcarolina.edu/nctomorrow/UNCT_Final_Report.pdf (accessed 19 August 2010).

Princen, T., 2005. *The Logic of Sufficiency*. Cambridge, MA and London: The MIT Press.

Rickard, J., Tayac, G., Chavez, C.L. and McMullen, A., 2005. Our Worlds. An exhibit of the National Museum of the American Indian, Washington, DC. Transcribed on site 5 December 2005; input to computer 8 December 2005.

Schmidt, P., 2002. States push public universities to commercialize research: conflict-of-interest fears take back seat to economic development. *The Chronicle of Higher Education*, March 29: A26–A27.

Seremetakis, C.N., 1994. *The Senses Still: Perception and memory as material culture in modernity*. Chicago, IL: The University of Chicago Press.

Stoller, P., 1997. *Sensuous Scholarship*. Philadelphia, PA: University of Pennsylvania Press.

Vizenour, G., 1994. *Manifest Manners: Postindian warriors of survivance*. Lincoln: University of Nebraska Press.

Walker, B. and Salt, D., 2006. *Resilience Thinking: Sustaining people and ecosystems in a changing world*. Washington, DC: Island Press.

Wilson, E.O., 1998. *Consilience: The unity of knowledge*. New York: Knopf.

EPILOGUE

Lucas F. Johnston

The sustainability educator and consultant Hunter Lovins once told me that "if you look at what's driving unsustainability, it is largely, I think, the absence of […] conversations across values structures" (interview 6 August 2008). The cases and examples collected here are drawn from educators and professionals from a host of different disciplines, and from different sizes and types of institutions. Those who have authored these chapters are thus beholden to different communities of accountability with different sets of values. Finding convergences among those values requires first that we are explicit about them and, of equal importance, that we can facilitate conversations about the usually implicit values that our educational institutions endorse through business-as-usual discipline-based educational arrangements.

Conversations exposing these institutional values and the types of unsustainable leaders and communities they generate have begun, as the chapters collected here illustrate. Colleges and universities, professional schools, and in some cases broader disciplinary associations have begun to attend to the importance of place-based and problem-based learning. Such approaches throw the focus onto the multi-scalar *relationships* between individuals, the built environment, and the rest of their habitats, creating a learning environment that is more attuned to its ecological impacts.

All education is ultimately environmental education, as David Orr rightly noted. But the sort of picture that most students are getting regarding "the environment" and their relationship to it does not facilitate the development of the skill sets that will be needed to provide complex and multi-scaled solutions to the variety of interlinked social–ecological–economic issues that face us today. As Edward Abbey once put it, a formal education can be broadening, "but more often merely flattens." Most of us have devolved; we have lost the ability to make distinctions about categories of plants and animals that quite literally provided the foundation for our evolution into the dominant animal on the planet. Studies by evolutionary psychologists and cognitive anthropologists have noted significant differences in the ability to form folk categorizations among those who live in industrialized locales, and some politically marginalized indigenous groups who depend on their habitats for subsistence (Atran and Medin 2008). The nature deficit disorder that is symptomatic of this devolution was perhaps first noted nearly 40 years ago in the work of the human ecologist Paul Shepard (1973, 1982, 1986; see also Louv 2005), but his point remains crucially important today: the human genome was formed in the late Pleistocene, and we are now decimating the species with which we co-evolved and which allowed us to flourish. The biologist E.O. Wilson, drawing on the psychologist Erich Fromm, called this affinity of living things for other life "biophilia" – and it is eroding. For Orr, without profound experiences with nature in childhood, human survival is in question: "We will not enter this new kingdom of sustainability until we allow our children the kind of childhood in which biophilia can put down roots" (quoted in Northwest Earth Institute 2001: VI-12).[1]

I would only add that sustainability also depends on encouraging such "root development" among adolescents and young adults.

Providing the proper growth medium and climate for student flourishing is a difficult task, and it is becoming increasingly clear that it will require transformational educational institutions and a radical revisioning of the purpose and scope of education, as Redman and Carp have suggested in their contributions to this volume. The approaches detailed here offer a wide variety of perspectives, approaches, and goals, and even different definitions or understandings of sustainability. And they are all valuable. Together they represent something like an "ecology" of the social movement toward education for sustainability – multiple individuals, populations, and communities working at different scales to integrate new forms of learning into our institutions. It is a task that could take generations to complete, and yet by some accounts, the biophysical deterioration of earth systems demands that it happen much more quickly than that. Opportunities abound, as do obstacles. It is the ways in which we navigate these obstacles, solving for patterns (not just for specific problems), and including currently marginalized constituencies in decision-making (not just providing expert-based solutions), that will determine the sustainability of our educational systems, and ultimately our intertwined political, social, economic, and ecological systems. This is the challenge set before us. Let us hope, for posterity's sake, that we are up to it.

Note

1   The selection was drawn from Orr's "The Coming Biophilia Revolution" in his book *Earth in Mind* (1994).

References

Atran, S. and Medin, D., 2008. *The Native Mind and the Cultural Construction of Nature.* Cambridge, MA: MIT Press.

Northwest Earth Institute. 2001. *Exploring Deep Ecology.* Portland: Northwest Earth Institute.

Louv, R., 2005. *Last Child in the Woods.* Chapel Hill: Algonquin Books.

Shepard, P., 1973. *The Tender Carnivore and the Sacred Game.* Athens: University of Georgia Press.

Shepard, P., 1982. *Nature and Madness.* Athens: University of Georgia Press.

Shepard, P., 1986. *The Others: How animals made us human.* Washington, DC: Island Press.

ABOUT THE CONTRIBUTORS

Brannon Andersen is Professor and Chair of Earth and Environmental Sciences at Furman University, where he has taught for 18 years. He holds degrees in geology from Texas A&M University, Miami University, and Syracuse University. He headed the design and implementation of the new Sustainability Science major and was involved in the development of the sustainability master plan at Furman. His research interests include application of ecological footprint analysis to problems of sustainability, biogeochemical remediation in constructed wetland wastewater treatment plants, and the impact of urbanization on the biogeochem-istry of streams and rivers. All his research involves undergraduate students, and he was named Howard Hughes Medical Institute Distinguished Research Mentor in 2010.

Braum Barber is a professional engineer instructing in the School of Engineering Technologies at Lethbridge College. He has a BSc in Mechanical Engineering, a Master of Distance Education, and a graduate Certificate in Renewable Energy.

Patricia D. Brackin is a Professor in mechanical engineering at Rose-Hulman Institute of Technology. She is also a licensed professional engineer. Her main research interests are design methodology. As she tried to determine what every mechanical engineering student should know about sustainable design, she real-ized a multidisciplinary and holistic approach is necessary. This realization led to collaborations across the disciplines at Rose.

Chris Brown is Assistant Director and Internship Coordinator for the PGA Golf Management Program at the University of Nevada, Las Vegas.

Jeremy Bruskotter is Assistant Professor in the School of Environment and Natural Resources at the Ohio State University. His research interests emphasize the application of social and psychological theory and methods to the study of fisheries and wildlife management. He is particularly interested in how people make decisions related to fisheries and wildlife management, and the origins of resource-related conflicts, especially those that involve wildlife. To that end, his research focuses on understanding the psychological foundations of attitudes and behaviors in the context of fish and wildlife management.

Jack Byrne is the Director of the Sustainability Integration Office at Middlebury College. Byrne is co-founder of the non-profit Foundation for Our Future at the Center for a Sustainable Future. While there, he oversaw a six-year $18 million US Department of Education project, Education for a Sustainable Future – a national and international collaboration to develop technology based, K-12 curriculum, training programs, software and on-line resources about sustainable development. He is a founder and was the first Executive Director of River Watch Network, an international non-governmental organization supporting community-based watershed conservation. He also serves on the Commission for Education and Communication of the World Conservation Union. Byrne holds a BS in Biology from the Honors College at Kent State University and a master's degree in environmental law from the Vermont Law School.

Richard M. Carp is Vice Provost for Undergraduate Academics at St Mary's College of California. He holds a BA in political science from Stanford University, an MA in religion and art from the Pacific School of Religion, and a doctorate in interdisciplinary studies from the Graduate Theological Union in Berkeley. He works in the interstices of the academic study of religion, performance, semiotics, anthropology, cognitive science, material culture studies, and visual art and design. Recent publications include "Religion and material culture: methodological considerations," in *Handbook of Research Methods in the Study of Religion* (2011) Michael Stausburg and Steven Engler, eds, Routledge; "Seeing is believing, but touching's the truth: religion, film, and the anthropology of the senses," in *Teaching Religion and Film* (2008) Gregory Watkins, ed., Oxford University Press; "Integrative praxis: learning from multiple knowledge formations" – *Issues in Integrative Studies* (2001); and "Art, education, and the sign(ificance) of the self," in *Semiotics and Visual Culture: Sights, Signs, and Significance* (2004), Debbie Smith-Shank, ed., National Art Education Association. He has also received grants from the National Endowment for the Humanities.

Cynthia Carruthers, PhD, is a professor in the Department of Educational and Clinical Studies at the University of Nevada, Las Vegas. She has served on both university and college sustainability committees. Carruthers was a member of a UNLV William F. Harrah College of Hotel Administration task force that received a grant to infuse sustainability into the curricular, extracurricular, and administrative activities of the college.

Brittany DeKnight has been the Associate Director of the David E. Shi Center for Sustainability at Furman University since 2009. After completing her degree in Earth and Environmental Sciences and Political Science at Furman in 2007, she obtained a Master of Arts in Sustainability from the School of Sustainability at Arizona State University.

Dedee DeLongpré Johnston is the director of Sustainability at Wake Forest University. She has a bachelor's degree in business administration from the University of Southern California with a concentration in entrepreneurial studies and a master's of business administration with an emphasis in sustainable management from the Presidio School of Management in San Francisco. She has 18 years of experience in nonprofit management, primarily in the areas of education, sustainability, and the environment. DeLongpré Johnston was a founding board member of the Association for the Advancement of Sustainability in Higher Education. She was also named one of the 10 Innovators of the Year in 2007 by *Florida Trend* magazine and was featured in a cover story in the October 2008 issue of *Sustainability: The Journal of Record.*

Rebecca DeVasher earned her PhD in Chemistry in 2004 from the University of Alabama in conjunction with the Center for Green Manufacturing. Since accepting a position as Assistant Professor in the Department of Chemistry & Biochemistry at Rose-Hulman Institute of Technology in 2005, Dr DeVasher has consistently introduced and incorporated the best practices of Green Chemistry in General and Organic Chemistry, including curricular reform and development in the General, Engineering and Organic Chemistry sequences. In addition to a full teaching load in a primarily service-based Engineering program, she has promoted an active research program, funding over 30 undergraduate engineering and science student scholars. Most recently, she has joined a multidisciplinary faculty team at Rose-Hulman to develop, implement, and execute a living-learning community of scholars called the Home for Environmentally Responsible Engineering (HERE) program. The first HERE cohort of freshman began classes in Fall 2011.

James J. Farrell is Professor of History, American Studies, Environmental Studies and American Conversations. As an interdisciplinary scholar and teacher, Jim's teaching has been weird, if not innovative, including courses on Environmental History, the Mall of America, Nuclear Weapons and American Culture, Walt Disney's America, Consuming College Culture, and Campus Ecology. Despite this record, Jim was chosen as St Olaf's first Boldt Distinguished Teaching Professor in the Humanities, proving that Norwegians have a rich and refined sense of humor. At the end of the millennium, Jim chaired the committee that wrote *St Olaf 2000: Identity and Mission for the 21st Century*. As "John Cummins," Jim performs a one-man Chautauqua show based on the life of a nineteenth-century Minnesota pioneer. As "Dr America," he was also curator of the magnificent (but wholly imaginary) American Studies Museum on public radio station WCAL. Recently, as a member of the college's Sustainability Task Force, he's had a hand in the greening of St Olaf. With colleagues at Carleton College, he's facilitated a series of sustainability workshops on "Cows, Colleges and Curriculum." Most recently, he served as a member of the Association for the Advancement of Sustainability in Higher Education's Summit on Sustainability in the Curriculum, held February 2010 in San Diego, CA.

Laura Fieselman is the Sustainability Coordinator at Meredith College in Raleigh, NC. Fieselman established the sustainability office for the college in 2008 in response to a student call for increased attention to the campus environmental footprint. She now chairs the Sustainability Committee, comprised of faculty, staff, students, and alumnae and also supports the Sustainability Teaching and Learning Circle, a group of faculty focused on integrating sustainability into the curriculum. She works with faculty on classroom-based projects and supports the Environmental Sustainability major and minor. Her work includes greening campus operations with particular focus on energy conservation, waste reduction and alternative transportation options. Fieselman is passionate about community-based food systems and is the co-founder of Raleigh City Farm, a project that transforms unexpected downtown spaces into beautiful and nourishing farmland. Fieselman graduated with first-class honors from McGill University with a BA in International Development Studies in 2005 and received a Certificate of Permaculture Design in 2008. Prior to her work at Meredith College, Laura was the Environmental Sustainability Educator at Pacific University in Forest Grove, OR.

Angela C. Halfacre is professor in the departments of Earth and Environmental Sciences and Political Science at Furman University in Greenville, South Carolina. She also serves as the director of Furman's David E. Shi Center for Sustainability. Before returning to Furman, her alma mater, in 2008, she spent 10 years at the College of Charleston as a political science professor and director of the graduate program in Environmental Studies. She earned her PhD from the University of Florida in 1997. At Furman, she teaches courses in environmental policy, conservation, sustainability, and research methods. Halfacre also coordinates several curricular and co-curricular programs related to sustainability on campus and in the local community. Her research and publications examine public perceptions of sustainability issues, community governance, and environmental decision-making. She has published several peer-reviewed journal articles, and has a University of South Carolina Press book titled '*A Delicate Balance': Constructing a Conservation*

Culture in the South Carolina Lowcountry (2012) (which examines environmental perceptions and associated social movements in the Lowcountry region of South Carolina). Halfacre co-coordinates Furman's Sustainability Planning Council and chairs The Duke Endowment Task Force on Community and Environmental Sustainability. Halfacre serves on several boards of local and national conservation and community organizations including nonprofit Greenville Forward, City of Greenville Green Ribbon Advisory Council, and the Association for the Advancement of Sustainability in Higher Education Steering Committee.

Erik Z. Hayes is the Director of Residence Life at the Rose-Hulman Institute for Technology. He is a member of the Facilities Sustainability Team there, whose purpose is to expand the inclusion of student, faculty, and staff representation, and to promote the responsible management of resources through the reduction of waste, shared learning, and community involvement.

Åsa Heiter holds an MSc in Sustainable Infrastructure and Environmental Engineering, and since 1998 has been a Lecturer in the Department of Urban and Rural Development at the Swedish University of Agricultural Sciences. She is the former Director of Studies for the MSc in Sustainable Development.

Gregory E. Hitzhusen is a lecturer in the School of Environment and Natural Resources at The Ohio State University; he was the founding director and now serves as board chair of Ohio Interfaith Power and Light. His work and research focus on the intersection of faith and the environment and on developing partnerships between scientific and faith communities; his teaching centers on environmental communications, sustainability, and religion and ecology. He is a member of the Faculty Learning Community on Sustainability Across the Curriculum at Ohio State, and serves as a faculty fellow for the Environment and Natural Resources (ENR) Scholars program at OSU. Dr Hitzhusen was previously the national coordinator and co-founder of the NatureLink program at the National Wildlife Federation (NWF); co-founder of the Outings Club and Creation Spirituality groups at Yale Divinity School; associate with the National Religious Partnership for the Environment; and land stewardship specialist for the National Council of Churches Eco-Justice Programs. Greg has a BS in ecology (Cornell, *with honors*), an MDiv concentrating in ecotheology (Yale, *cum laude*), and a PhD in faith-based environmental education (Cornell). He has taught courses on creation care and outdoor ministry at Yale Divinity School and Wesley Theological Seminary; he also spent many years teaching outdoor skills, aquatic ecology, and geology for NWF's Wildlife Camp and Teen Adventure programs in North Carolina and Colorado, and developing and instructing outdoor leadership, fishing, and canoeing courses for Cornell Outdoor Education. He lives with his wife, Erica, and two sons (ages 4 and 7) in Columbus, Ohio.

Michelle Horhota is an Assistant Professor in the Psychology Department at Furman University in Greenville, South Carolina. She earned her PhD from the Georgia Institute of Technology in 2008. At Furman, she is a member of Furman's Sustainability Planning Council and has been involved in developing workshops to help faculty members infuse sustainability into their courses. Her research and publications related to sustainability examine perceptions of sustainability issues at both the campus and community level.

Richard House is Associate Professor of English at Rose-Hulman Institute of Technology. In addition to Shakespeare and American literature, his professional interests include rhetoric in science and engineering. He has published numerous articles on communication practices and genres in engineering workplaces, and on engineering communication curriculum and pedagogy. As an advocate for environmental concerns, he is active in several community initiatives at Rose-Hulman, where he helped to found the Home for Environmentally Responsible Engineering (HERE) program, and in Terre Haute, where he serves on the board of Our Green Valley Alliance for Sustainability.

Nan Jenks-Jay is Dean of Environmental Affairs and teaches Environmental Studies at Middlebury College in Vermont. For over two decades she has been advancing environmental studies and sustainability programs within higher education and broadening academia's role within the greater community. Jenks-Jay has been immersed in a spectrum of environmentally related work as an administrator, educator, ecologist, trustee, and consultant. She was associated with Williams College in Massachusetts for 15 years and now Middlebury for 14 years. In between, she took a sojourn to the West Coast, developing new undergraduate and graduate environmental programs for University of Redlands. At Middlebury, Nan Jenks-Jay has inspired an institutional culture through strategic planning and implementation that has propelled the College's exemplary environmental academic program and award-winning sustainability program to new heights. She has held appointments on international and national committees, state boards, commissions, and with NGOs. Jenks-Jay writes and speaks on topics related to the environment, sustainability and transformative change within higher education.

Lucas F. Johnston is Assistant Professor of Religion and Environmental Studies, and a Faculty Associate in the Center for Energy, Environment and Sustainability (CEES) at Wake Forest University. Dr Johnston's interdisciplinary educational background includes degrees in Religion and Nature, Environmental Ethics, Theology, and Psychology (2012). His research focuses on the relationships between biocultural evolution and religion, with particular attention to contemporary sustainability-oriented social movements and cross-cultural political dialog related to ideas about nature. He is the author of *Religion and Sustainability: Social Movements and the Politics of the Environment* (Equinox Press, 2012), and is the

Book Reviews Editor and Assistant Editor for the *Journal for the Study of Religion, Nature, and Culture*. In addition, Dr Johnston is the At-Large Interdisciplinary member of the Board of Directors for the International Society for the Study of Religion, Nature, and Culture, is on the Steering Committee for the Religion and Ecology Group at the American Academy of Religion, and is a 2012 Academic and Community Engagement (ACE) Fellow at Wake Forest.

Sanaz Karim is Research Assistant at the division of Environmental Communication in the Swedish University of Agricultural Sciences. She has worked with improving and upgrading the syllabus of a master program in Sustainable Development. She has a background in control and systems theory and her current interest is mainly the implications of systems thinking for Education for Sustainable Development.

Yen-Soon Kim is Assistant Professor at the William F. Harrah College of Hotel Administration at the University of Nevada, Las Vegas.

Katherine Kransteuber serves as Program Coordinator at the Shi Center for Sustainability at Furman University. A graduate of Furman, she returned to her alma mater after spending several years teaching outdoor education and completing her MS in Natural Resources at the Rubenstein School of Environment and Natural Resources at the University of Vermont. At the Shi Center, she coordinates student and faculty fellowships and the Center's community-based programs.

Erin Lindquist is an Assistant Professor in the Department of Biological Sciences at Meredith College in Raleigh, NC. At Meredith she coordinates their new Environmental Sustainability major and minor. She teaches introductory biology courses for non-majors, and several courses for biology and environmental sustainability majors including plant biology, environmental science, and terrestrial field studies. She also leads a summer study abroad course, Tropical Ecosystems, in Costa Rica for Meredith students. Her research focuses on forest ecology and conservation. She has maintained a long-term tropical forest regeneration study in Costa Rica and coauthored a bilingual plant taxonomy book of the trees of her study area with undergraduate students. Lindquist has also collaborated with various international colleagues to study the role of land crabs in tropical ecosystems. In Raleigh she and her students study the ecology of an urban, fragmented forest on the campus in collaboration with the Ecological Research as Education Network (EREN) which Lindquist serves as co-PI. They have established a long-term forest plot to investigate such topics as small mammal ecology, tree community structure, and herbivory and have co-authored papers on their findings. Dr. Lindquist graduated *summa cum laude* from Cornell University with a BS in the Biological Sciences in 1997 and received her PhD in Ecology from the

University of Georgia in 2003. Prior to coming to Meredith College in 2006, Erin was a Resident Professor with the Organization for Tropical Studies in Costa Rica for their undergraduate and graduate field courses.

Michelle Millar is an Assistant Professor in the Department of Hospitality Management at the University of San Francisco. Her research areas include consumer behavior, in particular the wants and desires of travelers when selecting accommodation or tourism destinations, and why they make the decisions they do. Michelle is also interested in how hotels relate to and work within the environment, and how we can make companies more environmentally friendly. Her research has been published in the *Cornell Hospitality Quarterly, Journal of Travel Research, Journal of Hospitality Marketing and Management*, and *Journal of Hospitality and Tourism Education*. She has also presented her research at hospitality conferences throughout the world.

Mark Minster is Assistant Professor of English at the Rose-Hulman Institute of Technology. His research focuses primarily on environmental literature, and literature and religion.

Thomas Jones is an associate professor in the Department of Hotel Management at the W.F. Harrah College of Hotel Administration at the University of Nevada, Las Vegas. His research interests include the fields of environmental, facilities, and housekeeping management. Dr. Jones has authored three textbooks on housekeeping management for John Wiley & Sons, a textbook on convention management for the Educational Institute of the American Hotel & Lodging Association, and a textbook on hospitality facility management for Prentice Hall. He is also the author of several refereed articles, particularly in the area of indoor environmental quality. He serves on the board of directors of the Cleaning Industry Research Institute (CIRI), is a member of the International Council on Hotel, Restaurant and Institutional Education (ICHRIE), and the International Sanitary Supply Association (ISSA), and in the past, he has served on the board of directors of the International Executive Housekeepers Association (IEHA), and is a past President of the Las Vegas Chapter of IEH. He holds a Bachelor of Fine Arts degree from the University of South Dakota, a Bachelor of Science and a Master of Science degree in Hotel Administration from the University of Nevada, Las Vegas and a Doctor of Education degree from Arizona State University.

Carola Raab has been employed at the William F. Harrah College of Hotel Administration at the University of Nevada, Las Vegas since 2005. She holds a Bachelor of Science degree in Hotel Administration from the William F. Harrah College of Hotel Administration, a Master of Business Administration degree from UNLV, and completed her PhD in Hospitality Administration at UNLV. Dr Raab has approximately 15 years of experience in the restaurant industry and has published extensively on topics applied to restaurants and hotels. Furthermore, she worked as a controller and an internal auditor. She has published research articles in the *Cornell Hospitality Quarterly, Journal of Foodservice Business Research, International Journal of Hospitality Management, International Journal of Hospitality and Tourism Administration, Journal of Hospitality & Tourism Research, Journal of Hospitality and Tourism Education, International Journal of Contemporary Hospitality Management, Journal of Human Resources in Hospitality Tourism,* and the *Pakistan Journal of Nutrition.*

Charles L. Redman has been committed to interdisciplinary research since, as an archaeology graduate student, he worked closely in the field with botanists, zoologists, geologists, art historians, and ethnographers. Redman received his BA from Harvard University, and his MA and PhD in Anthropology from the University of Chicago. He taught at New York University and at SUNY-Binghamton before coming to Arizona State University in 1983. Since then, he served nine years as Chair of the Department of Anthropology, seven years as Director of the Center for Environmental Studies and, in 2004, was chosen to be the Julie Ann Wrigley Director of the newly formed Global Institute of Sustainability. From 2007–2010, Redman was the founding director of ASU's School of Sustainability. Redman's interests include human impacts on the environment, sustainable landscapes, rapidly urbanizing regions, urban ecology, environmental education, and public outreach. He is the author or co-author of 14 books including *Explanation in Archaeology, The Rise of Civilization, People of the Tonto Rim, Human Impact on Ancient Environments* and, most recently, co-edited four books: *The Archaeology of Global Change, Applied Remote Sensing for Urban Planning, Governance and Sustainability, Agrarian Landscapes in Transition,* and *Polities and Power: Archaeological Perspectives on the Landscapes of Early States.* Redman is currently working on building upon the extensive research portfolio of the Global Institute of Sustainability and teaching in the School of Sustainability which is educating a new generation of leaders through collaborative learning, transdisciplinary approaches, and problem-oriented training to address the environmental, economic, and social challenges of the 21st Century.

Carrie Rich is the Senior Director of Vision Translation and System Office Administrator for Inova Health System. As part of the executive leadership team, Ms. Rich's role is to develop a system wide vision for Inova in the context of a changing health care environment, then translate that theoretical construct from governance to operations. In addition to these duties, Ms. Rich is responsible for all Communications and the Executive Office leadership of Inova Health System. Ms. Rich also serves as the Scholarship Chair of the National Capital Healthcare Executives (2009-present), Chair of the Board of Everybody Eats DC (2010-present) as well as Co-Founder and CEO of The Global Good Fund (2011-present). As an adjunct faculty member at Georgetown University,

Ms. Rich developed a Healthcare Sustainability curriculum for higher education, the first of its kind to teach sustainable operations to future health care leaders. Her global pursuits include rural outreach, computer literacy training and social enterprise. Ms. Rich serves as a pro-bono consultant to international nonprofits seeking business expertise.

Leona Rousseau is the Sustainability Coordinator in the Green Leadership Office at Lethbridge College and faculty member in the School of Media and Design. She recently served as Development Chair for the Alberta Association of Colleges and Technical Institutes (AACTI), focusing on campus and community sustainability. She holds a first-professional Bachelor's degree in Interior Design, a Master of Design in Education and is a doctoral candidate in Educational Technology.

Debra Rowe is the President of the US Partnership for Education for Sustainable Development (www.uspartnership.org), the National Co-coordinator of the Higher Education Associations Sustainability Consortium (www.aashe.org/heasc), Founder of the Disciplinary Associations' Network for Sustainability (www.aashe.org/dans), and Senior Advisor to the Association for the Advancement of Sustainability in Higher Education (www.aashe.org). She helps higher education associations and institutions to integrate sustainability into mission, curricula, research, student life, purchasing and investments, facilities and operations, and community partnerships. A professor of energy management and renewable energy at Oakland Community College, she consults with colleges nationally, has numerous publications and is often a keynote speaker at conferences. Dr. Rowe received her PhD in Business, her MBA and an MA in Psychology from the University of Michigan, and a BA from Yale University.

Paul Rowland became the Executive Director of AASHE on 1 August 2009. Paul was one of the founders of the Ponderosa Project at Northern Arizona University where he served in a variety of capacities including Director of the Center for Environmental Sciences and Education, Coordinator of Environmental Education, and Director of Academic Assessment. More recently he has served as Dean of the School of Education at The University of Montana and Dean of the College of Education at the University of Idaho. He holds a PhD in Curriculum and Instruction from New Mexico State University and an MS in Ecology and a BA in Biology from Rutgers University.

Tamara Savelyeva, PhD, studied education at Virginia Tech University after receiving her training in sustainability and environmental education at Cornell University. Her teaching and research areas include sustainability education, sustainability curricular modeling, and design of Global Learning Environments in higher education. Savelyeva has taught and coordinated multiple research and educational projects since 1992, when she directed her first sustainability education initiative supported by UNESCO. An active member of the European Academy of Natural Sciences, she serves on an Education Task Force for the Earth Charter International, Costa Rica and assists sustainability-related projects for other academic and non-for profit organizations. This work, which is international in scope, has resulted in a book *Global Learning Environment: Innovative concept and interactive model for changing academia and academics* (VDM, 2009) and a more recent publication, entitled "Campus sustainability: emerging curricula models in higher education" (co-authored with Jim McKenna, *International Journal for Sustainability in Higher Education*, 2011). Currently, Savelyeva works as a research fellow in the Faculty of Education at the University of Hong Kong.

Nadarajah Sriskandarajah has been Professor of Environmental Communication at the Swedish University of Agricultural Sciences in Uppsala, Sweden since 2007. His current research and education activities are in natural resource management contexts and fall within the emerging field of environmental communication: understanding society's ways of constructing environmental problems and negotiating its responses to these problems. Designing experiential curricula and promoting systemic thinking has been his approach to providing education for sustainability.

Corey Taylor earned degrees in English from Ursinus College and the University of Delaware. He is an Assistant Professor of English in the Humanities and Social Sciences department at the Rose-Hulman Institute of Technology. In addition to co-founding and teaching in the Home for Environmentally Responsible Engineering (HERE) program, Dr Taylor teaches numerous courses in American literature and technical and professional communication.

Ken Teeters is Professor at the William F. Harrah College of Hotel Administration at the University of Nevada, Las Vegas.

Stephen Trombulak is a conservation biologist and landscape ecologist, with particular interests in (a) the field biology of mammals, birds, and beetles, (b) the use of geographic information systems (GIS) to develop science-based conservation planning tools, and (c) natural history education. Dr. Trombulak teaches in both the Biology Department and the Program in Environmental Studies at Middlebury, with a primary focus on environmental science, vertebrate natural history, and conservation biology.

William Van Lopik is a geography and sustainable development professor at the College of Menominee Nation, a tribal college in northern Wisconsin. He previously worked for an international development organization in Costa Rica and El Salvador. He received his doctorate at Michigan State University in Resource

Development. His research interests are in traditional ecological knowledge, indigenous land rights, sustainability in higher education, and political ecology in Latin America.

Seema Wadhwa created and oversees the Sustainability Department at Urban Ltd. where she leads healthcare and other industries in pursuing enhanced environmental practices that align with business imperatives. She is currently the Director of the Healthier Hospitals Initiative and Director of Sustainability for Inova Health System. Ms. Wadhwa's industry experience extends to advising best practices in green building as prescribed by her professional accreditation as a Leadership in Energy and Environmental Design (LEED AP), and enabling a sustainable approach to the design and implementation of healthcare projects. Prior to these roles, Ms. Wadhwa spent several years in engineering management, uniting industry experience in the areas of project management and logistical planning with technical leadership in water management, urban design and environmental engineering. Ms. Wadhwa's leadership in promoting healthcare sustainability initiatives include pending publication of a book on sustainability for leadership (fall 2012), featured publications on teaching sustainability, guest speaking at national industry venues, content submissions for national healthcare symposiums and co-founding the national region alliance on healthcare sustainability with member hospitals, design professionals and industry partners.

Arnim Wiek (PhD in Environmental Sciences) is an Assistant Professor at the School of Sustainability, Arizona State University. He is involved in sustainability research projects on emerging technologies, urban development, resource governance, and climate change in different European countries, Canada, USA, Sri Lanka, Mexico, and Costa Rica. He has had research and teaching engagements at the Swiss Federal Institute of Technology Zurich, the University of British Columbia, Vancouver, and the University of Tokyo.

Robyn Wilson is an Assistant Professor of Risk Analysis and Decision Science in the School of Environment and Natural Resources at The Ohio State University. Her research focuses on the individual decision making process under risk and uncertainty. Specifically, she studies how individuals process information, and the influence that this has on perceptions of risk and ultimately individual decisions. She also teaches courses about the psychology of environmental problems and best practices for communicating environmental risk.

Tarah Wright is Associate Professor in the Faculty of Science at Dalhousie University, Canada, where she currently serves as the Director of the Education for Sustainability Research Group and has played a pivotal role in the successful creation of the Environmental Science Program and co-creation of the university's new and innovative College of Sustainability. Dr Wright's research focuses on the emerging field of education for sustainable development and she has published numerous papers covering a wide range of issues in sustainability and higher education. She serves on the editorial boards of the *International Journal of Sustainability in Higher Education*, and the *Encyclopedia of Quality of Life Research*, is a Member of the Scientific Advisory Board for Environmental Management for Sustainable Universities (EMSU), and is a co-organizer for World Sustainable Development Teach-In Day. Dr Wright and her family make their home in the city of Halifax, on the traditional lands of the Mic Mac people, in the Acadian Forest Bioregion, at the edge of the Atlantic Ocean.

Li-Ting Yang joined the faculty at the University of Southern California in the fall of 2011. Prior to joining academia, she held executive positions in several upscale international hotels over 14 years. Because of her extensive hotel executive experience, Dr Yang has taught a wide range of hospitality management courses in several major hospitality programs in Taiwan and the US for many years. Before joining USC, she was an adjunct professor at University of Nevada, Las Vegas. In 2009, Dr Yang was awarded the title of Certified Hospitality Educator (CHE) by the American Hotel and Lodging Educational Institute.

Adam Zwickle is a PhD candidate in the School of Environment and Natural Resources at The Ohio State University. His doctoral dissertation research focuses on integrating social psychological theory into the communication of environmental risks. Specifically, Adam is interested in using risk messages to encourage individuals to construe environmental risks more abstractly and increase the weight placed on their long-term consequences in the decision-making process.

INDEX

AASHE (Association for the Advancement
of Sustainability in Higher Education):
credits 16; models 2–3; purpose 81;
survey 81–2
ABET, Inc. 112
academic programs *see* sustainability
programs; individual institutions
actions 172, 223–5
ACUPCC (American College and
University Presidents Climate
Commitment) 87
adaptive model 7, 187–8
Agenda 21 45
American College and University
Presidents Climate Commitment
(ACUPCC) 87
analytical thinking 55
Angels for the Environment 11–12
approach, holistic curricular 142–3,
149–50
Arizona State University (ASU): creation
of school of sustainability 215;
education design aspirations 215–16;
five elements of sustainability 217;
Global Institute of Sustainability (GIOS)
215; interdisciplinary approach 216,
221; program cornerstones 218–21;
sustainability curriculum 216–18
assessments: life-cycle 174–7; Sustainability
Literacy Assessment 19–21
assets, community 233–4

assignments: Global Seminar curriculum
146–7; open-ended 157–9; research
171–2
Association for the Advancement of
Sustainability in Higher Education
(AASHE): credits 16; models 2–3;
purpose 81; survey 81–2
Association of American Colleges and
Universities survey 103–4
ASU (Arizona State University) *see*
Arizona State University (ASU)
Asun 173
attitudes 125, 131–3

Barcelona, Declaration of 54, 55–6
behavior 173–4
Bernard, Ted 91
bodies 231–2
Bonn Declaration 48
Braaten, Elise 154–5

Cajete (Tewa), Gregory 230–1
Call to Action 3, 81
campus ecology 159, 162–3
campus greening 140–1
CAPs (Climate Action Plans) 188
careers 22, 103, 104
carryover skills 161
case study method, Global Seminar (GS)
model 148
Cedar Ridge Quality Homes 169

CFAES (College of Food, Agricultural and Environmental Sciences) 29
challenges: College of Menominee Nation 86–7; curriculum 86–7; Global Seminar (GS) model 150–1; healthcare sustainability 97; interdisciplinary approach 113, 186; sustainability 185, 218; sustainability major and minor 24
change: cultural 214; ecology 225–6; interaction 224–5; process 129; unpredictable 226
change agents 46–8, 56, 217
characteristics, student 170
Checkland, Peter 68–9
citizen change agents 46–8, 56, 217
City of Lethbridge 169
Climate Action Plans (CAPs) 188
club, environmental 11–12
CMN (College of Menominee Nation) see College of Menominee Nation (CMN)
codes of ethics, engineering 111–12
cognition, conspiratorial 170–1
coherence 70, 76–7
cohort approach 120–1
collaboration: cross-disciplinary 14–15; Global Sustainability model 149–51; industry leaders 95–7; interdisciplinary 142–3; learning 73–4; teaching partnerships 139–40
College of Food, Agricultural and Environmental Sciences (CFAES) 29
College of Menominee Nation (CMN): background 82–4; challenges 86–7; climate change 87; conferences 90–1; faculty hiring 88; Global Perspectives Inventory (GPI) 89–90; grants 88; learning objectives 84, 89–90; Menominee Model of Sustainable Development 84–5; project-based learning 88–9; survey 87; sustainable development course content 84–5; values 83–4; workshops 91
colleges and universities see individual institutions
communities: assets 233–4; residential 120–1; troubled 233–4
community versus independent solutions 178–9
community visioning model 25
competencies: examples 48–55; hospitality education 124–31; incorporating 134–5; practical 183; sustainability programs 220–1

conferences: Earth Summit (World Conference on Environment and Development) 45; Engineering Education for Sustainable Development 54; First Do No Harm 104–5; First Intergovernmental Conference on Environmental Education 46–7; Sharing Indigenous Wisdom: An International Dialogue on Sustainable Development Conference 90–1; Summit on Sustainability in the Curriculum 81; United Nations Decade of Education for Sustainable Development 80; Wake Forest University 4; World Conference on Education for Sustainable Development 48
conspiratorial cognition 170–1
construction materials 174
consumer culture 157
consumption 179, 228
Corcoran, Blaze 54
Corcoran, Wals 54
cornerstones of sustainability programs 218–21
Cortese, Anthony 80
Council for Higher Education Accreditation 46
course evaluations 109–11
course list 15–16
course requirement 208
criteria, accreditation 112
critical thinking 172
Crow, Michael 215–16
Cullingford, Cedric 186
cultural change 214
cultural patterns 156, 157–9
cultural transformation 214
culture: consumer 157; material 231–2

Dalhousie University: background 202–3; challenges 207–8; college location 210–11; curriculum 204; declarations 202; double major 204; environmental initiatives 202–3; experiential learning 205; governance structure 211; interdisciplinary approach 203–4; problems 203; program development 206; program rewards 212; student organizations 203; survey 212; sustainability undergraduate program 203–5; teaching partnerships 210
Dall'Alba 117
data, financial 97

David E. Shi Center for Sustainability 191
Davis, Tom 83
Decade of Education for Sustainable
Development (DESD) 47–8, 124
Declaration of Barcelona 54, 55–6
declarations: Barcelona 54, 55–6; Bonn
48; Talloires 12, 141; Tbilisi 46–7,
55–6, 57; United Nations 141
degree programs see sustainability
programs; individual institutions
Deloitte 97
DESD (Decade of Education for
Sustainable Development) 47–8, 124
despair 172
development, professional 117
devolution 239
dimensions of sustainability 23, 84–5
distinct discipline model 6
diversity: Global Seminar (GS) model
147–8; program 70; students and
teachers 76–7
doing and learning 161–2
Duncan, Arne 3

Earth Summit (World Conference on
Environment and Development) 45
ecological paradigm model 29
ecology: campus 159, 162–3; change
225–26; ideas and images 230–1; moral
155–6; socio-cultural 226–7
economics: educational investment 228–9;
interests 227–8; unsustainability 227–9
educating for a sustainable future (ESF) 45
education: design aspirations 215–16;
functions 173; hospitality 124–5;
indigenous 230–1; K-10 53; K-12 4,
53, 127
educational innovations 3
educational leadership 75
educational models 2–3
educational objectives: College of
Menominee Nation 84, 89–90;
Georgetown University 98–9; Global
Seminar curriculum 145; Tbilisi
Declaration 47; United Nations
Decade of Education for Sustainable
Development 80
Education for All 48
Education for Sustainability (EfS) 1–3,
140–1, 239
education for sustainable development
(ESD) 64–5, 72
Edwards, Andres 84

EfS (Education for Sustainability) 1–3,
140–1, 239
elements of sustainability 217
emergent model 7, 187–8, 196–7
emissions 177–8
Emory University, workshops 2–3
employment 22, 103, 104
empowerment 172
Energy Return over Energy Invested
(EROEI) 177–9
energy technologies, alternative 177–9
engineering codes of ethics 111–12
Engineering Education for Sustainable
Development 54
environmental club 11–12
environmental education: goals 128;
questions 172
environmental impact 157–8, 159, 174–6
environmental information 159–60
environmental programs see sustainability
programs; individual institutions
environmental responsibility 112–13
environmental values 157
EROEI (Energy Return over Energy
Invested) 177–9
ESD (education for sustainable
development) 64–5, 72
ESF (educating for a sustainable future) 45
evaluations: course 109–11; Global
Seminar curriculum 146–7
evolution 224
experiential learning 205
extracurricular sustainability efforts 88–9

faculty: Global Seminar curriculum 146;
survey 131–2; sustainability knowledge
125–6, 131–3
faculty-student interaction 224–5
field trips 158
financial data 97
Finger 173
First Do No Harm 104–5
First Intergovernmental Conference on
Environmental Education 46–7
five elements of sustainability 217
Focus the Nation's National Teach-Ins
12–13
Fowler, Verna 83, 87
fragmentation of knowledge
201–2, 203
Franklin Environmental Center 192
functions of education 173
funding 88, 227–8

Furman University: background 186–7; campus culture 190–1; curricular offerings 193; emergent model 187, 196; enhancing existing offerings 194; goals and strategies 190–1; interdisciplinary approach 193; learning outcomes 196; moral imperative 188; survey 193; workshops 195–6
futures 219–20

Georgetown University: employment 103, 104; faculty awareness 96; interdisciplinary approach 95–7, 99–100, 104; objectives 98–9; practitioner partnerships 100–1; student surveys 101, 103; sustainable healthcare management 95; undergraduate programs 99–100
GIOS (Global Institute of Sustainability) 215
Global Institute of Sustainability (GIOS) 215
Global Perspectives Inventory (GPI) 89–90
Global Seminar (GS) model: benefits 143; case study method 148; challenges 150–1; collaboration 149–51; diversity 147–8; features 140, 147–9; innovation 148–9; interaction 149; interdisciplinary approach 140, 147–8; international scope 147–8; learning cycles 148; teaching partnerships 148–9; technology 148–9
Global Seminar curriculum: assignments 146–7; evaluation 146–7; faculty 146; goals 145; grading 146–7; holistic approach 142–3, 149–50; institutional objectives 146; learning objectives 145; methodology 146; organization 146; stakeholders 146; structure 146
Global Seminar research: data analysis 145; data collection 144–5; design 143–4; goals 139–40; objectives 143
goals: education for sustainable development 72; environmental education 128; Furman University 190–1; Global Seminar curriculum 145; Global Seminar study 139–40; green home project 170; Middlebury College 192; "one university" 43; sustainability committee 126
governance structure 211

GPI (Global Perspectives Inventory) 89–90
grading, Global Seminar curriculum 146–7
grants 88, 215
Grass Roots 158
green careers 22
green home project 170
greening 11–12, 140–1
green jobs revolution 3
Greenprint, Meredith College 13–14
Green Team 25
green technologies 177–9
grief 172
Gruchow, Paul 158
GS (Global Seminar) model *see* Global Seminar (GS) model

healthcare management 95–9, 100–1
health spending 97
Hembree, Megan 12
HERE (Home for Environmentally Responsible Engineering) 120–1
holistic curricular approach 142–3, 149–50
holistic thinking 55
Home for Environmentally Responsible Engineering (HERE) 120–1
hope 162, 163–4, 212
Hope and Hard Times 91
hospitality education compentencies 124–31
hospitals 95

ideas and images, ecology of 230–1
identity, professional 111, 113–15, 118–19
impact, environmental 157–8, 159, 174–6
independent versus community solutions 178–9
indigenous education 230–1
information, environmental 159–60
infusion model 6
innovation 3, 148–9
Inova Health System 100–101
institutional objectives 146
integration: models 1, 7; sustainability 1, 42–3
interaction: change and 224–5; faculty–student 224–5; Global Seminar (GS) model 149; peer 119–20
interdependence 225
interdisciplinary approach: Arizona State University (ASU) 216, 221; challenges 113, 186; collaboration 142–3; Dalhousie University 203–4;

engineering programs 113; Furman University 193; Georgetown University 95–7, 99–100, 104; Global Seminar (GS) model 140, 147–8; importance of 55; Middlebury College 194; The Ohio State University 29–30, 43; recruitment 40; Uppsala University 64
interior materials 179–80
IUCN (World Conservation Union) 22–3

Jacobs, Michael 63
Jamieson 174
Jefferson, Thomas 161–2
jobs 22, 103, 104
Johns Hopkins University 116
justice, social 178

K-10 education 53
K-12 education 4, 53, 127
Keniry, Julian 141
knowledge: acquisition 72–3; faculty 125–26, 131–3; fragmentation 201–2, 203; practices 223–6, 229; universal 231
Kretzmann, John 233
Kübler-Ross 172

leadership 75, 91
learning: collaboration 73–4; cycles 148; and doing 161–2; experiential 205; laboratories 17; objectives see educational objectives; processes 73–5, 77; standards 127; transformative 54–5
learning outcomes: definition 46; examples 48–55; Furman University 196; hospitality education 124–31; incorporating 134–5; Meredith College 16–17, 23; Middlebury College 196; St. Olaf College 164–6; skills 46–8
Lethbridge College: course content 171–2; Energy Return over Energy Invested (EROEI) analysis 177–9; green home project 169; life-cycle assessment 174–7; product analysis 174, 179–80; product recommendations 176; project mission and goals 170; project stages 169–70; research assignments 171; student beliefs 170–1; student characteristics 170; student reactions 172
life-cycle assessment 174–7
list, course 15–16
The Living Home 169
living well 225

LOs (learning outcomes) see learning outcomes

management role 75
Master's program in SD (MSD) see Swedish University of Agricultural Sciences (SLU); Uppsala University
material culture 231–2
materials: construction 174; interior 179–80
McKnight, John L. 233
Menominee Indian Nation 85–6
Menominee Indian Tribe 82–4
Menominee Model of Sustainable Development 84–5
Menominee Tribal Enterprises (MTE) 85–6
Meredith College: background 11; environmental programs 27–8; "greening" of 11–12; Greenprint 13–14; Learning Laboratories 17–18; learning outcomes 16–17, 23; management role 16–17; sustainability curriculum 12–16; Sustainability Literacy Assessment 19–20; sustainability major and minor 21–5
messy human situations 67–9
methodology, Global Seminar curriculum 146
methods: The Ohio State University study 31–34; reflective practicum 173
Middlebury College: adaptive model 187, 196; background 186–7; campus culture 191–2; curricular offerings 193; enhancing existing offerings 194; goals and strategies 192; interdisciplinary approach 194; learning outcomes 196; moral imperative 188; workshops 195–6
Midgley 72
models: adaptive 7, 187–8, 196–7; community visioning 25; distinct discipline 6; ecological paradigm 29; educational 2–3; emergent 187–8, 196–7; Global Seminar see Global Seminar (GS) model; infusion 6; integration 1, 7; Menominee Model of Sustainable Development 84–5; necessity of 1–3; sustainability education 6–7, 139–40
money 227–8
moral ecology 155–6
moral imperative 188, 190

MSD (Master's program in SD) *see*
Swedish University of Agricultural
Sciences (SLU); Uppsala University
MTE (Menominee Tribal Enterprises)
85–6

National Teach-Ins, Focus the Nation
12–13
nature 156, 239
*The Nature of College: How a New
Understanding of Campus Life Can Change
the World* 162–3

objectives: College of Menominee Nation
84, 89–90; Georgetown University
98–9; Global Seminar research 143;
institutional 146; learning 145; The
Ohio State University study 30–1;
Tbilisi Declaration 47; United Nations
Decade of Education for Sustainable
Development 80
oecos 234–5
The Ohio State University (OSU):
background 29–30; interdisciplinary
approach 29–30, 43; "one university"
goal 43; study methods 31–4; study
objectives 30–1; study results 34–7,
39–41; sustainability programs 42–3
open-ended assignment 157–9
organization, Global Seminar
curriculum 146
organizations, professional 105
Orr, David 79–80
OSU (The Ohio State University) *see* The
Ohio State University (OSU)
Our Common Future 80
outcomes, learning: definition 46;
examples 48–55; Furman University
196; hospitality education 124–31;
incorporating 134–5; Meredith College
16–17, 23; Middlebury College 196;
St. Olaf College 164–6

partnerships: collaboration 139–40,
218–19; Georgetown University
100–101; *see also* teaching partnerships
Pascarella, Ernest 119–20
patterns, cultural 156, 157–9
pedagogy, transformative 149–51
peer interaction 119–20
perceptions 231–2
perspectives 55
practices, knowledge 223–6, 229

practicum 173
Presidents' Climate Commitment 30, 188
problematic human situations 67–9
problem-solving 116–17
process, change 129
processes, learning 73–5, 77
professional, definition of 115–16, 117–18
professional development 117
Professional Education 115–16
professional identity 111, 113–15, 118–19
professional organizations 105
programs, degree *see* sustainability
programs; individual institutions
programs, sustainability *see* sustainability
programs; individual institutions
project goals 170
purpose 72–3

questions: environmental education 172;
identity formation 114; sustainability
programs 4–5

real-world learning experiences
(RWLEs) 219
reflection-in-action 116–17, 173
reflective practicum method 173
The Reflective Practitioner 116
research, Global Seminar *see* Global
Seminar research
research assignments 171–2
residential communities 120–1
resilience: building 228–9; community
assets 233–4; destruction of 224;
indigenous education 230; knowledge
practices 225–6
responsibility, environmental 112–13
results, The Ohio State University study
34–7, 39–41
rewards, program 212
roles 75
RWLEs (real-world learning
experiences) 219

St. Olaf College: American Studies classes
155; Campus Ecology class 154–6;
carryover skills 161; environmental
information 159–60; environmental
values 157; field trips 158; hope 162;
learning outcomes 164–6; moral
ecology 156–7; *The Nature of College:
How a New Understanding of Campus Life
Can Change the World* 162–3;
open-ended assignments 157–9;

research assignments 159; social values 155; student feedback 160–1, 163–4; student-professor 161; survey 164–7
Sandberg 117
Schein, Edgar H. 115–16
Schön, Donald 116–17, 173
School of Environment and Natural Resources (SENR) 29–30, 42–3
science, sustainability 140–2
SD (sustainable development) 63–4
SENR (School of Environment and Natural Resources) 29–30, 42–3
sensory experiences 232–3
Seremetakis, C. Nadia 232
Sharing Indigenous Wisdom: An International Dialogue on Sustainable Development Conference 90–1
Shils, Edward 116
skills: carryover 161; change agent 54–6; learning outcomes 46–8
SLU (Swedish University of Agricultural Sciences) *see* Swedish University of Agricultural Sciences (SLU)
social justice 178
social norms 126
social responsibility 172
social values 155
socio-cultural ecology 226–7
Soft Systems Methodology (SSM) 68–9
SSM (Soft Systems Methodology) 68–9
stakeholders, Global Seminar curriculum 146
stand-alone program 209
standards, learning 127
STARS (Sustainability Tracking, Rating, and Assessment System) 16–17
Steinke, Pamela 23
Sterling, Stephen 141
STLC (Sustainability Teaching and Learning Circle) 14–16
stories 154–5, 167
strategies: environmental 98–9; Furman University 190–1; Middlebury College 192
structure, Global Seminar curriculum 146
student characteristics 170
student feedback 109–11
student-professor 161
studies: Global Seminar, goal 139–40; Global Seminar, objectives 143; The Ohio State University, methods 31–4; The Ohio State University, objectives 30–1; The Ohio State University,

results 34–7, 39–41; Sustainability in Business Today: A Cross-Industry View 97
Sullivan, William M. 117–18
Summit on Sustainability in the Curriculum 81
summits *see* conferences
Sundqvist, Bo 66
surveys: Association for the Advancement of Sustainability in Higher Education 81–2; Association of American Colleges and Universities 103–4; College of Menominee Nation (CMN) 87; Dalhousie University 212; faculty 131–2; Furman University 193; Georgetown University 101, 103; healthcare 97; St. Olaf College 164–7; sustainability 18–21, 81–2
survivance 230, 235
sustainability: challenges 185, 218; committee goals 126; courses, integration 1, 42–3; definition of 16, 185–6; dimensions 23, 84–5; education models 6–7, 139–40; efforts, extracurricular 88–9; elements 217; science 140–2; surveys 18–21, 81–2; Three Es 84; views 185–6; vision 13–14
sustainability-focused courses 16
Sustainability in Business Today: A Cross-Industry View 97
Sustainability Literacy Assessment 19–21
sustainability programs: Arizona State University (ASU) 215–21; competencies 220–1; cornerstones 218–21; Dalhousie University 203–11; Furman University 192–6; Georgetown University 96–104; Meredith College 21–5, 27–8; Middlebury College 192–6; models of 139–40; The Ohio State University 42–3; questions 4–5; St. Olaf College 154–67; *see also* interdisciplinary approach; individual institutions
sustainability-related courses 16
Sustainability Teaching and Learning Circle (STLC) 14–16
Sustainability Tracking, Rating, and Assessment System (STARS) 16–17
sustainable development (SD) 63–4
sustainable development, three pillars 125
Sustainable Furman 191
sustainable healthcare management 95–9, 100–101

Sustaining the Forest, the People, and the Spirit 83
Sverigeslantbruksuniversitet (Swedish University of Agricultural Sciences) *see* Swedish University of Agricultural Sciences (SLU)
Swab, Janice C. 12
Swedish University of Agricultural Sciences (SLU): background 64–5; challenges 69–73; development 65–7; interdisciplinary approach 64; orientation 76; transformation 73–5
systemic thinking 55, 63–5, 67–9, 77

Talloires Declaration 12, 141
Tbilisi Declaration 46–7, 55–6, 57
teachers 125–6, 131–2
teaching methodologies 56–7, 142–3
teaching partnerships: challenges 142, 150; collaboration 139–40; credit 210; defining features 142; holistic approach 142–3, 149–50; interaction 149; interdisciplinary approach 148; transformative pedagogy 149–50
team-teaching *see* teaching partnerships
technical rationality 116–17
technologies: alternative energy 177–9; Global Seminar (GS) model 148–9; green 177–9
Theory of Planned Behavior (TPB) 125
thinking: critical 172; holistic 55; systemic 55, 63–5, 67–9, 77
thinking processes 55
Three Es of sustainability 84
three legs of sustainability 198
three pillars of sustainable development 125
Thresholds in Education 91
TPB (Theory of Planned Behavior) 125
transacademic work 218–19
transformation: cultural 214; ecology 225–6; interaction 224–5; processes 73; unpredictable 226
transformative learning 54–5
transformative pedagogy 149–51
Trillium Workshop 17–18
triple bottom line 46, 98–9, 101–2, 169
troubled communities 233–4
truth 218, 225–6

UNESCO (United Nations Educational, Scientific and Cultural Organization) 80, 201
United Nations 47–8, 124
United Nations Decade of Education for Sustainable Development 80
United Nations declarations 141
United Nations Educational, Scientific and Cultural Organization (UNESCO) 80, 201
US Department of Education 3
US Department of Labor 3
United States' Partnership for Education for Sustainability 127
universal knowledge 231
unsustainability: cause 238; economics 227–9; history 226–7; knowledge practices 224–6
Uppsala University: background 64–5; challenges 69–73; development 65–7; interdisciplinary approach 64; orientation 76; transformation 73–5

values: environmental 157; social 155
variety 70, 76–7
vision for sustainability 13–14

Wake Forest University, conferences 4
WBCSD (World Business Council for Sustainable Development) 54
wicked problems 218
Woodhouse, Janice 91
work, transacademic 218–19
Work and Integrity 117–18
workshops 2–3, 17–18
World Business Council for Sustainable Development (WBCSD) 54
World Commission on Environment and Development 80
World Conference on Education for Sustainable Development 48
World Conference on Environment and Development (Earth Summit) 45
World Conservation Union (IUCN) 22–3
World Summit on Sustainable Development 80